CONTEMPORARY ISSUES IN

Zambian and English Company Law

A COMPARATIVE STUDY

CONTEMPORARY ISSUES IN

Zambian
and English
Company Law

A COMPARATIVE STUDY

Kenneth K. Mwenda

<teneo>
// press

Requests for permission should be directed to:
permissions@teneopress.com, or mailed to:
Teneo Press
PO Box 349
Youngstown, New York 14174

For my admirable son, Joseph T. Mwenda II,
and my dearest wife, Dr. Judith Mvula-Mwenda

"Therefore I prayed, and prudence was given me; I pleaded and the spirit of Wisdom came to me.

I preferred her to scepter and throne, And deemed riches nothing in comparison with her,

nor did I liken any priceless gem to her; Because all gold, in view of her, is a little sand, and before her, silver is to be accounted mire.

Beyond health and comeliness I loved her, And I chose to have her rather than the light, because the splendor of her never yields to sleep.

Yet all good things together came to me in her company, and countless riches at her hands."

Wisdom 7:7–11

TABLE OF CONTENTS

TABLE OF CASES

FOREWORD

In this book, Dr. Kenneth K. Mwenda has provided an authoritatively insightful analysis of contemporary issues in Zambian and English company law. There is perhaps no one better qualified to have engaged in such a magisterial treatment of the Zambian law in the context of its English law heritage than Dr. Mwenda, who is currently a Senior Counsel in the Legal Vice-Presidency of the World Bank and an Extra-Ordinary Professor of Law at the Faculty of Law of the University of Pretoria. Even before writing this book, Dr. Mwenda had already written extensively on a broad range of company law issues in the Zambian and English law contexts. This book and his scholarship represent the path that should be taken by future research on business law in Africa and elsewhere. The scholarly productivity of Dr. Mwenda, a full-time employee of one of the leading international financial institutions, also challenges scholars of and practitioners in Africa to develop resources for both teaching and practitioners' use. Materials such as this book which are written in a comparative context will also serve to inform further legal reform and judicial decision making.

As Dr. Mwenda explains in the preface, although the legal systems of developing countries such as Zambia share many features with those in common law countries in the West, legal solutions in developed economies do not necessarily provide exhaustive solutions or models for developing countries. That is why it is so welcome to read a book on Zambian company law that relies so much on Zambian statutory materials and judicial decisions, as well as on comparative materials from other common law jurisdictions. In doing so, the book is rigorously grounded in a law-in-context approach that is useful to students, practitioners, legal reformers, and judicial officers. Like Dr. Mwenda, I believe that local experts, both practitioners and scholars, as well as judges in developing countries ought not to blindly copy rules or judicial decisions from contexts that are different from those of their own country. Indeed, as the late Justice Nyarangi of the Kenyan Court of Appeal noted,

> Where there are Kenya decisions on point, and if there are no valid grounds for distinguishing [them] on facts, then the Kenya decision should be preferred and used to the exclusion of the others, with the exception of the neighboring countries of Uganda and Tanzania whose conditions are similar to Kenya ... If there are no Kenyan decisions on point, English or Commonwealth or USA authorities may be used as some sort of parameter. *Southern Engineering Company Ltd v. Mutia* [1985] KLR 730 at 747

Thus, a balance between locally relevant statutory and judicial materials on the one hand and persuasive foreign and comparative material on the other provides an ideal framework within which practitioners, judges, and students of law in Africa could operate productively in building the next generation of laws to help consolidate the growth of modern business structures. It is such engagement that Dr. Mwenda recommends throughout this book to fill in gaps in the Zambian Companies Act of 1994 as well as to make up for the limited participation of local expertise in its drafting. What Dr. Mwenda has done so well in this book is to achieve just such a balance, avoiding the pitfall of an inward-looking and parochial jurisprudence. I applaud Dr. Mwenda for this achievement and highly recommend this well-written and well-researched book to all readers.

James T. Gathii, LLB (Nairobi), LLM (Harvard), SJD (Harvard),
Associate Dean for Research and Scholarship and
Governor George E. Pataki Professor
of International Commercial Law,
Albany Law School, Albany, New York

PREFACE

The development of the financial and private sectors of many developing countries has not reached the levels of development that can be found in parallel sectors in many developed countries. This is a factor that law and institutional reformers should consider whenever they engage in the transplantation of legal, institutional, and regulatory models from developed countries to developing countries. Although some developing countries may have identical legal traditions to those of a particular developed country—as can be seen in many common law and civil law jurisdictions—that in itself is no guarantee that the developed country has exhaustive solutions or that it can serve as a single source for all of the model laws for developing countries.

It is true that certain norms of the common law system appear in much of the common law that is practiced around the world, irrespective of different countries' levels of financial and private sector development. (The same is true of civil law.) However, the importance of adapting various laws and regulatory models that are imported from abroad to a local, or host, environment cannot be overemphasised. This book is written based on that premise. As Lord Denning observed in *Nyali Ltd v. Attorney General*[1] regarding the applicability of English common law to the African continent, sounding a warning that extended to other parts of the world,

> Just as with an English oak, so with the English common law. You cannot transplant it ... and expect it to retain the tough character which it has in England. It will flourish indeed, but it needs careful tending ... In these far off lands the people must have a law which they understand and which they respect.[2]

Care and Haller argued that Lord Denning's dictum in *Nyali Ltd v. Attorney General*[3] highlights the difficulty that is inherent in applying the common law, which was developed over centuries in England, to foreign countries where very different circumstances prevail.[4] According to Care and Haller, the need to take these circumstances into account was recognised in the provisions for applying the common law to new settings.[5] Care and Haller pointed out that 'in many countries it was expressed to apply, *so far only as the circumstances [of the country] permit.*'[6]

Implicit in Lord Denning's dictum is the notion that developing countries that import or transplant model laws from abroad to their own local environments should consider not only the 'wisdom' of foreign technical experts but also the insights that local experts articulate about the particular conditions of the developing country. Even more worrying is the calibre and quality of some of the so-called foreign technical experts who come to Africa riding on the surfeit of Western ideological opulence. Although it is useful for law reformers or institutional reformers to be aware of developments pertaining to parallel legislation in different countries, they must also resist adopting a blind optimism about Eurocentric models of development which could cloud their judgment and objectivity.

It must be understood that the law does not operate or exist in a vacuum. Therefore, it must be situated in its proper socioeconomic and political contexts. Through an international and comparative study of contemporary issues in company law, this book aims to strike a balance between black-letter law and law-in-context. Legal scholars, law professors, law students, and legal practitioners, as well as judges and other people who are interested in company law and business law in general (e.g., accountants and accounting or business students), will no doubt find this book a resourceful, valuable, and informative read.

The law and information that are presented in this book are stated on the basis of the materials that were available to me as of 22 July 2010. However, the interpretations and conclusions expressed in the book are entirely mine. They do not represent the views of the World Bank, its executive directors, or the countries they represent.

Professor Kenneth K. Mwenda, PhD, LLD,
Washington, DC, USA

ACKNOWLEDGMENTS

Now that the writing of the book is complete, I am faced with a task which is by no means easy to fulfil. I would like to thank my dear wife, Dr. Judith M. Mvula-Mwenda, MD, MBA, MPH, and my admirable son, Joseph T. Mwenda II, for their unfailing love and support.

I would also like to acknowledge the inspiration that I continue to draw from my dear parents, the late Mr. Joseph T. Mwenda and Mrs. Esther M. Mwenda. My father in particular remains an unsung hero who taught me the virtues of truth, honesty, integrity, fairness, and love. He may not have been as famous as many of the hopelessly corrupt politicians of modern times or as ubiquitously conspicuous as many of the celebrities or supposedly influential business personalities whose associations are so often sought. However, as far as I am concerned, he was among 'the hidden righteous men who, according to Jewish mythology, are the only reason why the Almighty has refrained from destroying our sinful world'.[7] My father was a man of exceptionally well-cultivated values. That is where his wealth lay. A man of great character, he was a true gentleman. Although he has now crossed over, he remains my greatest role model. A humanely decent and God-fearing man whose life was guided by great moral and ethical values, my father gave his best and his all to the love of God and to the pursuit of knowledge. I have no doubt that he is in the goodness and presence of the Lord.

I now turn to express my gratitude to Professor James Thuo Gathii, the Associate Dean for Research and Scholarship and the Governor George E. Pataki Chair of International Commercial Law at Albany Law School in the United States, for honouring this book with an inspiring foreword as well as for his collegial and brotherly support over the years.

My intellectual interest in matters pertaining to corporate finance law grew when I read for the highly regarded postgraduate degree of Bachelor of Civil Law (BCL) at Oxford. Later, when I joined the Law Faculty of the University of Warwick in the United Kingdom as a full-time academic, it was corporate finance law, among other courses, that I taught in the Master of Laws (LLM) degree program. I have continued to write and publish in the area of international and comparative corporate law, including financial services regulation, culminating in the award of the esteemed Higher Doctorate Degree of Doctor of Laws (LLD) by Rhodes University in South Africa. Although higher doctorates generally are very rarely awarded, the LLD came through in a relatively short period of time—that is, within ten to twelve years of completing my PhD in Law at the University of Warwick.

More recently, the courts of law have cited as authority some of my scholarly publications—notably, the recent citation by the Supreme Court for the Republic of Zambia in the case of *Ventriglia and Ventriglia v. Eastern and Southern Africa Trade and Development Bank and Robert Simeza* SCZ NO. 13 OF 2010 (Appeal No. 11/ 2009). And, on 5 September 2009, at a ceremony held in Lusaka, Zambia, and hosted by the Bank of Zambia Governor, Dr. Caleb M. Fundanga— where the Hon. Chief Justice of the Supreme Court for the Republic of Zambia, Hon. Mr. Chief Justice Ernest Sakala, was in attendance as the Special Guest of Honour—I was honoured and humbled to be presented with distinguished courtesies in recognition of my scholarly contributions to the legal profession. It was a very humbling experience, especially because the ceremony was held specifically to honour my scholarly contributions as a leading Zambian scholar who has made significant and notable contributions to the advancement of the study and understanding of law at an international level. I must say that I owe it to the good Lord for continuing to guide me as I wade in the murky waters of erudition.

I would also like to thank my former law students at many leading universities where I have taught in Europe, North America, and Africa for their questioning minds on certain intellectual issues that form the core of this book. Some of my former law students have gone on to become prominent Supreme Court and High Court judges. Others are now distinguished political figures in their native countries—not forgetting, of course, those who are working in public international organizations as well as those who are heading the legal departments of such organizations. There is also a faction that comprises notable legal practitioners as well as one comprising emerging legal authorities in academia, including heads of academic departments and law practice institutes. Together, we have shared a common world. Their intellectual efforts have inspired me to succeed at receiving many academic and professional awards, including most recently the Mwape Peer Award 2010, celebrating the distinguished career of an individual whose world-class practice and commitment to law is an inspiration to the rest of the legal profession. The Mwape Peer Award 2010 is particularly important because the decision on this competitive award is arrived at by public vote and through the thoughtful deliberation of an eminent panel of assessors. In 1998, I also received a competitive graduate fellowship from Yale University Law School in the United States, which I later turned down to take up an appointment in the World Bank's Young Professionals Program.

I cannot stop without thanking my many other good friends, family members, and professional colleagues whose names, if I were to list them all, would occupy a whole chapter in this book. I thank them all for their support and friendship over the years. I am also grateful to the publisher and to the peer reviewers for the excellent work leading to the publication of this book.

CONTEMPORARY ISSUES IN

Zambian and English Company Law

A COMPARATIVE STUDY

CHAPTER 1

INTRODUCTION

1.0. MOTIVATIONAL STATEMENT

There has not been as much published scholarship on the practice and theory of company law in Zambia as there has been on that of the United Kingdom. In Zambia, many law students, as well as business and accountancy students, have to refer constantly to foreign textbooks on English company law in order to study Zambian company law. The irony is that although Zambia follows the English common law generally, there are a number of legislative departures in Zambia's Companies Act 1994. These legislative divergences will obviously affect the development of the common law in Zambia because judges have to take into account the subtle differences between English and Zambian statutory provisions when they pass court judgments. Practicing lawyers, too, must be awake to such realities.

In this book, valuable international and comparative perspectives on company law are presented. The book is a sequel to my earlier published scholarship in the fields of financial services regulation and international and comparative corporate law, reaffirming my sustained commitment to legal scholarship in these fields. Just as an artist developing a mosaic must have varied interests, so too a scholar must finesse his or her eclectic intellectual tastes. There is a certain quiet and loneliness that comes with indulging clairvoyantly in matters of erudition, especially when it comes to scholarly writing, albeit some warm and cordial intermissions may come from one's family, friends, and colleagues. However, with some commitment, applied competence, and perseverance, there is usually a sense of elated but humane decorum in the actual physical product of the mind.

In the sojourns of international legal practice, such as the road I have traversed over the last decade, I have come to understand that nothing is as practical as a good theory. Often, a good theory is both reflective of and a culmination of best practices. As such, there is no substitute for research when it comes to seeking the truth. The kernels of intellectual leadership cannot be divorced by any justifiable means from what obtains in practice, because there is a strong nexus between sound intellect on the one hand and best practice on the other. For example, in order for a development practitioner or policy maker to articulate or lead a policy dialogue proficiently, he or she cannot refer solely to some long-held dogmatic practice. Such dogmas or articles of faith do not often benefit from circumspection to determine the validity of the underlying theoretical or ideological premise. Yet, there are some people who claim— and proudly, too—to have many years of practical experience in doing the same thing over and over again, forgetting that they may have been doing that same thing incorrectly for much of their life. Such human failings, which are predicated on robotic and dogmatic intuitions, are often a result of a person treating lightly or paying insufficient attention to valuable and useful theories or ideas in a relevant discipline. Indeed, practice that is devoid of enlightenment is a good recipe for failure, as much as the carrying out of unintelligent repetitive tasks does not make one a genius. There can be no substitute for erudition, and thus, may our cooking places never grow cold.

By parity of reasoning, many theoretical and ideological constructs are developed on the basis of systematically and repeatedly observed facts. Therefore, a theory that subsists in the abstract only, without much relevance to concrete reality, is of little value to socioeconomic and political inquiry. In this vein, intellectual leadership should not be understood as being confined solely to the congenial habitats of classroom pedagogy. This form of leadership extends also to the practical implementation of policies, projects, and programmes, because it often points to evidence of best practice. Therefore, the argument that legal practice is entirely different from academia, for example—a charge that is made by some apologists who lack the necessary appetite or intellectual capacity to pursue knowledge fully—is clearly utopian and false. For those seeming friends who hold dear such myths, I say, as they would say in Russia, 'God save us from our friends; from our enemies we can defend ourselves'.[8] The argument that theory and practice are totally disconnected or that there is no correlation between the two indicates shortsighted laziness or simply the economical treatment of the truth. Academia and legal practice do fit together like a hand and a glove, or perhaps like the blossoming love between a bride and a groom. The particular combination of the two areas is a subject that some scholars have chosen to study. I can profess best only that which I have put to the test or practiced, as much as I can practice diligently only that which is grounded in sound and scientific theory.

1.1. CONTEXT OF THE DISCOURSE

Although a few academic theses and dissertations have been written on topics that range from the historical aspects of Zambian company law to the corporate governance aspects of parastatal companies in Zambia,[9] not much has been written about the black-letter law or the law-in-context approach to modern company law in Zambia. Striking a balance in considering the black-letter law and the law-in-context, this book endeavours to fill the lacuna of scholarship on modern company law in Zambia. Admittedly, company law in its broad sense covers many areas of study and practice. The book therefore focuses on the pertinent aspects of company law in Zambia arising from the enactment of the

Zambian Companies Act 1994. Not every single aspect of the Zambian Companies Act 1994 is examined here; the book deals mainly with contemporary legal issues that have resulted from the law's enactment. Such issues include the legal status of the *ultra vires* doctrine in Zambian company law; the liability of company directors for wrongful or fraudulent trading; and the issuing of shares of par value as well as of no-par-value, which can include share watering, allotting shares at a discount, and providing financial assistance in the acquisition of a company's shares.

There are other areas of company law in Zambia that have resulted from the enactment of closely related Zambian legislation. These include the Securities Act 1993; the Prohibition and Prevention of Money Laundering Act 2001; the Co-operative Societies Act 1970 (as amended up to 1994); the Competition and Fair Trading Act 1994, including the Competition Rules in Zambia that were promulgated under it; the Registration of Business Names Act 1931 (as amended up to 1994); the Small Enterprises Development Act 1996; the Self-Management Enterprises Act 1988; the Building Societies Act 1968 (as amended up to 2005); the Zambia Development Agency Act 2006; the Bankruptcy Act 1967 (as amended up to 1994, covering mainly unincorporated persons); and the Preferential Claims in Bankruptcy Act 1995 (also covering mainly unincorporated persons). These pieces of legislation, however, fall outside the scope of this study.

The enactment of Zambia's Securities Act 1993, for example, ushered in a new legislative framework in Zambia for the public distribution of securities on the stock market. At the time of the 1993 enactment, the Zambian Companies Act 1921 (which has since been repealed) had statutory provisions permitting public companies to issue shares to the public; however, when it was enacted, there was no stock exchange in Zambia. Thus, the repealed Companies Act 1921 did not cover such issues as insider dealing or the role and functions of a securities regulator in Zambia. Indeed, there was no securities regulator in the country. Much of what the repealed Companies Act 1921 included in regard to the public distribution of securities were statutory provisions pertaining to the preparation and issuance of a company prospectus.[10] It was only when the Securities Act 1993 was passed and the Lusaka Stock Exchange was set up that the stock exchange could prepare and issue listing requirements for the public distribution of securities on its market.[11] Elsewhere, I have examined the legal aspects of public distribution of securities in Zambia,[12] as well as the ways in which a number of market abuses, such as insider dealing, can be predicate offences of money laundering.[13] These discussions will not be repeated in this book, and the reader is encouraged to consult some of my earlier works.[14]

In regard to the legal framework for corporate financial reporting that was brought about by the enactment of Zambia's Companies Act 1994, the statute requires that financial statements of companies give 'a true and fair view',[15] but it does not require compliance with international financial reporting standards (IFRS) or any accounting standards. However, this feature alone should not be seen as a weakness or shortcoming of the statute, and it does not indicate that the Companies Act 1994 is now out of date. In many countries, accounting standards, like the standards for regulating other professions, are often treated as a living document. They change rapidly, and as such, it may not be advisable to codify IFRS into the provisions of principal legislation. It would be ill-advised to expect legislation such as the Companies Act 1994, whose function is not even directly related to the regulation of the accountancy profession, to codify IFRS. Indeed, how many times would such legislation have to be amended each time the international accounting standards are updated or revised? In contrast, the statute that regulates the accountancy profession in Zambia is the Accountants Act 2008. This statute has a short statutory provision stating that IFRS shall be applicable to Zambia, with possible adaptations to suit the Zambian context.[16] That way, even if IFRS are revised, the Zambian Accountants Act 2008 does not have to be amended. Prior to the enactment of the Accountants Act 2008, the statute that regulated the accounting profession in Zambia and which also provided for the establishment of the Zambia Institute of Certified Accountants (now referred to as the Zambia Institute of Chartered Accountants, or ZICA), was the Accountants Act 1982.

The reasoning articulated earlier for the adoption of IFRS in Zambia should be extended to situations in which Zambia's Companies Act 1994 appears to allow persons without a practicing license to audit private companies. Clarity on such matters must be made through secondary legislation or other codes of conduct that are promulgated pursuant to Zambia's Accountants Act 2008. Likewise, one would be misguided to expect that the Securities Act 1993 or the Lusaka Stock Exchange Listing Rules should provide explicitly for the application of IFRS by publicly traded companies. Accounting matters, as noted earlier, are best left to the principal and subsidiary legislation regulating the accountancy profession. In Zambia, it is ZICA that sets the accounting and auditing standards. This is the body which should be collaborating with various industry and sector stakeholders to promulgate subsidiary legislation or codes of conduct relating to such matters. If ZICA lacks the relevant institutional or compliance and enforcement capacities to manage this process, then an initiative must be put in place to strengthen the organization. One would exercise similar caution where there is no clear indication in Zambia's Public Finance Act 2004 regarding some state-owned enterprises' application of IFRS, international public sector accounting standards, or any other accounting standards.

But, then, does an external auditor owe a duty of care to the company that is being audited? Similarly, does the external auditor owe a duty of care to third parties that ultimately rely on those audited accounts?[17] The Companies Act 1994 is silent on these issues. One is left to look at the English common law. In *Re Kingston Cotton Mill*,[18] William J. Vaughan, examining the legal position of an auditor, ruled as follows: 'No doubt he is acting antagonistically to the directors in the sense that he is appointed by the shareholders to be a check upon them.'[19]

Woolf observed that the House of Lords in the United Kingdom has issued rulings to eliminate the open-ended liability to third parties faced by auditors.[20] The House of Lords, according to Woolf, has declared that auditors have a duty of care to a third party only if they have knowledge about the nature of the third party's transactions, know that their reports will be disclosed to the third party, and are aware that the decisions of the third party will be based on these reports.[21] However, these rulings have also made U.K. auditors apprehensive that the reduced likelihood of being sued will render the generality of accounts useless, thus reducing their credibility.[22] The changing trend of auditors' liability, Woolf argued, is also evident in case rulings in the United States and Australia. The 1992 *Security Pacific Business Credit v. Peat Marwick Main & Co* and the *AWA v. Deloitte* cases in the United States and Australia, respectively, provided examples of such court rulings.[23]

In the English case of *Re Kingston Cotton Mill (No. 2)*,[24] it was noted that an auditor is not required to prepare the audit report with suspicion but should prepare such a report on the basis that if suspicion does exist, then an obligation exists to 'probe it to the bottom.'[25] Accordingly, the standard of knowledge, skill, and care required of an external auditor is that expected of a reasonably competent auditor,[26] and the court should consider whether the act or omission departs from 'general practice'.[27] Citing the case of *Bolam v. Friern Mgmt Comm*,[28] Singh argued that in such a case, 'general practice' is interpreted to mean the typical behaviour of a skilled person accepted by a 'responsible body' of opinion.[29]

Commenting on a 2008 court ruling in the United Kingdom, Curd and Hare observed as follows:

> A recent case has considered the standard of care owed by auditors. The auditors were retained to prepare a report for the purposes of the 'whitewash' procedure under the Companies Act 1985, allowing a sale of shares by directors of the company to a new company incorporated for that purpose, with the purchase being funded by a loan from the company. The auditors prepared the report stating that they had enquired into the affairs of the company and that there was nothing to indicate that the opinion stated by the directors (*i.e.* that the company was presently solvent and would be able to pay its debts in full within the following 12 months, or within 12 months of being wound up if the winding up commenced within 12 months) was unreasonable. The company subsequently went into liquidation. It transpired that the company did not have sufficient distributable profits (as required by the statute) at the time the loan was provided. The directors

had significantly overvalued the worth of the company shares. The company, in liquidation, claimed against the directors for reimbursement of the purchase price, damages for breach of fiduciary duty and damages for negligence. It also claimed against the auditors for breach of contract and negligence, on the grounds that they had failed to deliver a competent report.

The court held,

- The directors were liable in respect of the claims against them as they had allowed the company to provide unlawful financial assistance and had preferred their own interests over those of the company.
- The court assessed the standard of care owed by the auditors against the best practice publication 'Audit Quality' published by the ICAEW. The court did not accept that the techniques that the auditors should have adopted to apply the standard would vary because of the size of the transaction. A proper analysis of the company's assets and business would have revealed it was in no position to advance the loan. The court also rejected the argument that, by analogy to negligent valuation cases, the auditors' opinion was not so far outside the reasonable range that they should be held liable for the entirety of the company's loss. The auditors were in breach of duty in that they failed to enquire into the affairs of the company to the extent that an auditor of reasonable competence would have done. If they had, the certificate would not have been signed and the loan would not have been provided.
- On the same basis, the auditors were liable to the director shareholders for breach of duty. The measure of damages was the loss in the value of their shareholdings.
- Both the directors and auditors were liable to the company for the same damage, therefore the court was entitled to apportion liability between them. The directors had received the whole of the sum advanced to the company, which was a personal 'windfall' to them, to the extent that it exceeded the true value of the shares at the date of completion. The directors were ordered to pay this difference in value to the company, and the auditors were required to pay the balance.[30]

In the chapters that follow, I will examine in greater detail some novel developments under Zambia's company law. For example, the legislative developments relating to the *ultra vires* doctrine and the capacity of a company to pursue its objectives have raised much debate in Zambian legal circles after the enactment of the Companies Act 1994. To many scholars, however, it is not clear whether the *ultra vires* doctrine has been abolished in Zambia or not. Not even Zambian case law has settled this issue convincingly.

Chapter 2 of the book delves into the intricacies of English and Zambian case law and provides sound legal arguments that the *ultra vires* doctrine in Zambia is still alive, despite the legislative efforts to water it down. The chapter also points out that the legislative draftsman's intention to abolish the *ultra vires* doctrine in Zambia's company law was not successful. A number of reasons help to explain that. Chief among them is that the legislative draftsman did not pay sufficient attention to the parallel legislative developments in other jurisdictions, and indigenous professionals and stakeholders had only limited participation in the preparation of the Zambian Companies Act 1994. A typical problem from which many developing countries have failed to extricate themselves is accepting the notion that every form of knowledge or advice that comes from the West is superior to indigenous knowledge or advice. In preparing the Zambian Companies Act 1994, the Zambian government should have consulted more widely both within and outside of Zambia, targeting those capable and well-established Zambian professionals who have expertise in the area of corporate law. Some of these individuals, if they had been encouraged to collaborate and work closely with the foreign experts who were hired to draft the act, could have produced a better product than what currently obtains for the Zambian Companies Act 1994.

In chapter 2, examples of developments of the *ultra vires* doctrine are drawn from countries such as the United Kingdom. A contrast is made between the position of the U.K. Companies Act 2006 and the less thoughtful position of Zambia's Companies Act 1994. In making a case for how the preparation of the Zambian Companies Act 1994 did not benefit much from a thoughtful consideration of the implications of not including in the statute some provisions for a company to have a memorandum of association, chapter 2 makes reference also to the Mauritius' Companies Act 2001. Like the U.K. Companies Act 2006, the Mauritius' Companies Act 2001 has elegant statutory provisions that deal with the *ultra vires* doctrine without creating uncertainties or obscurities.

In Zambia, the legislative draftsman, in a further attempt to do away with the *ultra vires* doctrine under the Zambian Companies Act 1994, abolished the common law doctrine of constructive notice. However, it is not clear if this development alone helps to resolve the conundrum that is associated with the *ultra vires* doctrine, because the mere absence of statutory obligations for companies to have memoranda of association cannot be interpreted as an abolition of the *ultra vires* doctrine. This view is explored in greater detail in chapter 2, which sets forth different scenarios that help to explain why the *ultra vires* doctrine has not been successfully abolished in Zambia.

Chapter 3 examines the concepts of par value in company law and paying up for shares. Arguments in favour of and against issuing shares of par value are advanced. Examples are drawn from different jurisdictions, including Ghana, the United States, and Australia, where shares of no-par-value can be issued. Chapter 3 questions the relevance of the par value concept in the modern world and, by parity of reasoning, its relevance to Zambian company law.

Some of the policy issues that underpin the statutory requirement in many jurisdictions for shareholders to pay up for allotted shares are also examined. Closely related to that, chapter 3 delves into the intricacies of the concept of share watering. Analogies are drawn from the United Kingdom and Zambia, examining issues such as the payment for shares using cash, the allotment of shares at a discount, the allotment of shares at a premium, and the allotment of shares for considerations other than cash. Exceptions to various general rules regarding the payment for shares are fleshed out, showing why in some instances a particular transaction may not amount to share watering. Chapter 3 concludes with an insightful discussion on the legal aspects of providing financial assistance in the acquisition of a company's shares. Again, analogies are drawn from the United Kingdom and Zambia, fleshing out the differences between the two jurisdictions and highlighting some areas of congruence. Exceptions to the statutory prohibition relating to financial assistance are also highlighted.

Chapter 4 examines the efficacy of the legal framework dealing with the liability of company directors for fraudulent trading and wrongful trading, including the salient and pertinent aspects of fraud that has been committed by the officers of companies that have gone into liquidation. A comparative study of the law in Zambia and the United Kingdom is set out. Chapter 4 argues that Zambia should consider enacting a statute that provides for the disqualification of persons from serving as company directors if they have been convicted of offences such as wrongful trading, fraudulent trading, or fraud by officers of companies that have gone into liquidation. Closely related to that idea is the argument that the absence of a legal framework in Zambia for licensing and regulating insolvency practitioners, as a means of protecting consumers and the market from malpractices of unlicensed and unauthorized persons who serve as insolvency practitioners, poses a great challenge to the development of corporate insolvency law in the country. Chapter 5 provides overall concluding remarks and sets forth some policy recommendations to improve company law in Zambia.

CHAPTER 2

CAPACITY OF A COMPANY AND THE *ULTRA VIRES* DOCTRINE

2.0. INTRODUCTION

Under the Zambian Companies Act 1994, incorporated companies, such as banks and financial institutions,[31] are not required to have a memorandum of association. This chapter examines the legal and policy reasons for doing away with this statutory requirement and seeks to find out if this means that banks and financial institutions in Zambia are no longer required to have an objects clause. This is particularly of interest given that prior to the repeal of the Zambian Companies Act 1921, a company that was incorporated under that statute was required to have an objects clause at its incorporation and at all times thereafter as a part of its memorandum of association.[32]

The introductory part of this chapter sets out the context of the study. The second part proceeds to define the terms *bank* and *financial institution*. In doing so, a legal analysis is provided of the statutory definition of terms such as *banking business* and *financial services business*.

The third part of the chapter delves into the jurisprudential aspects of the *ultra vires* doctrine in company law, highlighting the development of this doctrine in common law. The fourth part examines whether the *ultra vires* doctrine has been abolished in Zambia's company law or if it has simply been watered down. Preceding the conclusion, the fifth part of the chapter, which focuses primarily on banks and financial institutions as examples of some of the companies that are incorporated under Zambia's Companies Act 19994, explores the question of whether the *ultra vires* doctrine applies to banks and financial institutions in Zambia. Although the chapter draws on some analogous legislative and common law developments in the United Kingdom, no attempt is made to examine whether banks in the United Kingdom are also affected by the *ultra vires* doctrine. The focus of the chapter, it must be stressed, is on whether banks and financial institutions in Zambia should have an objects clause given that the Zambian Companies Act 1994 does not require companies that are incorporated under that piece of legislation to have a memorandum of association.

As evidenced from some of the data provided in interviews and e-mails by sources in Zambia, the dropping of the statutory requirement for a company that is incorporated under Zambia's Companies Act 1994 to have a memorandum of association was designed primarily to meet two objectives.[33] On the one hand, there was a policy shift to simplify the process and procedures for incorporating a company.[34] On the other hand, there was a botched intent on the part of the legislative draftsman to do away with the *ultra vires* doctrine in Zambia's company law.[35] According to the explanatory notes of the foreign consultant who was recruited by the Zambian government to provide leadership in drafting the Zambian Companies Act 1994,

> Removal of the '*ultra vires*' principle
>
> However, even if there are any such restrictions, the old doctrine of ultra vires will not apply. This is set out in section 23:
>
> 'No act of a company, including a transfer of property by or to a company, shall be invalid by reason only that the act or transfer is contrary to its articles or to the Act.'[36]

As shall be seen later in this chapter,[37] the legislative draftsman's view in this regard was somewhat misguided. Although he succeeded in dropping from the Zambian Companies Act 1994 the requirement for the incorporator(s) of a company to furnish a memorandum of association at incorporation, he incorrectly assumed that a company's principal business as well as its other business would be spelt out in the company's articles—say, through some 'restrictions'.[38] It must be observed that the Zambian Companies Act 1994 refers to what are generally known as articles of association as simply 'articles of the company'.[39] The change in nomenclature does not, however, point to any meaningful or substantive changes in the definitions of the terms. In this chapter, I thus continue to use the term *articles of association*.

Overall, a notable shortcoming of the view that was espoused by the legislative draftsman is that under the Zambian Companies Act 1994, there is no mandatory requirement for a company to have articles of association. Strictly speaking, the Companies Act 1994 allows also for a company without any articles of association to be incorporated. Section 7 of the Companies Act 1994 makes it optional for companies to have articles of association by using the term *may* instead of *shall*. Indeed, section 7 provides that 'a company *may* have articles' regulating its conduct, and that such 'articles *may* contain restrictions on the business that the company may carry on' (italics added).

Further, when a company with articles of association is incorporated, the Companies Act 1994 does not place any statutory obligation on the company to have in its articles of association any restrictions on the company's business. Such restrictions, I contend, are more of a company's right than its statutory duty. However, when a company decides to place some business restrictions in its articles of association, the company is prohibited by the Zambian Companies Act 1994 from carrying on any business or exercising any power that is disallowed by its articles as well as from exercising any of its powers in a manner that is contrary to the articles.[40] Be that as it may, there is very little incentive for a company to spell out its principal and other businesses in its articles of association because such information will already have been provided in the completed Form I, II, III, or IV, the models of which are outlined in the Companies (Prescribed Forms) Regulations.[41] I will examine later the type of information that should be filled in in Forms I, II, III, and IV.[42]

The legislative draftsman continued in his explanatory notes,

> So, a third party who deals with a company is entitled to assume that it has the power to do anything it wishes. If the officers of the company cause it to act in contravention of its articles, the members can take action against those officers, but the interests of the third party are not affected—unless, of course, the third party actually knew of the restrictions.[43]

First, it is not clear that the legislative draftsman had a full appreciation of the rule in *Foss v. Harbottle*[44] and the various exceptions to that rule. Indeed, it is the company, as a legal person, and not the members, that is entitled to take action against the directors, unless the directors have engaged in an *ultra vires* or illegal act or if the matter is one which could validly be done or sanctioned only by some special majority of members, or where the personal and individual rights of the plaintiff as a member have been invaded as well as where what has been done amounts to a 'fraud on the minority' and the wrongdoers are themselves in control of the company.[45]

Second, although the draftsman in his explanatory notes referred only to having knowledge in the phrase 'unless, of course, the third party actually knew of the restrictions', the concept of knowledge in law is different from that of notice.[46] Besides, the relevant statutory provision in the Zambian Companies Act 1994, as shall be seen in the following pages, refers to both knowledge and notice—in contrast to the draftsman's notes. Elsewhere, I have examined the concept of knowledge in greater detail;[47] the concept of notice is discussed in the latter sections of this chapter.[48] In Zambia, section 24 of Zambia's Companies Act 1994 abolishes the common law doctrine of constructive notice as follows:

> No person dealing with a company shall be affected by, or presumed to have notice or knowledge of, the contents of a document concerning the company by reason only that the document has

been lodged with the Registrar or is held by the company available for inspection.

In this regard, it would appear that the abolition of the doctrine of constructive notice by section 24 of the Companies Act 1994 was meant to complement and augment the botched efforts of the draftsman to abolish the *ultra vires* doctrine in Zambia. Indeed, an underlying premise might have been the notion that by abolishing the constructive notice doctrine, it would no longer be possible to impute any notice to a third party who was dealing with the company regarding the company's objects. In that way, the *ultra vires* doctrine would have a minimal or no effect whatsoever because the third party could not be presumed to have had notice of the objects of the company.

Third, the mere dropping from the Zambian Companies Act 1994 of the requirement for the incorporator(s) of a company to furnish the companies registrar with the company's memorandum of association is not in and of itself an abolition of the common law doctrine of *ultra vires*. Nothing in the Zambian Companies Act 1994 bars a company from having a memorandum of association, although some scholars believe that the registrar of companies, relying on section 370 of the Companies Act 1994, can refuse to admit a memorandum of association as a part of the documents that are being lodged to register the company.[49] Section 370 provides as follows:

1. Where this Act requires any document or particulars to be lodged with the Registrar, the Registrar shall register them in the manner prescribed or, if no manner is prescribed for the document or particulars, as determined by the Registrar.
2. For the purposes of this Act, a document or particulars shall be deemed not to have been lodged with the Registrar until any fee prescribed under section three hundred and seventy-seven has been paid to the Registrar.
3. Subject to this Act, where this Act requires a document or particulars to be lodged under this Act, each company concerned shall lodge a separate document or set of particulars.

4. All documents and particulars which are lodged with the Registrar shall be printed or typewritten on good quality paper to the satisfaction of the Registrar.

5. If the Registrar is of opinion that any document or particulars lodged with him—

    a. contain matter or matters contrary to law;
    b. by reason of any error, omission or misdescription have not been duly completed;
    c. are insufficiently legible;
    d. are written on paper insufficiently durable; or
    e. otherwise do not comply with the requirements of this Act; he may refuse to register the document or particulars in that state and direct that they be amended or completed in a specified manner and re-submitted.

6. If the Registrar gives a direction under subsection (5), the document or particulars shall be deemed not to have been lodged.

7. The Registrar may require that a document or a fact stated in a document lodged with him shall be verified by statutory declaration.

8. Where the Registrar is required or permitted under this Act to cause a copy or particulars of a document lodged with him to be published in the Gazette, he may require the lodgement with him of any such document in duplicate, or the provision of any such particulars, and may withhold registration of the document until the requirement has been complied with.

9. The Registrar may alter a document if so authorised by the person who lodged the document or his representative.

This statutory provision does not, however, place a mandatory obligation on the registrar of companies to decline the admission of such important corporate documents as a company's memorandum of association simply because the Companies Act 1994 is silent on the issue. Neither does the Companies Act 1994 say that the furnishing of a memorandum of association to the registrar at a company's incorporation is contrary to the law or that it does not comply with the requirements of the Companies Act 1994. The statute is simply quiet on the matter. Besides, the use of the words '*may* refuse' in subsection 5 of section 370 of the Companies Act 1994 indicates that the registrar of companies is not under a statutory obligation but instead has the option to either accept or turn down the documents. So, in theory, if it chooses, a company can have a memorandum of association.

Admittedly, the legislative draftsman should have considered more thoughtfully the parallel legislative developments in jurisdictions such as the United Kingdom, where the prospects for abolishing the *ultra vires* doctrine have been debated extensively.[50] The mere dropping from the Companies Act 1994 of the requirement for a memorandum of association is not good enough to convey the intended message of abolishing the *ultra vires* doctrine. Disappointingly, ten years after the enactment of Zambia's Companies Act 1994, Jamaica did the same thing when it enacted the long-awaited Jamaican Companies Act 2004.[51] In Zambia and Jamaica, there should have been more deliberate and conscious efforts to spell out more clearly in the respective acts the extent to which the *ultra vires* doctrine applies to company law in those countries. To illustrate, as a way of protecting an innocent third party who is dealing with a company in good faith, section 28 of Mauritius' Companies Act 2001 provides as follows:

1. Where the constitution of a company sets out the objects of the company, there is deemed to be a restriction in the constitution on carrying on any business or activity that is not within those objects, unless the constitution expressly provides otherwise.
2. Where the constitution of a company provides for any restrictions on the business or activities in which the company may engage—

    a.   the capacity and powers of the company shall not be affected by that restriction; and

    b.   no act of the company and no contract or other obligation entered into by the company and no transfer of property to or by the company is invalid by reason only that it was done in contravention of that restriction.

3. Subsection (2) shall be without prejudice to sections 169, 170, 174 and 176.

4. The capacity of the company to do an act shall not be affected by the fact that the act is not, or would not be, in the best interests of the company.[52,53]

Similarly, section 39 of the English Companies Act 2006 provides as follows:

1. The validity of an act done by a company shall not be called into question on the ground of lack of capacity by reason of anything in the company's constitution.

2. This section has effect subject to section 42 (companies that are charities).[54]

Section 40 of the 2006 English statute goes on to add:

1. In favour of a person dealing with a company in good faith, the power of the directors to bind the company, or authorise others to do so, is deemed to be free of any limitation under the company's constitution.

2. For this purpose—

    a.   a person 'deals with' a company if he is a party to any transaction or other act to which the company is a party,

    b.   a person dealing with a company—

        i.   is not bound to enquire as to any limitation on the powers of the directors to bind the company or authorise others to do so,

        ii.   is presumed to have acted in good faith unless the contrary is proved, and

    iii.   is not to be regarded as acting in bad faith by reason only of his knowing that an act is beyond the powers of the directors under the company's constitution.

3.   The references above to limitations on the directors' powers under the company's constitution include limitations deriving—

    a.   from a resolution of the company or of any class of shareholders, or

    b.   from any agreement between the members of the company or of any class of shareholders.

4.   This section does not affect any right of a member of the company to bring proceedings to restrain the doing of an action that is beyond the powers of the directors.

But no such proceedings lie in respect of an act to be done in fulfilment of a legal obligation arising from a previous act of the company.

5.   This section does not affect any liability incurred by the directors, or any other person, by reason of the directors' exceeding their powers.

6.   This section has effect subject to—

section 41 (transactions with directors or their associates), and section 42 (companies that are charities).[55]

Against this background, I submit that not much thoughtful consideration was accorded by the legislative draftsman to the implications of dropping from the Zambian Companies Act 1994 the requirement for the incorporator(s) of a company to furnish the registrar of companies with the company's memorandum of association at incorporation. As argued by one source, 'Generally, the drafting of legislation in Zambia is rushed and without adequate consultations of relevant stakeholders'.[56]

Indeed, many of the sources I contacted in Zambia about the policy bases for doing away with the requirement for the incorporator(s) of a company to furnish the registrar of companies with the company's memorandum of association had no clue that the legislative draftsman had actually intended, among other things, to abolish the *ultra vires* doctrine in Zambia's company law.[57] A number of them believed that the legislative changes had been introduced only to simplify the process and procedures for incorporating companies.[58] To resolve the conundrum that is associated with such legislative changes, I examine more critically in this chapter the issue of whether the *ultra vires* doctrine has been abolished in Zambia's company law or if it has simply been watered down.[59] Analogies are drawn from English common law because Zambia's jurisprudence, largely speaking, is based on and continues to draw upon English common law.[60]

I argue that a notable consequence of permitting a company without a memorandum of association to incorporate is that an investor could be misled to think that the Zambian Companies Act 1994 has done away with the requirement for companies to have an objects clause or at least some form of objects. However, one commentator observed that 'the Companies Act 1994 has not done away with the statutory requirement for companies incorporated thereunder to have an objects clause or some form of objects.'[61] According to that source,

> section 6(2)(i) of the Act makes it obligatory for the application for incorporation or '*the Incorporation Form*' to specify '*...the nature of [the company's] proposed business as the prescribed form may require*'...(incorporators are required to indicate, on completing the incorporation form, both the '*principal*' as well as any '*other business*' that the proposed company is to engage in). The view which I hold myself (which may not necessarily be consistent with whatever view (if at all) that the draftsman of the Act held) is that *the substance* of the Memorandum of Association under the repealed Act has been reduced to the various prescribed Companies Forms (Companies Forms 1 to 4) each one of which has all the features or elements which characterised the old Memorandum of Association, namely:
>
> a.   The Name Clause;
> b.   The Objects Clause;
> c.   The Capital Clause;

    d. The 'Association Clause' (This is contained on the page of the Incorporation Form where it is stated '*We, the several persons whose names and addresses are subscribed, wish to be formed into (type of company) and we respectively agree to take the number of shares in the capital of the company set opposite our respective names*'

    e. The company's registered office.[62]

More likely than not, I contend, the draftsman of the Zambian Companies Act 1994 did not give thoughtful consideration to such issues.[63] Thus, I argue that although the *ultra vires* doctrine continues to apply in Zambia, its significance has been watered down by the introduction of Forms I, II, III, and IV, as set out in the Companies (Prescribed Forms) Regulations,[64] to replace the statutory requirement in the Companies Act 1994 for an objects clause in the memorandum of association. Form I requires the incorporators of a public company to spell out the nature of the company's business. Form II covers the nature of a private company's business.[65] Form III relates to the nature of business of a private company limited by guarantee. Form IV deals with the nature of business of an unlimited company.[66]

Following is an examination of some definitional issues pertaining to the terms *bank* and *financial institution* in Zambia's Banking and Financial Services Act 1994. Elsewhere, I have examined in greater detail the common law position on what constitutes a bank and banking business.[67] Because of a lack of space here, I will not repeat that discussion, although the reader is encouraged to refer to some of my published work on the subject.[68]

2.1. SOME NOTABLE DEFINITIONAL ISSUES

In 2000, the Zambian parliament passed the Banking and Financial Services (Amendment) Act 2000 to amend the Banking and Financial Services Act 1994. Section 3 of the Banking and Financial Services Act 1994, as amended in 2000, provides that the act applies to 'all banks and financial institutions, whether or not constituted by any Act: provided that the requirements of this Act are not binding on the Bank of Zambia, except in so far as this Act expressly imposes a duty on that Bank.'

As noted in the following text, the statutory terms *bank* and *financial institution* in the Banking and Financial Services Act 1994 refer, respectively, to a legal person and an unincorporated association.[69] Examples of unincorporated associations in Zambia include partnerships.[70] Further, section 5 of the Zambian Companies Act 1994 provides that

1. Subject to this section, an association or partnership that—

    a. consists of more that twenty persons; and
    b. is not a body corporate;

    shall not carry on any business for gain by the association or partnership or individual members of the association or partnership.

2. Subsection (1) shall not apply to a partnership—

    a. formed for the purpose of carrying on a prescribed profession or calling; and
    b. having not more than the number of partners prescribed for the purposes of that profession.

3. If an association or partnership contravenes this section, each member of the association or partnership shall be guilty of an offence, and shall be liable on conviction to a fine not exceeding five hundred monetary units.

Whereas originally, section 2(1) of Zambia's Banking and Financial Services Act 1994 provided that the term *bank* meant 'a company that held a banking licence', section 2(c) of Zambia's Banking and Financial Services (Amendment) Act 2000 provides that a bank is 'a company conducting banking business'. The definition of a bank has been broadened. What this means is that the possession of a banking licence by any institution does not on its own form the criterion for determining whether or not an institution is a bank. It is important to look at the business an institution does in order to determine if it is a bank. To that end, one may need to ask whether a particular institution is carrying out banking business—and, for that matter, what constitutes banking business?

The statutory definition of banking business in section 2(1) of the Banking and Financial Services Act 1994 has also been amended to broaden its scope. Originally, this statutory provision provided as follows:

> 'Banking business' means the business of receiving deposits from the public and the use of such deposits, either in whole or in part, for the account of and at the risk of the person carrying on the business, to make loans, advances or investments, and includes any custom, practice or activity prescribed by regulation as banking business.

The statutory provision that was referenced earlier did not provide an exhaustive list of activities to be considered as banking business. It left room for constructive ambiguity, permitting, in addition to the aforesaid activities, 'any custom, practice or activity prescribed by regulation as *banking business*' (italics added) to be taken as such. However, it was not clear which body or office had the statutory authority to prescribe by regulation that a particular practice or activity constituted banking business. Could the minister of finance use any one or more of the statutory powers in the Banking and Financial Services Act 1994 that allow him to pass subsidiary legislation,[71] or was it the central bank that was vested with the statutory power to prescribe by regulation what constituted banking business?

Further, under the Banking and Financial Services Act 1994, the term *banking business* did not involve only the business of receiving deposits from the public. The term also included the use of such deposits, either in whole or in part, to make loans, advances, or investments. Thus, for an activity to be regarded as banking business under the Banking and Financial Services Act 1994, such an activity had to involve both the receiving and the use of deposits, as explained earlier. It was not good enough that the activity related only to the receiving or use of the deposits. There had to be both the receiving and the use of the deposits.

When the Banking and Financial Services (Amendment) Act 2000 was passed to amend the Banking and Financial Services Act 1994, its section 2(c) introduced the following changes:

'Banking business' means any of the following:

a.   the business of receiving deposits from the public including chequing account and current account deposits and the use of such deposits, either in whole or in part, for the account of and at the risk of the person carrying on the business, to make loans, advances or investments;
b.   financial services; and
c.   any custom, practice or activity prescribed by the Bank of Zambia as banking business.

Although many aspects of the statutory definition of banking business in the Banking and Financial Services Act 1994[72] were retained in section 2(c) of the Banking and Financial Services (Amendment) Act 2000, the inclusion of the words *chequing account*, *current account*, and *financial services* in the amendment statute goes beyond the scope of the original statutory definition.[73] Section 2(c) of the Banking and Financial Services (Amendment) Act 2000 now introduces financial services[74] as a part of banking business, although, as shall be seen later,[75] the respective statutory definitions of financial services and financial services business do not include banking business.[76] It is important to observe that prior to the enactment of the Banking and Financial Services (Amendment) Act 2000, the Banking and Financial Services Act 1994 did not include financial services in its statutory provision for banking business.[77] After the enactment of the Banking and Financial Services (Amendment) Act 2000, the determination of what constitutes a custom or practice of banking business shifted to become a responsibility of the Bank of Zambia. The minister of finance no longer has statutory powers to pass subsidiary legislation related to such matters.

A financial institution is described in section 2 of the Banking and Financial Services Act 1994[78] as 'a person other than a bank, conducting financial services business.' In the same statutory provision, however, a financial institution's licence is described as 'a licence under section 10 of the statute'; section 10 reads, 'a licence authorising the applicant to conduct any financial services business'. But, what is financial services business? The term is described in section 2 of the Banking and Financial Services Act 1994[79] as 'the business of performing or offering to perform any financial services to the public, *but does not include banking business*' (italics added).[80] The term *financial services* is defined in section 2 of the Banking and Financial Services (Amendment) Act 2000 as

> any one or more of the following services: (a) commercial or con-sumer financing services; (b) credit reference services; (c) deposit brokering; (d) factoring, with or without recourse; (e) financial leasing or finance leasing; (f) financing of commercial transac-tions, including forfaiting; (g) the issue and administration of credit cards, debit cards, travellers' cheques or bankers' drafts; (h) the issue of guarantees, performance bonds or letters of credit; (i) lending on the security of, or dealing in, mortgage or any inter-est in real property; (j) merchant banking services; (k) money transfer or transmission services or the payment of cheques or other demand payment orders drawn or issued by customers and payable from deposits held by the payer; (l) purchase and sale of foreign exchange; (m) issuance of debentures and money market instruments and the acceptance of six months (or such other period as prescribed by the Bank of Zambia) term deposits, other than current accounts and chequing deposits; (n) issuance of building society and mutual society shares, having characteristics simi-lar or identical to those of deposits; (o) venture capital funding; (p) secured or unsecured credit services; (q) any other services as the Bank of Zambia may designate, but does not include—(i) the underwriting, marketing or administration of contracts of insur-ance; or (ii)) any service excluded from the scope of this defini-tion by a provision of this Act or by the Bank of Zambia under this Act.

Before I delve into the intricacies of company law in Zambia, I will first examine the *ultra vires* doctrine in the United Kingdom because, as established earlier, the English common law is a major source of law in Zambia.[81] The focus here is on the *ultra vires* doctrine as it applies to company law and not administrative law. The following discussion is intended to provide a helpful background against which the efficacy of certain aspects of Zambian company law is analysed.

2.2. The Ultra Vires Doctrine under the English Common Law

Views have been expressed that in company law, the *ultra vires* doctrine refers to those acts attempted by a company that are beyond the scope of powers granted by the company's charter or in a clause in its memorandum of association.[82] Other documents that grant the company the capacity to pursue business objects can be found in the laws authorizing the company's formation. Commenting on the *ultra vires* doctrine, Davies observed,

> *Ultra vires* is a Latin expression which lawyers and civil servants use to describe acts undertaken beyond (*ultra*) the legal powers (*vires*) of those who have purported to undertake them. In this sense its application extends over a far wider area than company law. For example, those advising a Minister on proposed subordinate legislation will have to ask themselves whether the enabling primary legislation confers *vires* to make the desired regulations. In its application to bodies of persons, *ultra vires* is habitually used in three different senses which ought to be kept distinct. When used in the strict sense, essentially what is in question is whether the body as such has capacity to act. Unless the body is incorporated, and thus has a personality distinct from its members, this question will normally not arise; the body is simply an association of human beings all or most of whom will have full capacity. Hence *ultra vires* in this sense does not arise in relation to partnerships. And the early case of *Sutton's Hospital*[83] is generally taken to have established that it also has no application to chartered corporations despite the fact that they do have a legal personality distinct from that of their members.[84]

Addressing the case of chartered corporations, Davies went on to say,

In these cases the only question is whether those have acted are deemed to be authorized to do so in accordance with the normal agency principles ... Nevertheless, it is customary to say that when those so acting (for example, the governing body) have exceeded their authority they have acted *ultra vires*. Thirdly, the courts have an unfortunate habit of describing as *ultra vires* any activity which a company cannot lawfully undertake (for example one which infringes the capital maintenance provisions...).[85]

From a policy point of view, the *ultra vires* doctrine arose historically due to two main reasons.[86] First, shareholders who invested money in a company were entitled to see that the money was applied 'for the purposes for which they were presumably induced to invest and not to see it dissipated in uncontemplated ventures.'[87] Second, those people who advanced credit to a company were entitled to rely on its creditworthiness so far as that could be ascertained from, inter alia, its statement of objects and powers.[88]

The *ultra vires* doctrine, it must be stressed, is a rule that is concerned with the capacity of the company.[89] It imposes artificial limitations on the acts and things which a company is regarded in law as being capable of doing.[90] To illustrate, in the English case of *Ashbury Rly Carriage & Iron Co Ltd v. Riche*,[91] a company was incorporated under the Act of 1862. Clause 3 of the memorandum provides as follows:

> The objects for which the company is established are to make and sell, or lend on hire, railway-carriages and waggons, and all kinds of railway plant, fittings, machinery, and rolling-stock; to carry on the business of mechanical engineers and general contractors; to purchase and sell, as merchants, timber, coal, metals, or other materials; and to buy and sell any such materials on commission, or as agents.

Clause 4 of the articles then states, 'An extension of the company's business beyond or for other than the objects or purposes expressed or implied in the memorandum of association shall take place only in pursuance of a special resolution.'

The company agreed to provide Riche and his brother with financing for the construction of a railway in Belgium. Later, the company decided to repudiate the agreement. When Riche sued it for damages, the company pleaded that it was *ultra vires* for it to enter into such a contract. In the lower courts, the argument centred mainly on whether the contract, though it was unauthorised, had been approved by the shareholders under clause 4. However, in the House of Lords, it was ruled that the contract was void and that ratification, even if it had taken place, would have been wholly ineffective. In this House of Lords ruling, one of the reasons why the court showed little sympathy to Riche and his brother, although it was not articulated in the speeches of their lordships, could be that it had by then been established that persons who dealt with a company should discover for themselves the contents of the memorandum and articles of association.[92]

A leading authority on this point is the case of *Re Jon Beauforte*.[93] In that English case, a company had been incorporated with an objects clause that authorised the company to carry on business as a maker of ladies' clothes, hats, and shoes. The company later decided to manufacture veneered panels. In the furtherance of this latter business, the company contracted with a builder to construct a factory, entered into a contract with a supplier of veneer, and ordered coke from a coke supplier to heat the factory. All three of these sources remained unpaid when the company went into liquidation and the liquidator rejected their proofs in the winding-up on the ground that the contracts were to further an *ultra vires* activity and were therefore void. In his ruling, Roxburgh J. upheld the liquidator's contentions. The rejection of the coke supplier's proof was 'particularly harsh, since whereas the builder conceded that the contract was *ultra vires*, the coke supplier was unaware of the purpose for which the coke would be used and it could easily have been used to further legitimate objects.' But, as Roxburgh J. pointed out, 'they had received orders for the coke on letter-head notepaper which made it clear that the company was now a veneer panel manufacturer and the objects clause, of which the coke supplier would have constructive notice, did not authorise the company to carry on this business.'[94]

Commenting on the *Re Jon Beauforte*[95] case, Goulding acknowledged the 'justification' put forward by Roxburgh J. that the letterhead notepaper made it clear that the company was a veneer panel manufacturer and that there was also constructive notice that the objects clause did not authorise the company to carry on the business of dealing in coke. However, he noted, if a contract was void for being *ultra vires*, then notice on the part of the third party, whether it was actual or constructive, was irrelevant to the result.[96]

Goulding observed further that the problem of the *ultra vires* doctrine was exacerbated by the fact that the objects clause could be altered only within certain specified limits and in any event not so as to affect retrospectively any transaction which was in question.[97] 'It could prove to have disastrous consequences for a person dealing with a company who was in good faith and was totally innocent apart from failing to obtain and interpret the company's objects clause.'[98] Thus,

> companies responded to the *ultra vires* doctrine by drafting very wide and lengthy objects clauses which attempted to include every conceivable form of commercial activity.[99] Eventually the Court of Appeal was even prepared to give effect to a clause which provided that the company could 'carry on any other trade or business whatsoever which can, in the opinion of the board of directors, be advantageously carried on by the company in connection with or as ancillary to any of the above businesses or the general business of the company' and held that a particular transaction was *intra vires* even though it had no objective connection with a relationship to the company's main business.[100,101]

There are some acts, as Sealy observed, which by nature a company or any other kind of corporation simply cannot perform (e.g., marrying or committing the crime of rape).[102] In addition to these natural limitations on a company's capacity, the company is also to be regarded as being incapable of doing anything which is not within the scope of its objects clause or reasonably incidental thereto.[103] The doctrine, in other words, as Sealy observed,

> restricted the powers of the company to matters covered by its stated objects, and any act which was outside those objects was not simply beyond the authority of the directors as a corporate organ, but beyond the capacity of the company itself—in the eyes of the law a nullity, having no effect whatever. It followed that not even the unanimous decision of the shareholders could authorise or ratify such an act, as the House of Lords established in the leading case of *Ashbury Rly Carriage & Iron Co Ltd v Riche* in 1875.[104]

Although in general, the *ultra vires* doctrine is intended to confine the activities of a company within its stated objects, it necessarily has had the effect also of restricting the company's powers.[105] But, in reality, the distinction between the objects and the powers of a company is not an easy one to make. In *A–G v. Great Eastern Rly Co.*,[106] the House of Lords made the concession that a company should be deemed to have the implied powers to do anything that is reasonably incidental to its declared objects. That said, it has long been recognised that not all of the contents of the objects clause provide for separate, free-standing objects which constitute the purposes for which the company was formed.[107] In *Cotman v. Brougham*,[108] there were powers which were ancillary in the sense that they were present to support the substantive objects of the company. It could be argued that other examples of ancillary powers include the power for a company to borrow money or give guarantees.[109] In the past, the English courts have accepted the existence of such ancillary powers as long as these powers are fairly incidental to achieving the company's objects.[110] Indeed,

> it was at first held that even if express powers were used to further an *ultra vires* purpose, the exercise of the power itself was *ultra vires*. For example, borrowing money to fund an activity not stated in the objects clause.[111] But the most recent cases, most

notably *Rolled Steel Products (Holdings) Ltd v. British Steel Corp*, narrowed the scope of *ultra vires* and held that the use of an express power could not be beyond the capacity of the company but rather it was an act done in excess or abuse of the powers of the company.[112] The practical difference of this finding was that an act which was *ultra vires* the company was void and a nullity irrespective of the notice of the third-party, whereas an act done in excess or abuse of the company's powers was unenforceable only if the third party had notice of this fact. Further, an *ultra vires* act could not be ratified by the shareholders whereas an act done in excess or abuse of powers could be.[113,114]

As far back as 1945, recommendations for the reform of the law that was applicable to the *ultra vires* doctrine in the United Kingdom had started gaining ground.[115] Views had been expressed through the Cohen Committee that the *ultra vires* doctrine served 'no positive purpose' and was 'a cause of unnecessary prolixity and vexation.'[116] According to Goulding,

> The Jenkins Committee also recommended reform, but only to provide protection for third parties contracting with companies in good faith.[117] No action was taken on these recommendations until the UK became a member state of the EEC and was required to implement the First Directive of Company Law. This reform of the law was originally contained in s. 9(2) of the European Communities Act 1972 and subsequently became s. 35 of the 1985 Act. But a number of difficulties came to light, and after a report was produced by Dr. Prentice for the DTI,[118] a much more thorough reform was implemented. This is now contained in ss. 35, 35A, 35B 322A and 711A of the 1985 Act as substituted and provided by the 1989 Act.[119]

> Article 9(1) of the first EEC Directive on Company Law 1972 stipulated that

> acts done by the organs of the company shall be binding upon it, even if those acts are not within the objects of the company, unless such acts exceed the powers that the law confers or allows to be conferred on those organs.

The United Kingdom's domestication of article 9(1) of the first EEC Directive on Company Law came through the enactment of sections 35 and 35B of the English Companies Act 1985.[120] According to Rose,

> The *ultra vires* doctrine became less of a protection for members and creditors and more of an obstacle that might have arisen unexpectedly to invalidate an apparently *intra vires* transaction. Following Prentice's D.T.I. Consultative Document 'Reform of the *Ultra Vires* Rule' (1986), it was, therefore, effectively abolished by the C.A. 1989 (substituting C.A. 1985, ss. 35–35B). The stated objects in the memorandum may, therefore, be specific and detailed (statement of a wide range of objects was formerly a useful way of avoiding the limitations of the *ultra vires* doctrine). However, the memorandum may state that the object of the company is to carry on business as a general commercial company, in which case the object of the company is to carry on any trade or business whatsoever and the company has power to do all such things as are incidental or conducive to the carrying on of any trade or business by it (C.A. 1985, s.3A).[121]

With the enactment and coming into force of the relevant provisions of the English Companies (Amendment) Act 1989, the *ultra vires* doctrine was effectively preserved only for the internal purposes of the company.[122] It was used as a means of enabling the shareholders to control the activities of the company directors.[123] In line with section 35 of the English Companies Act 1985, the directors had to observe any limitations on the powers of the company as stipulated in the company's constitution. Section 35A stated that if the directors acted in excess of the said powers and in excess of their authority, a third party could only enforce the resulting transaction if it were in good faith.

On 8 November 2006, a new legislative framework for company law was introduced in the United Kingdom.[124] The U.K. Companies Act 2006 received royal assent on the date,[125] and some major changes were made to English company law.[126] As noted in the earlier parts of this chapter,[127] sections 31 and 39 of the U.K. Companies Act 2006 greatly reduce the applicability of the *ultra vires* doctrine to company law in the United

Kingdom. The doctrine continues to apply in relation to charities,[128] and a shareholder can also apply for an injunction—in advance only—to prevent an act which is claimed to be *ultra vires*.[129] Sulkowski and Greenfield observed that the *ultra vires* doctrine has historically allowed 'a shareholder to sue to prevent a company from engaging in an activity outside of the specific parameters of its corporate charter.'[130] This view is echoed in an exception to the general rule in *Foss v. Harbottle*,[131] which allowed for an individual shareholder to bring a derivative action on behalf of the company to prevent the company directors from committing the company to an *ultra vires* action.[132]

Section 31 of the U.K. Companies Act 2006, dealing with the statement of a company's objects, provides for a novel approach to the subject. Under the Companies Act 1985, all companies were required to have objects, and these objects were to be specified in the memorandum of association.[133] The Companies Act 1985 also made provisions for a company to be specific about its objects when the company was going to be carrying on business as a general commercial company (see section 3A of the 1985 act).[134] However, based on a recommendation of the Company Law Review[135] (*Final Report*, paragraph 9.10), the Companies Act 2006 provided a different approach.[136] Instead of companies being required to specify their objects,

> companies will have unrestricted objects unless the objects are specifically restricted by the articles (see subsection (1)). This will mean that unless a company makes a deliberate choice to restrict its objects, the objects will have no bearing on what it can do. Some companies will continue to restrict their objects. Companies that are charities will need to restrict their objects (under charities legislation) and some community interest companies may also choose to do so.[137]

Section 39 of the U.K. Companies Act 2006 provides that the validity of a company's acts is not to be questioned on the ground of a lack of capacity related to anything in a company's constitution.[138] This statutory provision replaces subsections 35(1) and 35(4) of the

English Companies Act 1985, which made a similar provision for the restrictions of capacity that are contained in the memorandum of association.[139] However, section 39 of the U.K. Companies Act 2006 does not contain provisions corresponding to subsections 35(2) and 35(3) of the English Companies Act 1985. These provisions are considered to be unnecessary in light of the facts that the U.K. Companies Act 2006 allows a company to have unrestricted objects (and when it has restricted objects, the directors' powers are correspondingly restricted) and that its section 171 provides a specific duty for directors to abide by the company's constitution.[140] Subsection 2 of section 39 of the Companies Act 2006 indicates that that section, like section 35 of the English Companies Act 1985, is modified in its application to charities.[141]

Finally, section 40 of the U.K. Companies Act 2006 restates sections 35A and 35B of the English Companies Act 1985 and provides safeguards for a person who is dealing with a company in good faith.[142] The power of the directors to bind the company, or to authorise others to do so, is deemed not to be constrained by the company's constitution.[143] This means that a third party that is dealing with a company in good faith need not concern itself about whether a company is acting within its constitution.[144] Under the U.K. Companies Act 2006, subsection (2)(b)(i) of section 40 replaces part of section 35B of the English Companies Act 1985, stating that

> an external party is not bound to enquire whether there are any limitations on the power of the directors. The first limb of section 35B (which refers to the memorandum) has not been carried forward. This is concerned with restrictions in a company's constitution that limit a company's ability to act and consequently the powers of the directors to bind the company (the so called 'ultra vires rule'). Under the UK's Companies Act 2006, the objects no longer affect the company's capacity to act and so this limb is not necessary.[145]

A moot question remains, however: What does the statutory phrase 'dealing with a company in *good faith*' (italics added) mean?[146] The concept of good faith may have different meanings to different people. However, in day-to-day ordinary parlance, the term *good faith* may be understood as simply complying with some standards of decency and honesty.

Keily argued that good faith is not a principle which can be adequately defined; it has been described vaguely as a rechristening of the fundamental principles of contract law and as a phrase that has no general meaning but which operates to exclude various forms of bad faith.[147] Good faith is also seen as a discretionary standard that prevents parties from recapturing opportunities that were foregone when contracting.[148] In addition, good faith has been compared with unconscionability, 'fairness, fair conduct, reasonable standards of fair dealing, decency, reasonableness, decent behaviour, a common ethical sense, a spirit of solidarity, community standards of fairness',[149] and 'honesty in fact'—indicating that good faith is an extremely versatile concept.[150] Commenting on good faith, Keily observed,

> Its versatility is an essential characteristic because, as stated by Aristotle, 'there are some cases for which it is impossible to lay down a law, so that a special ordinance becomes necessary. For what is itself indefinite can only be measured by an indefinite standard.' However, good faith is not an obligation to act altruistically. Regretfully, Lücke writes, 'one must leave the universal adoption of such a noble motive to some far-distant and much more enlightened age.' Good faith does not require the abandoning of self-interest as the governing motive in contractual relations. However, it may prevent a party from abusing a legal right.[151]

Having examined the *ultra vires* doctrine in the United Kingdom, I now turn to examine the *ultra vires* doctrine in Zambia.

2.3. THE *ULTRA VIRES* DOCTRINE IN ZAMBIA'S COMPANY LAW

I have already established that in the United Kingdom, the coming into force of the provisions of the English Companies (Amendment) Act 1989 related to the *ultra vires* doctrine meant that that doctrine was effectively preserved only for the internal purposes of companies.[152] Further, it was established that the enactment of the U.K. Companies Act 2006 saw the retention of a number of statutory provisions of the English Companies Act 1985 regarding the *ultra vires* doctrine.[153] It was also pointed out that sections 31 and 39 of the U.K. Companies Act 2006 greatly reduce the applicability of the *ultra vires* doctrine to company law in the United Kingdom. However, the doctrine continues to apply in relation to charities, and a shareholder, as established earlier, can apply for an injunction—in advance only—to prevent an act which is claimed to be *ultra vires*.[154]

In contrast to the position in the United Kingdom, the Zambian Companies Act 1994 presents some interesting challenges. With regard to the *ultra vires* doctrine, the relevant provisions of the Zambian Companies Act 1994 are not drafted in an intelligible manner. By reading the statute alone, it is not immediately clear whether the *ultra vires* doctrine has been abolished through its enactment. Indeed, it is not clear what the legal and policy bases are for doing away with the statutory requirement that companies incorporated under Zambia's Companies Act 1994, such as banks and financial institutions, have a memorandum of association. Section 7 of the Companies Act 1994 merely states that

1. A company may have articles regulating the conduct of the company.
2. The articles *may* contain restrictions on the business that the company may carry on.
3. Where a provision in the articles is inconsistent with this Act or any other written law, the provision is invalid to the extent of the inconsistency.
4. The articles of a company may adopt the regulations of the Standard Articles, or any specified regulations thereof.
5. The articles of a public company or a private company limited by shares shall be deemed to have adopted the regulations of the Standard Articles except insofar as the articles exclude or modify those regulations.

6. The articles of a company shall be divided into paragraphs numbered consecutively. (italics added)

There is nothing in the statute to indicate why the provision for a memorandum of association was dropped. Section 8 of the Companies Act 1994 continues,

1. Subject to this Act, and to its articles, a company may amend its articles if it passes a special resolution approving the amendment.
2. If a company passes a special resolution approving the amendment of its articles, it shall within twenty-one days after the date of the resolution lodge a copy of the resolution with the Registrar together with a copy of each paragraph of the articles affected by the amendment, in its amended form.
3. The articles have effect in their amended form on and from the day of their lodgment with the Registrar or such later date as may be specified in the resolution.
4. If a company fails to comply with subsection (2), the company, and each officer in default, shall be guilty of an offence, and shall be liable on conviction to a fine not exceeding three monetary units for each day that the failure continues.

In 2008, the Supreme Court of Zambia passed a ruling confirming, in part, that the *ultra vires* doctrine still applies to company law in Zambia.[155] In the Zambian case of *Freshint Ltd and Others v. Kawambwa Tea Company*,[156] (PW2) Hemant Kumar Jalan (the second plaintiff), a director of both Freshint Limited (the first plaintiff), and Kawambwa Tea Company Limited (the defendant company), negotiated for a loan of US$100,000 from Thompson Lloyd and Ewart Limited (the third plaintiff on behalf of the defendant company). The loan was duly advanced to the defendant company. The condition under which the loan was granted was that the defendant company was to export its tea through the third plaintiff. The loan was to be recovered from the proceeds of the exported tea. The guarantor of this loan was the second plaintiff. The defendant company was, however, put under receivership. George Sokota and Nobert H. C. Chiromo were appointed joint receivers/managers by HSBC, which was owed some money by the defendant company. The receivership was as a result of the floating charge, dated 26 June 2000, that was created between the defendant company and HSBC.

The loan of US$100,000 was not repaid by the defendant company. The receiver/managers acknowledged the loan, but they refused to repay it to Thompson Lloyd and Ewart. The loan was, however, paid off by Freshint Limited as per the memorandum of understanding between the second plaintiff and the third plaintiff. The documents relating to this loan were signed by the second plaintiff on behalf of the defendant. The plaintiff's first witness, one Edward Kenneth Clive Foster, confirmed the payment of the loan by Thompson Lloyd and Ewart to the third plaintiff. The second plaintiff made a personal guarantee for the full payment of the loan on 22 November 2000.

The defendant company called one witness (DW1) Nallan Chakravarty Narasimhan, its financial director. Narasimhan stated that the defendant was a stranger to the documents purporting to be a memorandum of understanding between the second plaintiff and the third plaintiff. At the time the document was executed by the parties, the defendant company was already under the receivership of Sokota and Chiromo. On examining the documents that were held by the defendant company, Narasimhan observed that the US$100,000 loan which was obtained through the loan agreement dated 28 November 2000 had not in fact been applied to purchase machinery or as working capital for the defendant company. The defendant company was forced to carry out some investigations against the second plaintiff and other codirectors for the breach of their fiduciary duties to maintain its assets' value or to advance its commercial interests. The records further revealed that the defendant company had paid a total sum of US$265,558 from its tea export sales to third parties from which the defendant company derived no benefits.

Making reference in passing to the common law rule in *Turquand*'s case[157] as well as to the Zambian case of *Zambia Bata Shoe Company v. Vin-Mas Limited*,[158] the Supreme Court of Zambia ruled that

> in this instant case now before us we are not satisfied that the 2nd plaintiff acted with the authority given to him by the defendant company. He acted without authority hence his failure to produce evidence to that effect. It was not for the defendant company to prove that it had, in fact, not given him such power. Since this was a pleaded issue in its defence it was for the plaintiffs to have been on guard to prove that the 2nd plaintiff had in fact acted within the authority given to him. The defendant company adduced sufficient evidence through its witness who said the loan was not used for the purpose it was obtained. As he acted without authority from the company the loan agreement he entered into, purportedly on behalf of the defendant, was therefore 'ultra vires' and so it was not binding on the defendant. The trial Judge was therefore on firm ground when he so found. The plea of subrogation did not apply here and so it fails.[159]

Although one might think that the Supreme Court of Zambia should have explored also the possibility of a *Quistclose* trust in this case of *Freshint Ltd and Others v. Kawambwa Tea Company*,[160] there was hardly any reference, obiter dictum or otherwise, to the concept.[161]

Some views have been expressed, however, that the drafting of the Zambian Companies Act 1994 has benefited from some models of parallel legislation in different jurisdictions such as New Zealand.[162] Also, as observed earlier, it has been asserted that a primary goal of enacting the Zambian Companies Act 1994 was to simplify the process and procedures for incorporating a company in Zambia.[163] To that end and in the light of the ruling in *Freshint Ltd and Others v. Kawambwa Tea Company*,[164] although the original intent of the legislative draftsman in dropping from the Zambian Companies Act 1994 the requirement for incorporators to furnish a company's memorandum of association at incorporation was to abolish the *ultra vires* doctrine,[165] the doctrine has not been abolished and continues to apply to company law in Zambia.[166]

Following are a number of theses premised on the view that this doctrine still applies to company law in Zambia.

Thesis 1

The *ultra vires* doctrine continues to apply to Zambia because Form II in the Companies (Prescribed Forms) Regulations[167] requires the incorporators of a private company to submit to the registrar of companies a completed form bearing, inter alia, a summary statement regarding the principal business of the company. An underpinning but misleading assumption inherent in this statutory provision is that every individual incorporating a company has the competence and skill to spell out accurately and sufficiently a summary statement regarding the principal and other businesses of the company[168] or/and that, as shall be seen in the following pages, some restrictions or limitations on the objects and powers will obviously be imbedded in the articles of association. But, does the Zambian Companies Registry (PACRO) have the capacity to scrutinise all of this information to ensure that the incorporators of private companies provide sufficient and accurate information in Form II as well as in the articles of association? A view has been expressed that given the laxity in some quarters of the Companies Registry, it is quite likely that some incorporators of companies do not always document sufficiently and accurately this type of information and that this weakness presents a challenge.[169]

> Section 9(1)(a) of the Zambian Companies Act 1994 provides that
>
> an application for incorporation shall be accompanied by a statutory declaration that the requirements of this Act in respect of registration and of matters precedent and incidental thereto have been complied with, made by: (a) a *legal practitioner* having a practising certificate who was engaged in the formation of the company. (italics added)

It is not immediately clear that the legal practitioner described in this section has to personally draft the summary statement in Form II of the

Companies (Prescribed Forms) Regulations[170] regarding the business of the company. It appears that all that is required is for the legal practitioner to make a statutory declaration that there has been some compliance with the law and that he or she was in some manner—remotely or otherwise—involved in the incorporation of the company.

In cases where a company has already been incorporated and then there happens to be some irregularity affecting the articles of association—for example, in regard to the manner in which the directors have taken a particular decision that affects a bona fide third party that is dealing with the company—the Supreme Court of Zambia, sitting in the case of *Zambia Bata Shoe Company v. Vin-Mas Limited*,[171] ruled that

> in practice most people dealing with companies rely on the rule in *Turquand*'s case and do not bother to inspect the articles. Applying the fiction of constructive notice both the vendor and the purchaser were aware of the need for a special resolution and the binding contract for sale was entered into on that basis. The company's authorized agents bound the company to comply with the contract and such liability cannot be avoided.[172]

The Zambian Companies Act 1994 does not have any statutory provisions requiring the incorporators of a company to furnish the registrar of companies with a memorandum of association—in which document, as was the case under the repealed Companies Act 1921 of Zambia, the objects clause would be stipulated. However, it has been argued that the provision of such information by an incorporator in Form II of the Companies (Prescribed Forms) Regulations[173] suffices for the purpose of stating the company's business in a simplified manner.[174] In short, Form II, like Forms I, III, and IV, is said to serve the same function that a statutory requirement for an objects clause in the memorandum of association would serve in those common law jurisdictions with such statutory provisions.[175]

There are a number of shortcomings associated with this argument. First, although Form I deals with public companies, Form II deals only with private companies that have share capital. Yet, section 6 of the

Companies Act 1994 allows also for the incorporation of companies limited by guarantee. Such companies can be only private companies because section 14 of the Companies Act 1994 and Form I in the Companies (Prescribed Forms) Regulations[176] both stipulate that a public company must have share capital. In essence, what this means is that Form II does not cover a private company limited by guarantee. These companies are instead covered separately by Form III.

Second, Form II does not cover unlimited companies, though such companies are required, like private companies with share capital, to have share capital and articles of association.[177] Unlimited companies are, however, covered separately by Form IV.

Third, the relevant section of Form II (including Forms I, III, and IV, respectively) is drafted in such a way that a company can have a broad set of objects or multiple unrelated objects. The section reads as follows:

2. General nature of business:

    a. Principal business:...
    b   Other business:...

3.* The articles do not restrict the business that the company may conduct
    OR
    *The articles restrict the business that the company may conduct as follows:...
    *Delete whichever is not applicable.

The asterisk is a reflection of section 7(2) of the main statute—that is, the Zambian Companies Act 1994—which provides that 'the articles *may* contain restrictions on the business that the company may carry on.' Additionally, section 22(1) of the Companies Act 1994 states that 'a company shall have, subject to this Act and to such limitations as are inherent in its corporate nature, the capacity, rights, powers and privileges of an individual.'[178] I have described earlier Sealy's view that there are some acts which by nature a company or any other kind of corporation simply cannot perform.[179] This view is reflected in section 22(1) of the Zambian Companies Act 1994.[180]

Section 22(3) of the Zambian Companies Act 1994 provides that 'a company shall not carry on any business or exercise any power that it is restricted by its articles from carrying on or exercising, nor exercise any of its powers in a manner contrary to its articles.'

In contrast, section 23 of that same statute provides that no act of a company, including any transfer of property to or by a company, will be invalid by reason only that the act or transfer is contrary to the company's articles or the Companies Act 1994. It appears that these two statutory provisions, namely, sections 22(3) and 23, contradict each other. Let me take a reasoned look.

Whereas section 22(3) requires a company to avoid engaging in business that is prohibited by its articles of association, section 23 says that where a company engages in an act that is prohibited by its articles, such an act will not be considered invalid even though the act is prohibited by the company's articles of association. So, what is the purpose of section 22(3) if a company can engage in conduct that is prohibited by its articles of association and yet that conduct will still be valid in spite of the company's transgression? Mindful that under the Companies Act 1994 there is no requirement or provision for a company to have a memorandum of association, I am inclined to think that the purpose of section 23 is not to preempt or water down section 22(3). Rather, the articles of association are no longer just a contract between the shareholders and the company and amongst the shareholders themselves. But, under the Companies Act 1994, the articles of a company can also regulate some of the functions that were previously regulated by the memorandum of association under the repealed Companies Act 1921. One of those functions is captured in section 22(3) of the Companies Act 1994, regarding the prohibition for a company not to carry on business or exercise powers that it is restricted by its articles of association from carrying on or exercising. Against this background, section 23 of the Companies Act 1994 seeks only to protect bona fide third parties that have given value to the company where unscrupulous or fraudulent directors of a company decide that the company will not honour its side of the deal because the business at stake infringes upon the company's articles. Without section 23, some dubious companies would be engaging in all sorts of businesses that are not provided for in their articles of association. These companies would be collecting money from unsuspecting bona fide customers and thereafter refusing either to deliver goods or to provide services to the purchasers. In such situations, it is expected that the defaulting company would argue that the contract is outside its articles of association and should thus not be honoured. So, section 23 of the Companies Act 1994 does not contradict section 22(3), but merely qualifies it.

Another thorny issue in Zambia's Companies Act 1994, regarding the *ultra vires* doctrine, can be found in section 7(5). Whereas under section 7(1) of the Companies Act 1994, there is no mandatory requirement for a company to have articles of association (i.e., because the said section 7(1) uses the word *may* in the requirement for a company to adopt articles of association), section 7(5) of the Companies Act 1994 states that the articles of association of a public company or private company limited by shares will be deemed to have adopted the regulations of the standard articles in the Companies Act 1994, except insofar as the company's articles exclude or modify those regulations. But, section 7(5) applies only to public companies and private companies limited by shares, and it does not create a mandatory requirement for all companies to have articles of association. A possible explanation for restricting the application of section 7(5) to public companies and private companies limited by shares is that the rights and duties of shareholders of such companies are often attached to the respective classes of shares in the company's share capital and are expected to be found in the company's articles. This feature is in contrast to companies limited by guarantee that have no share capital, but have only guarantees provided by the various members of the company. Indeed, those guarantees do not have to adopt the regulations of the standard articles in the Companies Act 1994. There is no share capital, and there are no classes of shares to talk about.

Notwithstanding the foregoing, the provision for 'other business' in Form II in the Companies (Prescribed Forms) Regulations can indeed mean anything but illegal or unlawful objects. To that end, how is one to tell the extent of the limitation on the objects to which the company directors can commit the company if the relevant section of Form II on 'other business' refers to a whole range of issues and the articles of association do not place a restriction on the objects? What would happen if, without spelling out in the articles of association any limitations or restrictions on the objects or powers, a resourceful individual were to come up with a clause such as the following:

> to carry on any other trade or business whatsoever which can, in the opinion of the board of directors, be advantageously carried on by the company in connection with or as ancillary to any of the above businesses (*i.e.* the 'principal' business) or the general business of the company.

In terms of distinguishing between a power and an object, how easy is it for company directors to determine the extent of the limitations on the power if the objects are so broadly defined and the articles do not place restrictions on the powers? It would appear that if there are no restrictions or limitations on the objects and the powers, it would not be easy to determine what objects could be deemed *ultra vires* for the company or what power could be deemed to exceed the powers of the directors. In that sense, it is doubtful that the *ultra vires* doctrine can be invoked successfully under the circumstances stated earlier.

Thesis 2
The second thesis is that where a public company is being incorporated, one should be mindful that Form I in the Companies (Prescribed Forms) Regulations bears great resemblance to Form II. Form II has already been discussed.[181] So, the arguments that were presented earlier in relation to Form II apply mutatis mutandis to Form I and in regard to public companies.

Thesis 3

Third, when a company limited by guarantee is being incorporated, Form III should be completed. When an unlimited company is being incorporated, Form IV should be completed. Both of these forms bear great resemblance to Form II. Because I have already discussed Form II,[182] the arguments presented earlier in regard to Form II apply mutatis mutandis here.

Thesis 4

The fourth thesis is that those companies that were incorporated prior to the repeal of the Zambian Companies Act 1921 will continue to have a memorandum of association as well as an objects clause unless they decide to adapt to the framework of the Companies Act 1994 and do away with the memorandum of association and its attendant objects clause. If these companies retain their memorandum of association and the attendant objects clause, the *ultra vires* doctrine will apply as it did in the United Kingdom prior to the enactment of the English Companies Act 1985.

To illustrate, in a leading Zambian case, *J. P. Karnezos v. Hermes Safaris Limited*,[183] the plaintiff claimed from the defendant a sum of money for goods that had been sold and delivered. By an oral agreement with the manager of the defendant company, the defendant had agreed with the plaintiff to purchase burnt maize. Under the objects clause of the memorandum of association of the company, the goods the company could buy did not include burnt maize. It was contended by the defendant that the purchase of the burnt maize was not within the power of the company. Sakala J., sitting in the High Court of Zambia, ruled in favour of the defendant. His ruling was based on the following observations: (1) whether any given transaction is or is not within the powers of a company is a question of law depending on the construction to be placed on the objects clause of the memorandum of association, and (2) in construing any memorandum of association in which there are general words, care must be taken to construe those general words so as not to make them a trap for unwary people.[184] According to Sakala J., general words must be taken in connection with what are shown by the context to be the dominant or main objects of the company. In his ruling, Sakala J. noted the following:

> Before leaving this case, I wish only to observe that the facts of this case are a clear example of the hardship that the doctrine of *ultra vires* may cause to an unsuspecting third party dealing with a large company. It is in cases of this nature that I entirely agree with the suggestion of the Jenkins Committee (Cmnd, 1949–1962) recommending the virtual abolition of the doctrine and protection to third parties who might have acted reasonably in the circumstances. I hope that any future changes to the Companies Act will take into account the hardships caused by the doctrine of *ultra vires* and make provisions to modify it.[185]

However, when a company that was incorporated under Zambia's Companies Act 1921 decides to adapt to the framework of Zambia's Companies 1994, doing away with the memorandum of association and its attendant objects clause, that company will have to abide by the requirements that are set forth in the applicable Form I, II, III, or IV of the Companies (Prescribed Forms) Regulations. In that regard, the arguments that were presented under thesis 1 apply mutatis mutandis here.

2.4. DOES THE ULTRA VIRES DOCTRINE APPLY TO BANKS AND FINANCIAL INSTITUTIONS IN ZAMBIA?

Now that I have established the different circumstances under which the *ultra vires* doctrine applies to company law in Zambia, can this analysis be extended to banks and financial institutions that are licensed under the Banking and Financial Services Act 1994 because most of these entities are legal persons incorporated under the Companies Act 1994?[186] I pointed out at the beginning of this chapter that due to a lack of space, I will not draw any analogies about whether banks in the United Kingdom are affected by the *ultra vires* doctrine. The focus here, as established already, is on whether banks and financial institutions in Zambia should have an objects clause given that the Zambian

Companies Act 1994 does not require companies incorporated under that piece of legislation to have a memorandum of association.

Providing for the continuous existence of companies that were incorporated prior to the repeal of the Zambian Companies Act 1921, section 4 of the Zambian Companies Act 1994 states as follows:

> Subject to this Act, this Act applies to an existing company as if it had been duly incorporated under this Act as—
>
> a. a public company, if it was a public company under the former Act;
> b. a private company limited by shares, if it was a private company limited by shares under the former Act; or
> c. a company limited by guarantee, if it was a private company limited by guarantee under the former Act.[187]

The term *former Act* points to the repealed Zambian Companies Act 1921.[188] To ensure that the articles of association of companies that were incorporated prior to the repeal of the Companies Act 1921 are not inconsistent with the provisions of the Zambian Companies Act 1994, section 391 of the 1994 statute provides as follows:

1. An existing company shall be deemed to have, on and from the commencement of this Act, articles consisting of—

    a. those provisions of the memorandum of association and articles of association of the company, within the meaning of the former Act, which regulate the operation of the company and are not inconsistent with the former Act; and
    b. any provisions of Table A of the former Act which, under the former Act, applied to the company; whether or not the articles so deemed are consistent with this Act.[189]

The statutory provision continues,

2. The articles of an existing company under subsection (1) shall be valid, and this Act shall not apply to the company to the extent of any inconsistency with them, until—

    a.   the company adopts new articles in accordance with subsection (3); or

    b.   the last day of the first financial year of the company to commence after the commencement of this Act; whichever is earlier.

3.   An existing company shall, not later than the last day of the first financial year of the company to commence after the commencement of this Act, in accordance with section eight, adopt articles expressed in terms of and consistent with this Act.

4.   Where an existing company has lodged with the Registrar new articles for the purposes of subsection (3), the Registrar shall issue to the company—

    a.   a replacement certificate of incorporation; and

    b.   a replacement certificate of share capital, in the case of a company with share capital; worded to meet the circumstances of the case.

5.   An existing company shall not amend its articles unless, after the amendment, the articles are expressed in terms of and consistent with this Act.

6.   Until subsection (3) has been complied with, an existing company may satisfy the requirements of section twenty-nine in relation to the articles of the company and the certificate of share capital by supplying to a member a copy of its memorandum of association and articles of association within the meaning of the former Act.

7.   If an existing company fails to comply with subsection (3), the company, and each officer of the company in default, shall be guilty of an offence, and shall be liable on conviction to a fine not exceeding ten monetary units for each day that the failure continues.[190]

All in all, four major categories of companies can apply to the Bank of Zambia for a licence to operate as a bank or a financial institution.

The first category relates to companies that are incorporated under the 1921 Companies Act. The second category applies to companies that are incorporated under the 1994 Companies Act. The third category involves companies that are incorporated under the 1921 Companies Act but have adapted to the framework established by the Companies Act 1994. The fourth category pertains to a statutory body corporate, such as the Development Bank of Zambia, that is set up under a separate piece of legislation from the Companies Act 1994.[191]

It has already been established that unincorporated entities such as partnerships do not meet the statutory requirement of being a separate legal personality in order to get licensed under section 4(1) or section 10(1) of the Banking and Financial Services Act 1994.[192] In essence, banks and financial institutions in Zambia are subject to two main layers of regulation. The first layer relates to meeting the statutory requirements for a company to be incorporated under the Companies Act 1994. The second layer of regulation can be seen in the regulatory framework that was established pursuant to the Banking and Financial Services Act 1994, including the terms and conditions of licenses that are issued to banks and financial institutions. Linking the two layers is section 399 of the Companies Act 1994, which provides that nothing in the statute will abrogate or affect any special legislation, such as the Banking and Financial Services Act 1994, pertaining to companies carrying on the business of banking, insurance, or any other business.

In Zambia, for an entity to be licensed as a bank it must first be incorporated as a company under the Zambian Companies Act 1994.[193] The legislative framework that guides the incorporation of companies is the Zambian Companies Act 1994,[194] or in the case of companies that were incorporated prior to 1994, its predecessor, the repealed Zambian Companies Act 1921.[195] When a foreign company intends to conduct any type of business in Zambia, it has to meet the requirements of part 12 of the Zambian Companies Act 1994. Only then can a foreign company be eligible to be considered for a banking licence under Zambia's Banking and Financial Services Act 1994.[196]

In contrast, for an entity to be licensed as a financial institution under Zambia's Banking and Financial Services Act 1994, it need not necessarily be a company incorporated under the Zambian Companies Act 1994 or the repealed Zambian Companies Act 1921.[197] The entity can be a body corporate, a category that was created under a separate piece of legislation but is recognized by the Bank of Zambia as an acceptable form for a financial institution.[198] This additional option—allowing for a body corporate that is created under a separate piece of legislation but recognized by the Bank of Zambia—came about prior to the passing of the Banking and Financial Services (Amendment) Act 2000, when the central bank (i.e., the Bank of Zambia) faced insurmountable challenges in its attempt to subject the Development Bank of Zambia to its supervisory role.[199] The Development Bank of Zambia objected to such jurisdictional claims, arguing that it was a legal entity that had been created by the Development Bank of Zambia Act 1972,[200] a separate piece of legislation from that under which the BoZ operates as a banking regulator and supervisor, and that it was therefore not subject to the licensing, regulatory, or supervisory jurisdiction of the central bank.[201]

In this chapter, however, the focus is not on statutory bodies such as the Development Bank of Zambia but on those financial institutions that are incorporated as companies under the Zambian Companies Act 1994, including those foreign companies that are recognised as companies under part 12 of the act. At this point, cognisance should be made of the fact that the Zambian Companies Act 1994, like its predecessor, the repealed Zambian Companies Act 1921, is an independent piece of legislation from Zambia's Banking and Financial Services Act 1994.

In Zambia, banks and financial institutions, as incorporated companies,[202] are subject to the legal framework of the Companies Act 1994. In addition, they are subject to the legal framework of the Banking and Financial Services Act 1994 because they are licensed by the central bank, pursuant to provisions of the Banking and Financial Services Act 1994, to conduct business in the financial sector.[203] Indeed, whereas the registrar of banks and financial institutions,[204] in consultation with the minister of finance, has the statutory power to issue a licence or authorise a company to conduct banking or financial services business,[205] it is the central bank—that is, the Bank of Zambia—which is empowered by law to act as the competent authority for supervising banks.[206] However, the distinction is an artificial one because the registrar of banks and financial institutions is actually an officer of the Bank of Zambia.[207] As the Bank of Zambia points out on its website,

> To operate a bank in Zambia, it is a requirement that the bank be licensed by the Registrar of Banks and Financial Institutions ('the Registrar') whose office is based at the Bank of Zambia. The decision to licence the bank lies with the Registrar. The applicant must first submit its proposed name to the Registrar for clearance prior to making its application for a licence.[208]

The document goes on to add, 'Upon receipt of a complete application, the Bank of Zambia shall, within 180 days, review the application and determine whether a license should be granted to the applicant or not'.[209]

As a general rule, a person is not allowed to conduct or offer to conduct banking business unless he or she holds a licence for that purpose.[210] Similarly, a person other than a licensed bank or a licensed financial institution is prohibited from conducting or offering to conduct financial services business.[211] Banks and financial institutions are permitted to engage only in business that is covered by a banking license or a financial services licence as well as the statutory provisions of the Banking and Financial Services Act 1994.[212] So, what does this entail? Under the Banking and Financial Services Act 1994, can an *ultra vires* action or conduct of a bank or financial institution be construed as unsafe and unsound practice?[213] Given the broad definitions of financial services and banking business in the Banking and Financial Services Act 1994,[214] can it not be argued that the Banking and Financial Services Act 1994 has in principle introduced the concept of universal banking in Zambia? Indeed, where should one draw the line on what falls within or outside of the statutory definition of financial services? The same questions can be raised in relation to the statutory term *banking business*.

An opportunity arose in 2003 for the High Court of Zambia to examine critically the concept of unsafe and unsound practice under Zambia's Banking and Financial Services Act 1994, but the court missed its chance.[215] In the Zambian case of *Access Finance Services Limited and Access Leasing Limited v. Bank of Zambia*,[216] the central bank, the Bank of Zambia (BoZ), had taken over the possession of both Access Finance Services Limited (AFSL) and Access Leasing Limited (ALL) in early 2003.[217] The two companies were alleged to have been involved in criminal activities that included unsafe and unsound practices.[218] Contesting the decision of the BoZ, the applicants, AFSL and ALL, applied for judicial review to the High Court of Zambia.[219]

The applicants challenged the decision of the BoZ to place them into compulsory winding-up. The BoZ argued that both AFSL and ALL not only breached the law but also operated their businesses recklessly, prompting the bank to place them under liquidation. According to the BoZ, the two institutions were closed down on the grounds that they violated the Banking and Financial Services Act 1994 and other written laws and because they were insolvent.[220] The BoZ submitted before High Court Judge Japhet Banda that the wording of sections 81, 84(B), and 101 of Zambia's Banking and Financial Services Act 1994 made it clear that parliament left it to the BoZ to determine and establish the facts that might compel it to take supervisory actions against any bank or financial institution.[221] The BoZ contended that parliament had entrusted it to determine the insolvency or solvency of any financial institution as well as what action was necessary to enable the BoZ to carry out its functions under Zambia's Banking and Financial Services Act 1994.[222] The BoZ was also of the view that as a supervisory agency, it had exercised its powers properly upon examining the business activities and financial books of AFSL and ALL. According to the BoZ, 'It's not open to the applicants under judicial review application to challenge the merits of BoZ's decision. All they could do is to call into question the decision making process that BoZ followed.'[223]

The BoZ argued further that although as a supervisory agency, it did not prescribe the accounting systems and software packages that were to be used by banks and financial institutions, AFSL and ALL had engaged in obscure accounting practices that were designed to disguise the sources of funds that were attributed to certain credit accounts, thereby obstructing the audit trail.[224] According to the BoZ, AFSL and ALL had been using journal vouchers to post the receipt of funds to general accounts with confusing or misguiding narrations, and this practice 'was obviously contrary to the spirit of Zambia's Banking and Financial Services Act.'[225]

AFSL and ALL were quick to counterargue that the unsafe and unsound practices they had allegedly committed were not defined anywhere in Zambia's Banking and Financial Services Act 1994.[226] Indeed, section 77(1) of Zambia's Banking and Financial Services Act 1994 provides as follows:

> Where, in the opinion of the Bank of Zambia, a bank or financial institution is *committing* or *pursuing* or *is about to commit* or *pursue* on behalf of the bank or financial institution *any act* or *course of conduct* that is *considered by the Bank of Zambia as unsafe or unsound practice*, the Bank of Zambia may enter into one or more written agreements with the bank or financial institution or its board of directors to establish a programme of action to counteract the unsafe or unsound practice and to establish or maintain safe and sound practices in the conduct of the business of the bank or financial institution.[227] (italics added)

Section 77(1) does not provide a definition of unsafe and unsound practice but merely uses the term and highlights the steps that the BoZ should take whenever, at its discretion, it determines that an act or course of conduct of a particular bank or financial institution constitutes such behaviour.[228] Considering this, can an *ultra vires* action or conduct by a bank or financial institution be construed as unsafe and unsound practice?

Notwithstanding the submissions made by the parties to the *Access* case,[229] not much thought was accorded by the court to the concept of unsafe and unsound practice under Zambia's Banking and Financial Services Act 1994. In the United States, by contrast, the judiciary has often deferred to the expertise of bank regulatory agencies to define what constitutes unsafe and unsound practice, limiting the judiciary's review to a determination of whether the regulatory agency's action was arbitrary, capricious, or otherwise unsupported by substantial evidence in the record.[230]

In contrast, in the Zambian case of *Access Finance Services et al v. Bank of Zambia*,[231] Judge Banda merely alluded to section 77 of Zambia's Banking and Financial Services Act 1994 on pages J13 and J19 of his ruling. He did not explain, obiter dictum, what would constitute, for example, arbitrary or capricious action by a regulatory agency such as the BoZ or what would otherwise constitute an action that was unsupported by substantial evidence in the record. An order for certiorari was granted on the grounds that the BoZ had misdirected itself in determining that AFSL and ALL were insolvent and that the two companies should be placed under compulsory liquidation. However, the court did not address fully the issue of whether AFSL and ALL had engaged in unsafe and unsound practices that would have entitled the BoZ to take punitive or corrective measures against the two companies. Neither was the issue of whether the BoZ, as the bank regulator, had acted arbitrarily or capriciously addressed in greater detail.

No doubt it would have been helpful if the BoZ had in its policies or regulations promulgated some examples of unsafe and unsound practice. Such examples could have included tax evasion, money laundering, anticompetitive banking practices, predatory lending, insider lending, and the payment of excessive management fees. The BoZ should have made an effort to interpret the statutory term *unsafe and unsound practice* through, for example, a policy statement. Such a policy statement would not need to provide an exhaustive list of examples, but it should allow for constructive ambiguity so that the BoZ could, with time, include other incidents that were not listed as unsafe and unsound practice.

Turning back to the issue of a memorandum of association under the Zambian Companies Act 1994, I have already observed that the Companies Act 1994 neither forbids nor requires a company to have a memorandum of association. It was pointed out that the incorporators of a private

company must file with the Companies Registry (PARCO) a completed
Form II (or in the case of a public company, a completed Form I) to
incorporate the company.[232] Companies that intend to obtain a banking
license from the central bank have to furnish the Bank of Zambia with,
inter alia, the full particulars of the business that they propose to conduct
under the authority of the banking licence that is being sought.[233] Against
this background, can a bank or financial institution be licensed to conduct
banking business or financial services business even if such an entity
does not have a memorandum of association? From an economic point
of view, there is little incentive for an applicant for a banking licence to
have a memorandum of association because the applicant's line of business will already have been disclosed in Form II as well as in the particulars that are furnished to the Bank of Zambia in the application for a
banking license.[234] That said, it should be noted that both the Companies
Act 1994 and the Banking and Financial Services Act 1994 do not bar
or prohibit a bank or financial institution from having a memorandum of
association. Legally speaking, therefore, a bank or financial institution
can be licensed to conduct banking business or financial services business whether or not it has a memorandum of association. What, then, are
the implications of such innovations in Zambia's company and financial
services law?

One view is that because banks and financial institutions must be
incorporated lawfully as companies before they can be licensed under
the Banking and Financial Services Act 1994, these entities are under
no statutory obligation under Zambia's Companies Act 1994 to have a
memorandum of association. Therefore, they are less likely to have elab-
orately stated objects than mere short 'layman-like' summary statements
on Form I, II, III, or IV, whichever is applicable. That said, one is still
left to look at Forms I, II, III, and IV, depending on whether the entity
is a private company, a public company, a company limited by guarantee, or an unlimited company. Under Zambian company law, as noted
already, the information that is spelt out in Form I, II, III, or IV regarding
the principal business or the other business of the company cannot be
presumed through constructive notice.[235]

Prior to the enactment of the Banking and Financial Services (Amendment) Act 2000, an applicant for a banking licence under Zambia's Banking and Financial Services Act 1994 was required to provide the particulars of its memorandum and articles of association.[236] With the coming into force of the Banking and Financial Services (Amendment) Act 2000, that statutory requirement has been dropped. Today, a company applying for a banking licence is required to furnish the registrar of banks and financial institutions with, inter alia, the following items:

- its articles of association;
- the physical and postal address of its head office and the permanent residential addresses of its directors, chief executive officers, managers, and shareholders;
- the name and permanent residential address of every subscriber for any class or series of shares issued by the company in a number that exceeds 1 percent of all the shares of that class or series, whether such shares carry the right to vote in all circumstances or not;
- the full particulars of the business the company proposes to conduct under the authority of the banking licence that is being sought; and
- the amount of that company's capital.[237]

Elsewhere[238] and earlier in this book, I have argued that although the Zambian Companies Act 1994 requires a company to provide articles of association at incorporation, that statute neither prohibits nor requires a company to provide a memorandum of association at any time. The legal implications of this seemingly purposeful omission have been explored at some length.[239] Here, suffice it to say, between 1994 and 2000, the Banking and Financial Services Act 1994 required applicants for a banking or financial services license to furnish the registrar of banks and financial institutions with, inter alia, their memorandum of association, yet the Companies Act 1994 did not require these companies to have a memorandum of association. This anomaly was redressed only when the Banking and Financial Services (Amendment) Act 2000 was passed. Prior to the enactment of that amendment, the requirement for an applicant of a banking licence to provide a memorandum of association invited the following possible interpretations:

1. Although the Companies Act 1994 was (and still is) silent on whether or not a company must furnish a memorandum of association at incorporation, the requirement under the Banking and Financial Services Act 1994 directed an applicant for a banking licence to prepare a memorandum of association solely for the purposes of licensing and supervision.

2. Alternatively, it could be argued that the requirement under the Banking and Financial Services Act 1994 was meaningless because the Companies Act 1994, under which the company was incorporated, did not require a memorandum of association at incorporation or at any time thereafter.

After making a close examination of the law, it could be argued that the repealed licensing requirement that an applicant for a banking licence should provide a memorandum of association was meant solely for the purposes of facilitating the licensing and supervision of banks. There are three main reasons that support this view. First, the preamble of the Banking and Financial Services Act 1994 stresses the importance of providing safeguards for investors (which could take the form of licensing and supervision). Second, the Banking and Financial Services Act 1994 is an independent piece of legislation and cannot therefore be superseded by a competing statute which has no provisions of an overriding nature.[240] Third, and most convincing, the Zambian parliament has now amended the Banking and Financial Services Act 1994, and the statutory requirement that an applicant for a banking licence should furnish a memorandum of association has been removed.[241]

What are the consequences of this statutory amendment on the *ultra vires* doctrine insofar as banks and financial institutions are concerned? A consequence of permitting banks and financial institutions to be incorporated without a memorandum of association is that an investor might be misled to think that the Zambian Companies Act 1994 has done away with the statutory requirement for companies to have an objects clause. But, I will take a more reasoned look at this question.

It would be interesting to find out what will happen to those banks and financial institutions that were incorporated before the Companies Act 1994 was enacted. I submit here that thesis 4, as presented earlier, should apply. Further, is the repeal of the Banking and Financial Services Act 1994's requirement for a banking or financial services licence applicant to provide a memorandum of association to the registrar of banks and financial institutions tantamount to a statutory prohibition on all banks and financial institutions having a memorandum of association? What happens to the memoranda of association of banks and financial institutions that were licensed before the statutory requirement was abolished? Should the law simply turn a blind eye to such matters, or should the business of these banks and financial institutions be confined solely to what is specified in their objects clauses (which can be found in the memoranda of association)? What happens when the actions of a bank's directors exceed the powers of the bank as stipulated in the memorandum of association? Can such bank directors evade the *ultra vires* doctrine by hiding behind the concept of universal banking and claiming that after all, under the Banking and Financial Services Act 1994 (as amended in 2000), there is no need for any bank or financial institution to have a memorandum of association? One is left to look at the contents of each and every license that is issued to a bank or financial institution as well as the statutory definitions of a bank and a financial institution in the Banking and Financial Services Act 1994 (as amended in 2000) in order to determine the objects and powers that are implicit in the legal and regulatory framework.

In a typical situation, such as that under the Zambian Companies Act 1994, there is not much incentive for a bank or financial institution to go beyond the letter of the statute and provide a memorandum of association.[242] Indeed, why would a bank or financial institution do so if that would limit it to performing only the business activities that are spelt out in the objects clause? Besides, as I have pointed out earlier,[243] Forms I, II, III, and IV of the Companies (Prescribed Forms) Regulations,[244] like section 4(2) of the Banking and Financial Services Act 1994,[245] do make provisions for a bank or financial institution to state the nature of its business.

So, legally speaking, as already established, a company such as a bank can, if it chooses, have a memorandum of association.[246] There is nothing illegal or unlawful about such a decision. Indeed, as pointed out earlier, the Zambian Companies Act 1994 neither prohibits nor requires a company to have a memorandum of association at any time. In theory, it is up to the company itself to decide whether or not to have a memorandum of association. However, the introduction of this document might not serve much purpose because a number of items that should have been covered by the memorandum of association are likely to be covered by the articles of association[247] as well as by Form I, II, III, or IV in the Companies (Prescribed Forms) Regulations. Assuming that a company opts to have a memorandum of association in addition to its articles, what would happen if the articles of association and the memorandum of association are seen to be inconsistent or contradictory?

In common law, as held in the English case of *Guinness v. Land Corporation of Ireland*,[248] the general rule is that where there is a conflict between the terms of the memorandum of association and those of the articles of association, the terms of the memorandum of association should prevail.[249] In the *Guinness* case,[250] the memorandum of association stated that the objects of the company were the cultivation of lands in Ireland and things that were incidental thereto, and that the capital of the company was £1,050,000, divided into 140,000 A shares of £5 each and 3,500 B shares of £100 each. The articles of association (by article 8) provided that the capital representing the B shares should be invested in a fund that was set up to guarantee the payment of a 5 percent preferential dividend to the holders of the A shares. One of the B shareholders brought these proceedings against the company to test whether it was allowable for the company to apply its funds in the manner prescribed by article 8. The Court of Appeal held that the articles of association cannot modify the memorandum of association and that where there is some inconsistency between the two, the terms of the memorandum should prevail.

In another English case, *Re Duncan Gilmour & Co. Ltd.*,[251] the memorandum of association (as construed by the court) gave the company's preferential shareholders the right in a winding-up to a preferential return of their capital but nothing more, although the articles purported to give all of the company's shareholders a right to participate in any surplus assets on a pro rata basis. Wynn-Parry J. held that the articles of association could not be referred to 'to vary that which would be the result of the memorandum standing alone.'[252]

In Zambia, however, unlike in the United Kingdom, the memorandum of association is not a statutorily mandated document under the Zambian Companies Act 1994. As established earlier, only the articles of association are required under this statute. Against this background, should one allow a document that is not premised on a legislative requirement to take precedence over a legal document that is mandated and required by legislation? It would appear that in Zambia's case, for those companies that are incorporated under the Zambian Companies Act 1994, the articles of association should take precedence over the memorandum of association when the provisions of the two documents conflict with or contradict one another. This approach could help also to resolve matters pertaining, for example, to the alteration of the objects clause when a company opts to have a memorandum of association in addition to its articles. For those companies that were incorporated prior to the repeal of the Zambian Companies Act 1921, the memorandum of association should take precedence over the articles of association in accordance with the common law.[253]

In the case of a company that is incorporated under Zambia's Companies Act 1994 and has a memorandum of association, it is imperative that the objects clause in the memorandum of association is drafted closely in line with the summary statement regarding the business of the company that is given in Form I, II, III, or IV, whichever is applicable. However, given that the memorandum of association is not provided for (but is also not prohibited) by the Zambian Companies Act 1994, can the objects clause in such a memorandum be altered without a special resolution of the company, or does the company have to obtain a court order before it can alter the objects clause? Or, is everything entirely up to the company itself to determine, either in the articles or the memorandum of association, including the procedure of altering the objects clause? What happens when these provisions for the alteration of the objects clause turn out to be deliberately and purposely prejudicial to minority shareholders? Can the courts intervene, and if so, what would be the legal authority for such an intervention? In general, when a company such as a bank or financial institution has no memorandum of association but has furnished the registrar of companies with a completed Form I or Form II, whichever is applicable, that company will not be expected to have a separate objects clause.[254]

2.5. CONCLUSION

This chapter has examined the legal and policy bases for doing away with the statutory requirement for companies that are incorporated under the Zambian Companies Act 1994, such as banks and financial institutions, to have a memorandum of association. It was pointed out that a notable consequence of permitting the incorporation of companies without a memorandum of association is that an investor could be misled to think that the Zambian Companies Act 1994 has done away with the statutory requirement for companies to have some form of an objects clause. I have argued that although the *ultra vires* doctrine continues to apply in Zambia, its significance has been watered down by the introduction of Forms I, II, III, and IV in the Companies (Prescribed Forms) Regulations to replace the statutory requirement in the Companies Act 1994 for an objects clause in the memorandum of association.[255] These legislative changes, it was observed, were meant not only to simplify the incorporation of companies but also to abolish the *ultra vires* doctrine in Zambia's company law.[256]

In general, as alluded to in the chapter, banks and financial institutions in Zambia are subject to two main layers of regulation. The first layer relates to meeting the statutory requirements for a company to be incorporated under the Companies Act 1994. The second layer of regulation is the framework that was established under the Banking and Financial Services Act 1994, including the terms and conditions of licenses that are issued to banks and financial institutions.

The chapter highlighted four related theses regarding the *ultra vires* doctrine in Zambia. The first was that the *ultra vires* doctrine continues to apply in Zambia because Form II in the Companies (Prescribed Forms) Regulations requires the incorporators of a private company to submit to the registrar of companies a completed form bearing, inter alia, information about the principal business of the company. It was argued that this approach assumes that the principal business will be defined reasonably well enough or that some restrictions or limitations on the objects and powers will be imbedded in the articles of association.

The second thesis was that when a public company is being incorporated, one should be mindful that Form I in the Companies (Prescribed Forms) Regulations bears a great resemblance to Form II and that the arguments pertaining to Form I apply to Form II mutatis mutandis. The third thesis focussed on unlimited companies and those companies limited by guarantee, arguing that by parity of reasoning, some threads of the second thesis can be extrapolated and applied, mutatis mutandis, to Forms III and IV. The fourth thesis was that those companies that were incorporated prior to the repeal of the Companies Act 1921 of Zambia will continue to have a memorandum of association as well as an objects clause unless they decide to adapt to the framework of the Companies Act 1994 and thus do away with both. However, if these companies retain their memorandum of association and the attendant objects clause, the *ultra vires* doctrine will apply as it did in the United Kingdom prior to the enactment of the English Companies Act 1985.

CHAPTER 3

THE PAR VALUE CONCEPT
AND PAYING UP FOR
COMPANY SHARES

That subscribers to a company's share-capital must pay up for their shares is a well-known feature of the common law.[257] However, the policy objectives underpinning this precept are often not well understood. This chapter seeks to examine such policy bases before delving into the intricacies of the legal aspects of paying up for company shares. It begins by examining the relevance of the par value concept in Zambian company law and then turns to examine the legal aspects of share watering and financial assistance in the acquisition of company shares. These three areas of the law are interrelated and interconnected in that they all pertain to the central theme of the legal aspects of paying up for company shares.

The first part of the chapter examines some leading theories on why shareholders are required to pay up for their shares. Are there any legal justifications, for example, upon the verge of a company's insolvency, for the company's creditors to enforce such shareholder obligations?[258] What about the ruling in the U.S. Supreme Court case of *Handley v. Stutz*[259] which says that shareholders are exempt from the obligation to pay up for shares at a par value equal to that of newly issued shares when the company is in financial distress and the market value of the shares at the time of their issue is less than par?[260] An underscoring view in this chapter is that

> in the commercially sophisticated world in which developing countries increasingly find themselves, their financial legislation may demonstrate weaknesses which result in part from a limited number of indigenous professional specialists, in particular lawyers, and in part from paying insufficient attention to parallel legislation in other jurisdictions.[261]

The second part of the chapter deals with the relevance of the par value concept in the modern world and, by extension of reasoning, its relevance to Zambian company law. The third part turns to look at the Zambian legal framework for an allottee of shares to pay up for the allotted shares. This discussion then leads into a critical analysis of the pertinent legal aspects of share watering and financial assistance in the acquisition of a company's shares.[262]

In this chapter, only aspects of the common law are examined. Due to a lack of space, no attempt is made to look at parallel developments in civil law countries. The chapter argues, inter alia, that the concept of par value has little relevance in the modern world of commerce and that shares of no-par-value often reflect the true value of the shares. An argument is also made that the legal justification for a creditor to enforce the share-payment obligation of shareholders rests not only on one premise but on a number of reasons. One of the reasons is to protect investors from the consequences of a company going out of business; that is, there is a need to ensure that at least the share-capital account of the debtor company is well maintained and that the called-up share-capital has been paid up in full. Following is a discussion of some notable reasons why shareholders should pay up for their shares.

3.0. FRAUD THEORY

The fraud theory, often referred to as the 'holding-out theory' of shareholder liability, was first postulated in the case of *Hospes v. North-Western Manufacturing and Car Co.*[263] This case held that the tort of misrepresentation provides the ground upon which the liability of shareholders to pay up for the allotted shares is based. As Manning and Hanks observed,

> The basic rationale of the Hospes court was that the creditor had somehow received a representation from the corporation to the effect that the shares had been fully paid for; if in fact the shares had not been paid for, and if the company later became insolvent the creditor could claim that he had been misled and could compel shareholders who had not paid in the par value of their shares to do so ... The most immediate effects of this beautifully representative expression ... were to make it absolutely clear that (i) the creditor had no cause of action against shareholders unless the company became insolvent (since no damage had been shown to the creditor) and that (ii) any creditor who extended credit to the corporation before the relevant stock (share) was issued was barred from complaining.[264]

A major shortcoming of the fraud theory is that it places the liability for share payments on the shareholders when, in fact, it is the corporation that makes the representation about the paid-up share capital. The law simply makes out a presumption of shareholder liability and does not even require the creditor to show that the shareholders made the representation which the creditor then relied upon. Despite these anomalies, it is clear that under the fraud theory, the liability of the shareholders crystallises only when the company becomes insolvent and when a creditor who has extended value after the shares have been issued institutes proceedings.[265]

3.1. TRUST FUND THEORY

> Justice Story in his landmark opinion in *Wood v. Dummer*[266] said
> that shareholders are not permitted to take their assets out of a
> corporation, thus rendering the company insolvent, because the
> shareholders' equity (the 'capital stock') is in the nature of a 'trust
> fund' for creditors.[267]

But, can the obligation of shareholders to pay up for the shares be
extended to subsequent transferees if, in fact, the shares that have been
transferred are 'watered' shares?[268] This issue pushes interesting judicial
opinions to the fore. One view is that 'the creditor's remedy, if he has
one at all, must be against the initial share purchaser who underpaid—if
the creditor can find him.'[269] Laudable as this view may seem, it does
not resolve the polemic. I have argued elsewhere that under the English
Companies Act 1985, whereas a public company faces restrictions in
the way it deals with non-cash considerations, a private company does
not generally face such constraints.[270] Thus, a private company may, by
agreement, allot shares as fully or partly paid up otherwise than in cash
in return for the transfer of property or the rendering of services to the
company.[271]

In the English case of *Re Wragg Limited*,[272] Wragg and Martin was
a partnership that was managed by two persons. It was later registered
as E. J. Wragg Limited, a private company, whereby the two partners
and another person became directors. The company then bought the
property of the partnership, and an agreement was executed and registered. The company went into liquidation, and the liquidator filed a
misfeasance summons to obtain payment for the shares. It was held that
since the agreement could not be impeached the adequacy of the consideration could not be gone into.[273] Similarly, in *Brownlie and Others,
Petitioners*,[274] which was decided after *Re Wragg*, Darling L. J. ruled
that where a company, in good faith, issues shares as fully paid-up in
consideration of property transferred or services rendered, the court will
not inquire into the value of that which was accepted by the company as
an equivalent of money.[275]

What all of this evidence shows is that the trust fund theory can be appreciated only in a context which argues against the depletion of assets that have already been paid in, and not assets that have not yet been paid in. Indeed, this view was the original construction of Justice Story in *Wood v. Dummer*,[276] although later cases took a departure which has since faced heavy criticism from the proponents of the fraud theory.[277]

3.2. CONTRACT THEORY

When shareholders subscribe for shares and the company agrees to allot them the shares, a contractual arrangement of mutual obligations is established. It is pursuant to such contractual obligations that the shareholder must pay up for the allotted shares. Under the contract theory, shareholders must be held to the terms upon which they have acquired the shares, and the creditor of the insolvent company must be permitted to enforce the obligations of the shareholders. According to Hamilton,

> the charter of a corporation represents a contract (a) between the state and the corporation, or (b) between the corporation and its shareholders, or (c) among the shareholders themselves. This theory is most likely to surface today in disputes between different classes of shareholders, or in disputes in which one class of shareholders claims that the class is being discriminated against in some way.[278]

3.3. LEGISLATIVE INROADS

It must be noted that there are cases in which shareholders are under a general statutory obligation to pay up for the allotted shares in cash. As I have argued elsewhere,[279] the position of public companies in the United Kingdom provides a helpful example. It will be shown later and in greater detail how legislation in countries such as the United Kingdom permits exceptions to the general statutory obligation of shareholders to pay up for shares in cash.[280]

> Stock (shares) which was issued without a corresponding pay-in of assets valued at an amount equal to par was called 'watered stock'—stock issued not against assets but against water ... It must be emphasised that concepts of watered stock..., and the doctrines that came to surround them, were and are limited in application to the *issue* of stock, that is, sales by the *corporation* of its own stock. The doctrines do not in any way inhibit the *shareholder's* freedom to sell his stock at any price he can get, or to give it away if he wishes. Similarly, a corporation holding shares of another corporation may, like any other shareholder, dispose of them at any price it wishes or can get. The reason why shareholders were held to pay in the par value of their shares is that that was the price exacted by the law for the corporate advantage of limited liability.[281]

The concept of par value of company shares denotes the minimum amount by which the shares can be purchased.[282] However, even if the law exacted a price for the advantage of providing limited liability to the shareholders, taking into account the net worth of the company, it is not easy to maintain a constant equilibrium between the nominal capitalisation of the company and the value of its assets. Over time, the value of the assets could depreciate or appreciate. Indeed, if this were to happen, then the value of the assets of the company could cease to have a corresponding value to the original share-capital that was employed. It could be argued that any monetary pricing that is introduced as a signal to the market of the value of a share in the equity of a company is almost always a fictional and may be not only meaningless but also misleading. As Manning and Hanks observed,

> A number of serious analytical problems flaw this argument, as they also flaw contractual theories and other approaches that litigants and courts tried in efforts to assert shareholder liability to contribute capital to the incorporated enterprises. And all sorts

of remedial and procedural questions arose ... But in time, this much became clear:

1. The courts came to recognise that purchasers of shares from the corporation have some obligation to invest in the corporate enterprise;
2. It came to be understood (perhaps 'assumed' is a better word) that the measure of the investment liability of such a shareholder was the number of shares issued to him times the par value of the shares; and
3. It came to be recognised that at least some creditors could in at least some circumstances enforce this obligation of the purchasing shareholder in some way.[283]

Manning and Hanks continued,

Statements may be occasionally found in the literature to the effect that the *reason* why shareholders were held to pay in the par value of their shares is that that was the price exacted by the law for the corporate advantage of limited liability. While some such idea may have occurred to some nineteenth century court or legislative draftsman, the history of the matter will not bear out this theory. Limited liability arose in American corporation law as an almost incidental by-product of corporateness, and did so independently of the development of the par and stated capital scheme in the statutes.[284]

I now turn to examine the par value concept and the legal aspects of allotting shares in Zambia.

3.4. THE PAR VALUE CONCEPT AND THE ALLOTMENT OF SHARES

Under the Companies Act 1994 of Zambia, a company without a memorandum of association may be incorporated in the same manner as a company with a memorandum of association.[285] As noted in chapter 2, the Companies Act 1994 of Zambia, repealing the Companies Act 1921, neither prohibits nor requires companies to have a memorandum of association.[286] Unlike its predecessor, the Companies Act 1994 does not have any statutory provision relating to a requirement for a company to have a memorandum of association. Therefore, when a company decides to provide a memorandum of association, it is not clear if the memorandum must state the division of the share-capital into shares of a fixed amount.[287] The nominal amount of each share is what is known as the par value.[288] As Hamilton observed, in the case of the United States,

> *par value* or *stated value* of shares is an arbitrary or nominal value assigned to each class of shares issued under par value statutes. At one time par value represented the selling or issuance price of shares, but in modern corporate practice, par value has little significance and serves only a limited role. The Model Business Corporation Act (1984) and the statutes of many states have eliminated the concept of par value.[289]

In the case of the United Kingdom, Ferran pointed out that as well as stating the total amount of the authorised share capital, a company's memorandum of association must also state the division of the share capital into shares of a fixed amount.[290] The stated fixed amount of each share, according to Ferran, is what is known as the nominal, or par, value of the share.[291] The phrase *fixed amount* was examined closely in *Re Scandinavian Bank Group plc*,[292] where it was held that although this phrase had to point to a monetary amount, that amount did not have to be capable of being paid in legal tender; thus, it could be a ½ p or some other fraction or percentage of currency. It was further held that the fixed amount could not be stated in two currencies—that is, a share of US$1 or £1—but it could be stated in different currencies for different shares.

The shortcomings of the Zambian Companies Act 1994 related to the absence of statutory obligations for a company to have a memorandum of association can be attributed in part to the argument that was advanced in chapter 2—that is, they are a result of the limited participation of indigenous experts and other stakeholders in the law-making process.[293] Regarding the document or place where the share-capital of a company is to be found, section 6 of the Zambian Companies act 1994 merely states that

1. Subject to this Act, any two or more persons associated for any purpose may form an incorporated company by subscribing their names to an application for incorporation that satisfies this section and lodging it with the Registrar, together with—

   a. any proposed articles of the company;
   b. a statutory declaration in accordance with section nine;
   c. a signed consent from each person named in the application as a director or secretary of the company to act in the relevant capacity; and
   d. a declaration of guarantee by each subscriber, if the company is to be limited by guarantee.

2. An application for incorporation shall be in the prescribed form, shall be signed by each subscriber and shall specify—

   a. the proposed name of the company;
   b. the physical address of the office to be the registered office of the company;
   c. a postal address to be the registered postal address of the company;
   d. the type of company to be formed;
   e. if the company is to have share capital—

      i. the amount of share capital of the company;
      ii. the division of the share capital into shares of fixed amount; and
      iii. the number of shares each subscriber agrees to take.

Although not every private company in Zambia will have share-capital,[294] because other private companies could be limited by guarantee and not by shares,[295] section 20(1) of the Zambian Companies Act 1994 places a mandatory obligation on all unlimited companies to have a share-capital. Similarly, section 14 creates a mandatory obligation on all public companies to have a share-capital, although this provision goes further to add that the shares of a public company must actually be transferable. Section 14 reads as follows:

1. A public company shall have share capital.
2. The articles of a public company shall state—

    a. the rights, privileges, restrictions and conditions attaching to each class of shares, if there are two or more classes; and
    b. the authority given to the directors to determine the number of shares in, the designation of, and the rights, privileges, restrictions and conditions attaching to each series in a class of shares, if the class of shares may be issued in series.

3. All shares shall rank equally apart from differences due to their being in different classes or series.
4. Where a public company is wound-up, a member shall be liable to contribute, in accordance with Part XIII, an amount not exceeding the amount, if any, unpaid on the shares held by him.
5. The articles of a public company shall not impose any restriction on the right to transfer any shares of the company other than—

    a. a restriction on the right to transfer any shares on which there is unpaid liability; or
    b. a restriction on the right to transfer shares issued to directors or other officers or employees exercising any rights or options granted under section seventy-three, or issued in pursuance of any scheme adopted under that section; or
    c. a provision for the compulsory acquisition, or rights of first refusal, of shares referred to in paragraph (b), in favour of other members of the company or trustees appointed under any scheme adopted under section seventy-three.[296]

Although the concept of par value might be relevant to the primary issues of securities in both private and public companies (e.g., at incorporation), that is not necessarily true for the secondary trading of securities. In the case of secondary trading, par value might be useful only to issues in private companies, not to issues in public companies. One of the reasons supporting this view is that in many countries, shares in a public company are traded on a stock exchange. Because for most of this stock market trade the public can purchase shares in such companies, it is the market itself that will be expected to set the price of the shares. Further, the concept of par value might have some significance if it gave some indication of the market value of the company's assets. However, it usually does not do so and instead may turn out to be a source of confusion.[297]

BonBright, however, argued that the purpose of the par value concept is not to reflect the market value of the enterprise, which is constantly shifting and which therefore cannot be set by the face value of the share certificate, but to indicate the capital that the shareholders have agreed to contribute.[298] This feature is alluded to by BonBright as being historical and therefore fixed.[299] In *Orregun Gold Mining Company of India v. Roper*,[300] Lord Halsbury ruled that certain requirements—that is, stating par values with respect to the individual shares into which the authorized share-capital is divided and not allotting shares at a price that is less than their individual par values—are necessary because every creditor of the company is entitled to expect a fixed and certain amount of capital as his security. Also, Halsbury added, a company should not be allowed to mislead potential shareholders and creditors about the amount of its real capital. Ferran, however, argued that

> to suggest that par values prevent creditors and shareholders from being misled about the amount of the company's capital ignores the fact that there are remedies in tort and contract in respect of false or misleading statements. Regardless of whether shares have a par value or not, creditors and shareholders would be entitled to look to these remedies in the event of a company making inaccurate statements about the amount of finance it has raised through share issues. With regard to the argument that a minimum par value prevents one group of shareholders

acquiring shares more cheaply than other groups, this is negated by the practice of issuing shares at a premium to their par value. The price that investors are willing to pay for a company's shares from time to time will fluctuate in accordance with market conditions, and it is perfectly proper for the company to adjust the issue price to meet investor demand ... The effect of par value requirements is to impose an arbitrary limit on the company's ability to adjust issue prices in response to investor demand and market conditions.[301]

Another view supporting the policy basis of having the par value system is that in order for the creditors of a company to be confident that the corporation will pay off its debts when it is in financial distress, the par value is seen as a basis upon which the share-capital account of the debtor company can be based. Also, the par value prevents the arbitrary valuation of shares in excess of their true value. Pennington observed that the nominal value of shares is useful in declaring dividends (which are usually expressed as a percentage of the nominal value) and determining voting rights at shareholders' meetings. In the case of preference shares which have priority for the repayment of capital, he added, it is also helpful in determining the amount which must be paid to the preference shareholder in winding-up before the company's remaining assets are shared between the ordinary shareholders.[302] It has been noted that in America,

> no-par stock (shares) is common in the world of contemporary corporate finance. It is interesting, however, that it has not pre-empted the field, and par stock continues to be in majority use. This is true for several reasons. For a long time, the computational method of the federal stamp tax on stock issuance favoured par as against no par stock and some state franchise tax provisions still do. Additionally, for a careful lawyer concerned about such things, it is appealing that a lower par value on a share of stock sets the outer limit of liability of a subscriber-shareholder as against a creditor's claim, whereas in the case of no par stock the subscriber's liability would appear inevitably—for want of any other criterion—to be measured by the full amount that he agreed

to pay for each share of the stock. The use of low par values, and the ease of shareholder amendment to reduce par in situations where the par proved not to have been low enough, combine to make par stock a usable tool in the hands of the experienced corporate practitioner—and the market is used to it.[303]

3.4.1. Arguments Against the Par Value Concept

The concept of par value has received some strong criticisms from a number of scholars.[304] Among these criticisms is the problem associated with issuing shares for considerations other than cash. What happens when shares are issued in return for services or goods? How does one determine if the services or goods are on par with the nominal value of the shares?

Another difficulty facing the concept of par value is the attitude of the courts towards this concept.[305] In the American case of *Commonwealth v. Leigh Av. Ry. Co.*,[306] the court overlooked the applicable par value and adopted an arbitrary value based on the amount that was paid to the company. In that case, a company was capitalised at US$1,000,000 altogether. The charter of the company provided that the company could not issue bonds in excess of 50 percent of the par value of the shares. A suit was brought to enjoin an issue of US$250,000 of bonds, and an injunction was then granted. The court declined to recognise the $50 par value that was established by the charter and instead held that the $5 per share that was received by the company was the real par value—the other figure was merely a 'nominal' value.

The courts have also disregarded the par value in instances where recognising it would prejudice the interests of the company. In *Handley v. Stutz*,[307] a coal company was capitalised at US$200,000, and with US$120,000 of the shares unissued, it became obliged to raise US$50,000 in order to continue business. The issued shares had depreciated significantly in value, and no investor could offer the full value for the unissued shares. Therefore, bonds to the amount of the required sum, although they were not marketable by themselves at their principle value, were sold by giving out an equal amount of the previously unissued shares at a bonus. The remaining US$30,000 of the shares was then distributed among the old shareholders as a present. In a creditor's bill to compel payment in cash to the corporation at the par value of the new shares, the court declared that 'an active corporation may, for the purpose of paying its debts and obtaining money for the successful prosecution of its business, issue the stock (shares) and dispose of it for the best price that can be obtained.'[308] The ruling meant that if a company is in a state of 'economic emergency', it can, without generating the risk of liability to new stock purchasers, issue stock at the best price it can get, whether or not that is below par.

> A legal prophet at the time would have predicted that because courts are by and large sensible, they would gradually expand the *Handley* concept of 'economic emergency' to cover any situation where the going market value of the stock was below the par value. But in fact that proposition never fully developed, for other ways were found to deal with the problem.[309]

What the *Commonwealth v. Leigh* and *Handley* cases show is that American courts are slowly developing a common law that discourages the idea of par value shares. However, these cases also point to a critical weakness in the use of the par value concept as a yardstick to measure the limited liability of shareholders. Generally, an investor could be attracted to subscribe for the shares on the basis of their represented value, and often, it is this represented value that bolsters the price of the shares above their real value.[310] A great discrepancy between the value of the holdings of a corporation and the nominal value of capitalisation usually lends an opportunity to defraud inexperienced purchasers. Therefore, a shift towards abandoning the par value system and adopting a non-par-value system might be more efficient because it would put the investor on guard and thus avoid creating a false sense of investors' protection. Hamilton, however, cautioned,

> It is important to distinguish conceptually between 'no par shares' in states that retain the par value structure, and shares issued in states with statutes that have eliminated par value. The issuance

of 'no par shares' in par value states affect the stated capital and capital surplus accounts, may create a watered stock liability in certain circumstances, and may affect the distributions a corporation may lawfully make. States that have eliminated the par value structure have also eliminated the mandatory capital accounts and have established rules relating to distributions that are independent of any allocation of the consideration received when the shares are issued.[311]

3.4.2. The No-Par-Value Concept

Under the common law, the notion of issuing shares at no-par-value can be traced to the joint stock companies of the Elizabethan period, when shares were used 'in the natural sense, namely, as an appreciable part of the whole undertaking not as a multiple of units of the capital.'[312] Harmen, however, observed that the concept of no-par-value originates from American jurisprudence.[313] He argued that in the United States, company promoters often found themselves engaged in lawsuits to prove that some of the shares which had been allotted, although they were treated as being fully paid up, were in fact not fully paid up. These lawsuits constrained the functions of promoters, and thus, to avoid such bottlenecks, companies were permitted to issue shares of no-par-value.[314] Indeed,

> if a corporation may have stock (shares) with a par value of 1 cent per share, why not abandon the par concept entirely and permit the issuance of stock with no dollar amount printed on the share certificate? Why not have no par value stock? It was not until 1912 [in the United States] that analysis of the matter had reached a sufficiently wide circle to produce the first statutory authorisation of no par stock. The advent of no par stock did not, however, have the effect of eliminating the concept of legal capital. It was, and still is, statutorily necessary to designate some dollar number on the corporate bank sheet as 'capital'. Since, with no par stock, it is no longer possible to calculate what the 'capital' is by multiplying the number of shares issued times the par value, a 'capital' number can be arrived at for this purpose only by fiat—by declaration—by stating it.[315]

In the *Gedge Report on Shares of No-Par Value*, the following three instances were identified as typical cases in which shares can be issued for no-par-value under the American legal system:

a. where the law only requires the certificate of incorporation to state the number of shares of no-par value to be issued, leaving it to the corporation to determine how much of the proceeds of issue of such shares should be allocated to capital and how much to distributable surplus;

b. where the law requires the certificate of incorporation to state the amount of the capital of the corporation which must include some minimum amount (for example US$1.00) in respect of every issued share of no-par value. In such cases, any excess of the proceeds of issue of such shares over the minimum amount may in general be treated as a distributable surplus; and

c. where the law requires that the amount of capital stated must include the whole consideration received on the issue of shares of no-par value. In such cases there can be no distributable surplus. This system is permissible in New York and certain other states. But in Wisconsin, for example, an amount up to 25% of the proceeds of issue may be allocated to surplus.[316]

The Gedge Committee acknowledged the need for safeguards against abuse. However, it concluded that provided the proceeds of any issue of shares having no-par-value were treated as capital money and not as distributable reserves, the position would be neither more nor less open to abuse than if the shares had a par value.[317] In 1962, the Jenkins Committee also recommended that legislation should be introduced to permit shares with no-par-values.[318] According to Ferran,

> This Committee [i.e., the Jenkins Committee] went one step further than the Gedge Committee by recommending that no-par-value preference shares, as well as no-par-value ordinary shares, should be permitted. Despite these various recommendations, no reform has to date been enacted in the UK. This is

in contrast to the position in countries which historically had company law systems that largely followed the English model but which, latterly, have moved closer to the position under the corporations laws of the US states. No-par-value shares are widely recognised in US states.[319]

In New Zealand[320] and Canada,[321] the issuance of no-par-value shares is permitted. In Ghana, following the Gower report on the development of that country's company legislation,[322] the issuing of shares of no-par-value is no longer forbidden. The cases of Ghana and New Zealand show that company legislation in those two countries now requires all company shares to be issued at no-par-value.[323] Indeed, section 40(1) of Ghana's Companies Code 1963 explicitly provides that 'all shares created or issued after the commencement of this Code shall be shares of no-par value', whereas section 28 of New Zealand's Companies Act 1990 stipulates unequivocally that 'no share shall have a nominal or par value'. Australia, too, has a statutory requirement that makes it mandatory for all shares to be issued at no-par-value.[324] Further, in Ghana's case, the Gower report notes,

> the main obstacle in rendering the true nature of a share in a company readily comprehensible to the man-in-the street is that fact that the present law insists that a nominal value should be attached to it … At the commencement of a company's life par-value may be arbitrary and misleading, since shares may be issued at a premium or even (through an issue for a consideration other than cash) at a disguised discount. Thereafter they become totally arbitrary; a so-called $G1 share may if the company has made losses be worth anything from $G1 to infinity. The retention of the misleading $G1 symbol is an endless source of complication and confusion both to the sophisticated and especially, to the unsophisticated investor who is apt to think that he is getting a bargain if he buys a $G1 share for 10 cents. And that he has been cheated if he is able to buy 30 cents. If Ghanaians are to be encouraged to invest in shares everything should be done to make it clear to them that a share is simply a share in the fluctuating value of a business and not a piece of paper worth the value endorsed upon it.[325]

In the United Kingdom, the abolition of the par value concept may not be easy to achieve given that article 8 of the Second Company Law Directive under the European Union laws requires public companies to attribute par values to their shares.[326] That said, in other jurisdictions, companies can, if they so desire, issue shares of no-par-value.[327]

3.4.3. Arguments in Support of the No-Par-Value System

Generally, shares that are issued without par value afford a more realistic approach to the appraisal of profits in relation to the assets that are employed in a business.[328] Such an approach avoids the problems that are associated with determining profits and dividends by reference to a nominal value.[329] Also, the issuance of shares of no-par-value affords flexibility, which makes capital reorganizations much simpler.[330] Because no-par-value shares can be issued for any amount of consideration that is specified by the directors, there is no floor below which the price cannot be set.[331] As a result, the issuing company is usually free from the threat of a possible breach of the statutory prohibitions against share watering. Indeed, in a troubled economy, such as where there is war, companies may wish to issue shares at lower prices as a way of raising capital. Companies should be able to do so without being afraid of judicial consequences. At the same time, it must be acknowledged that it is in furtherance of good business practice that companies must be permitted to raise finances by selling their shares in accord with the true and fair view of the company's business. If such a view were overlooked, companies could begin to engage in overleverage to raise finances. Overleverage could indeed increase the risks and costs that are associated with insolvency.

Countering the school of thought that supports the no-par-value system, Berle argued that the concept of no-par-value could be open to abuses by some company directors.[332] This view assumes somewhat that no remedial measures will be taken by the company because the legal system is not transparent enough for the shareholders to access the relevant information about the abuses. Berle observed that in dealing with corporations that have non par-value shares, an investor must ascertain whether the shares without a visible dollar mark on the share certificate are in fact true no-par-value shares or whether they are 'stated value' no-par-value shares—in substance, merely a par value share with a different name.[333]

Adding to the criticisms, BonBright argued that the removal of par value is likely to lead to a serious danger in corporate finance—that is, the danger that the stated capital will be fixed far below the real capital.[334] BonBright observed further that the law would lead to a conclusion that creditors have been stripped of their long-recognised rights to hold the shareholders liable for partially paid shares and to hold the directors of the issuing company liable for an impairment of capital.[335] However, this view has its own limitations. As was held in the U.S. case of *American Co. v. Staples*,

> it has been said that while non par value stock corporations have no nominal value—no dollar mark—stated in the face of their stock certificates, yet the general rules regarding the liability of the subscribers for non-payment of the full amount of their subscription, and the general rules regarding the declaration of dividends, apply as in the case of a par-value corporation, the liability of the shareholders depending upon whether he has paid or delivered, the amount in money, or its equivalent for the stock that was sold while the capital stock of a non par-value corporation cannot be lawfully invaded by the declaration of dividends any more than the capital stock of a par value stock corporation.[336]

Having examined the par value concept, I now turn to look at the legal aspects of share watering in Zambian company law.

3.5. THE CONCEPT OF SHARE WATERING

Watered stock—or share watering, so to say—is a generic term that is used to describe the issuance of shares at a price below par value.[337] According to Hamilton, there are three subtypes of watered stock:

1. 'Bonus' shares are shares issued for no consideration at all. Bonus shares are usually issued in connection with the valid issuance of senior securities as an inducement to invest in the senior securities (*e.g.* preferred shares);

2. 'Discount' shares are shares issued for a consideration that is less than the legally established price, either the par value or the price set by the directors; and

3. 'Watered' shares are technically shares issued for property the value of which has been artificially inflated. Historically, many fraudulent transactions took the form of shares issued for over-valued property.

The phrase 'watered stock' generally refers to all three types of watered shares.[338]

In common law, a share is generally understood to mean the interest of a shareholder in the company as measured by a sum of money for the purpose of liability, first, and interest, second. It also consists of a series of mutual covenants that are entered into by all of the shareholders inter se.[339] From this definition, it is clear that whereas a share, as an interest, entitles a shareholder to a number of rights—such as the right to vote at meetings and the right to participate in the profits of the company by way of dividends—the share will also attract liability on the unpaid-up share-capital of the company in the event that the company goes into liquidation.[340] These rights and liabilities represent some of the contractual relationships among the shareholders[341] and between the shareholders and the company.[342] As Astbury J. observed in the *Hickman* case,

> An outsider to whom rights purport to be given by the articles in his capacity as such outsider, whether he is or subsequently becomes a member, cannot sue on those articles, treating them as contracts between himself and the company, to enforce those rights.[343]

The relationships among the shareholders and the shareholders and the company are regulated mainly by the articles of association. The articles are contractual rules and can thus be amended.[344] However, in a strict commercial sense, the equity interests held by the shareholders in the company are like commodities. As such, the allotted shares must be paid for.[345] A share, as a commodity, has both economic and investment value.[346] Indeed, shares can yield dividends.[347]

The concern of this section is not to address the legal aspects of paying up for shares that are purchased from an individual shareholder, but rather to examine the legal aspects of paying up for shares that are purchased from an incorporated company (more so in the case of primary issues). In Zambia, the bulk of the law governing the payment for shares is found in the Companies Act 1994. However, the Zambian Companies Act 1994—unlike the English Companies Act 2006 and its predecessor, the English Companies Act 1985[348]—has fewer rules relating to the payment for shares. For example, whereas the rendering of financial assistance in the acquisition of a company's shares is regulated under the Zambian and English Companies Acts,[349] the allotment of shares at a discount—or 'share watering', as it is commonly known—is not covered under the Zambian Companies Act 1994. At the time the Zambian Companies Act 1994 was enacted, the United Kingdom's primary piece of legislation related to the administration of its company law was the English Companies Act 1985. Consequently, I will refer in many instances to the English Companies Act 1985, especially to aspects that the legislative draftsman in Zambia could have easily considered as parallel company law statutory provisions in the United Kingdom. A number of the statutory provisions that are set forth in the English Companies Act 1985 are repeated verbatim in the U.K. Companies Act 2006, although with some novel developments included in the later statute.

A further notable difference between the company law developments in the United Kingdom and Zambia is that in the former country, section 100 of the English Companies Act 1985 prohibits the allotment of shares at a discount.[350] This statutory provision, now carried forward as section 580 of the English Companies Act 2006, reads as follows:

1. A company's shares must not be allotted at a discount.
2. If shares are allotted in contravention of this section, the allottee is liable to pay the company an amount equal to the amount of the discount, with interest at the appropriate rate.

In contrast, there is no statutory provision in the Zambian Companies Act 1994 prohibiting the allotment of shares at a discount. In Zambia, as long as the common law or the articles of association do not prohibit share watering, companies have the liberty to engage in the practice. I have already defined the term *share watering* when I looked at the historical origins of the par value concept.[351]

The standard articles of association that are found in schedule 1 of the Zambian Companies Act 1994 provide the rules governing the issuance of shares at a discount. I will look at these rules later. Here, suffice it to say that when a company has adopted the standard articles in schedule 1, it can alter the articles in the same manner as if it had formulated its own articles.[352] That said, not all companies will adopt the standard articles because there is no obligation whatsoever to do so.

In discussing the legal aspects of share watering, I will examine the allotment of shares for cash, the allotment of shares for considerations other than cash, the allotment of shares at a discount, and the issuance of shares at a premium. Some notable restrictions, exceptions, and risks that are associated with making payments for shares will also be discussed. I now turn to look at the legal aspects of allotting shares for cash.

3.5.1. Allotment of Shares for Cash

Under the United Kingdom's Companies Act 1985, a company limited by shares was required to state in its memorandum of association the division of the share-capital into shares of a fixed amount.[353] The general rule under that statute was that when shares were allotted, they had to be paid up in full.[354] The payment had to be in money or money's worth, which could include goodwill and know-how.[355] The latter mode of payment will be discussed in the next section when I deal with non-cash considerations. Here, suffice it to say that shares would be deemed paid up in cash if the payment that was received by the company was either in cash or was a cheque received in good faith which the directors had no reason for suspecting would not be paid.[356] Payment in cash could also involve an undertaking to pay cash to the company at a future date.[357]

Today, under the U.K. Companies Act 2006, a company can, if so authorised by its articles, (1) make arrangements for a difference between the shareholders in the amounts and times of the payment of calls on their shares; (2) accept from any member all or part of the amount that remains unpaid on any shares he or she holds, although no part of that amount has been called up; or (3) pay a dividend in proportion to the amount that is paid up on each share, where a larger amount is paid up on some shares than on others.[358] Also, shares that are allotted by a company, and any premium on them, can be paid up in money or money's worth (including goodwill and know-how).[359] However, the U.K. Companies Act 2006 does not prevent a company from allotting bonus shares to its members or from paying up, with sums that are available for the purpose, any amounts that are for the time being unpaid on any of its shares (whether on account of the nominal value of the shares or by way of a premium).[360]

In other words, shares cannot be issued as fully paid up at a consideration below their nominal value. When shares are paid up at a discount, the allottee will be liable to pay the allotting company an amount equal to the amount of the discount, with interest at an appropriate rate.[361] If the allottee has already sold the shares, the subsequent holder of the shares will be liable to pay the company an amount equal to the amount of the discount, with interest at an appropriate rate.[362] The subsequent holder is, however, allowed a defence if he can show that he is a bona fide purchaser for value and without actual notice.[363] Directors and any officer of the allotting company who are responsible for the discounted allotment will be liable to a fine.[364]

The principle that shares must be paid up in full must be seen as important not only in safeguarding any efforts to raise company finances but also in ensuring that fair trade in securities takes place. To hold otherwise would amount to condoning share watering and thereby putting the existing shareholders and the creditors at a disadvantage. If a case of collusion between an allottee and the directors of the allotting company were to occur for the purposes of issuing shares at a discount (while the company is a going concern), I argue that the remedy should consist of more than making the allottee pay an amount equal to the discount. The allottee must also be made to forfeit his or her right to hold shares—only in regard to those shares that were acquired through the transaction—because he or she has demonstrated the ability to undermine the company by entering into dubious transactions. This proposal is made in the light of the fact that the law in the United Kingdom is silent on the fate of an allottee who subsequently makes a payment that is equal to the discount on the share price. It is submitted further that although the U.K. Companies Act 2006, as well as its predecessor, the English Companies Act 1985, provides statutory provisions governing the payment for shares, neither statute deals with situations relating to share-price discounts on a single share. Section 580(1) of the U.K. Companies Act 2006 and section 100 of the English Companies Act 1985 cover only those situations relating to the allotment of more than one share: 'A company's shares must not be allotted at a discount.'[365]

What happens if only one share is allotted at a discount? It is my view that because an issued share is part of the share-capital, the directors of the company, as the people who manage or are custodians of the company's assets, have unquestionable fiduciary duties towards the corporation they direct.[366] On that basis, the directors can be held liable for the breach of their fiduciary duties if they allot one share at a discount.[367] Alternatively, under section 583(2) of the U.K. Companies Act 2006, it could be argued that the phrase *payment in cash*, in relation to the acquisition of company shares, includes any payment that is made for a single share. Indeed, section 583(2) provides, 'A share in a company is deemed paid up (as to its nominal value or any premium on it) in cash, or allotted for cash, if the consideration received for the allotment or payment up is a cash consideration.'

The term *cash consideration* is defined in section 583(3) of the U.K. Companies Act 2006 as (a) cash received by the company, (b) a cheque received by the company in good faith and that the directors have no reason to suspect will not be paid, (c) a release of a liability of the company for a liquidated sum, (d) an undertaking to pay cash to the company at a future date, or (e) payment by any other means that gives rise to the present or future entitlement (of the company or a person acting on the company's behalf) to a payment in cash or credit equivalent to the payment. Section 583(3) of the U.K. Companies Act 2006 repeats much of what is contained in section 738(2) of the English Companies Act 1985. The exception is paragraph (e) in the former statutory provision, which states that cash consideration includes 'payment by any other means giving rise to a present or future entitlement (of the company or a person acting on the company's behalf) to a payment, or credit equivalent to payment, in cash.'

3.5.2. Allotment of Shares for Considerations Other Than Cash

Although people consider paying for shares in cash to be an ideal and often preferred arrangement, there used to be an exception to this general rule under the English Companies Act 1985. According to its provisions, a private company was not prohibited from allotting shares for non-cash consideration.[368] The shortcoming of this option, however, was that such flexibility could be abused. In the case of public companies, the English Companies Act 1985 provided that

1. A public company shall not allot shares as fully or partly paid up (as to their nominal value or any premium on them) otherwise than in cash unless—

    a. the consideration for the allotment has been independently valued…

    b. a report with respect to its value has been made to the company by a person appointed by the company (in accordance with that section) during the 6 months immediately preceding the allotment of the shares; and

    c. a copy of the report has been sent to the proposed allottee.[369]

This statutory provision is repeated in section 593(1) of the U.K. Companies Act 1994. It is designed to protect existing shareholders and creditors from possible share watering whenever public companies are making non-cash considerations. This rule is now examined in greater detail.

3.5.3. Non-cash Considerations in the Case of Public Companies

Under the English Companies Act 1985, two mandatory provisions prohibited public companies from allotting shares for a non-cash consideration.[370] The first provision applied to situations in which shareholders undertook to do work or perform services in return for shares.[371] The second provision related to the allotment of shares as fully or partly paid up for a consideration to transfer property to the company after five years from the date of allotment.[372] In the case of the latter prohibition, a public company could allot its shares if the transfer of property was to occur within five years from the date of the allotment. That statutory prohibition is repeated in section 587(1) of the U.K. Companies Act 2006. However, the policy basis underpinning these prohibitions is somewhat unclear. Perhaps the rule is intended to ensure that the public is given enough time to pay up for the shares. The criteria for measuring a five-year period are not easy to discern.

Whenever a breach of one of the two mandatory provisions under the English Companies Act 1985 prohibiting public companies from allotting shares for non-cash considerations were to occur, the allottee was under a statutory obligation to pay up an amount equal to the share price discount.[373] In addition, each of the directors of the allotting company that was responsible for the allotment would be liable to a fine.[374] These statutory obligations are repeated in the U.K. Companies Act 2006.[375]

Under the English Companies Act 1985, in order for a public company to accept a non-cash consideration as payment for the shares, the consideration had to be valued.[376] The same rule holds under the U.K. Companies Act 2006.[377] However, the valuation is not required in a case where the shares are allotted by a company in connection with its proposed merger with another company—that is, when one of the companies proposes to acquire all of the assets and liabilities of the other in exchange for the issue of shares or other securities of the first company with those of the other, with or without any cash payment to the shareholders.[378]

The independent valuation of a non-cash consideration is important in order to avoid some unscrupulous person placing an inflated value on such a consideration. However, assuming the valuation report were to disclose that the non-cash consideration was of less value than the value of the shares that were being allotted and the directors issued the shares anyway, could it not be argued that both the directors and the allottee connived in the allotment of the shares at a discount? I submit that in the course of normal day-to-day transactions, both the directors and the allottee might have had notice of the valuation report and its contents. If the directors, however, decided to ignore the report and issue shares at a discount, both the directors and the allottee (who has notice) should be held liable. This, it is argued, would be a clear case of conspiracy to defraud the company of its capital.[379] A notable shortcoming in this regard could be that in the case of a conspiracy to defraud the company of its capital, the burden of proof would lie on the prosecution to prove beyond reasonable doubt that there was a common intent to defraud.[380]

3.5.4. Non-cash Considerations in the Case of Private Companies
Under the English Companies Act 1985, a public company faced restrictions in the way it dealt with non-cash considerations, but a private company did not generally face such constraints.[381] The same applies under the U.K. Companies Act 2006.[382] Thus, a private company can, by agreement with the allottee, allot shares as fully or partly paid up otherwise than in cash in return for the transfer of property or the rendering of services to the company.[383] Illustratively, as was seen earlier in *Re Wragg Limited*,[384] Wragg and Martin was a partnership that was managed by two people. It was later registered as E. J. Wragg Limited, a private company, whereby the two partners and another person became directors. The company then bought the property of the partnership, and an agreement was executed and registered. The company went into liquidation,

and the liquidator filed a misfeasance summons to obtain payment for the shares. It was held that since the agreement could not be impeached the adequacy of the consideration could not be gone into. Similarly, as noted earlier in *Brownlie and Others, Petitioners*,[385] decided after *Re Wragg*, Darling L. J. ruled,

> Where a company, in good faith, issues shares as fully paid-up in consideration of property transferred or services rendered, the court will not inquire into the value of that which was accepted by the company as an equivalent of money.[386]

What are the lessons to be learnt from these cases? Under the law of contract, the freedom to contract is guaranteed. Once the parties have agreed on the property or services to be exchanged for fully paid-up shares, the courts will not look into the adequacy of the consideration.[387] As a consequence, it may not be possible to tell whether the shares have been issued at a discount or at a premium. Such anomalies in the law could lead to share watering. In addition, the company will not know whether or not its shares have been issued at a premium, and of course, a premium account will not have been created and set aside.[388] Such is the position for a private company.

Generally, a private company, as the name suggests, does not distribute its securities to the public. In many common law jurisdictions, private companies are perceived as small companies whose shareholding is composed of close friends or relations who know each other very well. This means that when shares are allotted, the allottees will usually be close friends or family relations.[389] Such a closely knit 'family of shareholders', whose relationship is anchored upon mutual trust and confidence, will not be too willing to accept people from outside the family circle buying shares in the company.

The position is different for many public companies. The relationships among the shareholders within a public company can be of a personal, business, or other, nonpersonal nature. For example, if a public company is listed on a stock exchange, it means that members of the public could bid for shares in the company. In order to protect the public as well as the creditors, it is a matter of public policy that such companies must be protected by legislation from share watering which could arise from poorly valued, unvalued, or undervalued non-cash-considerations.[390]

In Zambia, the standard articles of association that are contained in schedule 1 of the Companies Act 1994 do not provide for the payment of shares through non-cash considerations. The Zambian Companies Act 1994 is similarly silent on the matter. Thus, a company might end up not adopting any articles that address non-cash consideration payment for its shares. However, to attract more investment, particularly in the case of public companies, these companies should consider adopting certain aspects of the U.K. legislation about non-cash considerations as a part of their articles of association.

3.5.5. Allotment of Shares at a Premium in the United Kingdom

In the United Kingdom, before the enactment of the Companies Act 1948, share premiums were not treated as a part of the share-capital.[391] As Harman J. observed in the case of *Henry Head & Co. Ltd. v. Ropner Holdings Ltd*,

> The question which I have to determine is whether the defendants were obliged to keep their accounts in that way. That depends purely on s.56 of the Companies Act 1948 [CA 1985, s.130], which is a new departure in legislation and was, it is said, intended to make compulsory that which had long seemed to be desirable, namely, the practice of putting aside as a reserve and treating in the ordinary way as capital cash premiums received on the issue of shares at a premium.[392]

In the *Henry Head & Co. Ltd v. Ropner Holdings Ltd* case, a holding company acquired two companies by means of a share-for-share exchange. The actual value of the shares that were acquired was much greater than the nominal value of the shares that were issued as consideration, and the directors of the holding company were counselled that they had to account for this excess by crediting it to a share premium account.

This view was upheld by the court. It has been observed, however, that despite this ruling, 'some practitioners continued to believe the obligation to create a share premium account in this type of situation could be avoided.'[393] According to Ferran,

> The arguments on which that practice was based were finally considered by the court in *Shearer v. Bercain Ltd.*[394] Essentially, those arguments were: (i) it was for the company to determine the terms of issue and it was not obliged to obtain a premium merely because investors might be willing to pay it; and (ii) if the sale and purchase agreement provided for the assets to be sold at a price equal to the par value of the shares to be issued as consideration, there was no obligation on the company to create a share premium account. Walton J rejected these arguments. In his view it was the prima-facie duty of directors to obtain the best possible price for the shares.[395] The obligation to create a share premium account was not optional and could not be avoided by stating that the shares were issued at their nominal value; if the assets acquired in consideration of the issue of shares had an actual value greater than the nominal value of the consideration shares then, irrespective of the terms on which those shares had been issued, the company was subject to a mandatory requirement to create a share premium account.[396]

The reasoning behind the old view that share premiums were not a part of the share-capital was based on the argument that because par value was the nominal value of each share, any value of the issued shares above the par value was not considered to be a part of the share-capital. The excess amount was considered to be part of the distributable profits which the company could return to the shareholders as dividends.[397] After 1948, the law changed when a new Companies Act was passed in the United Kingdom. A company can issue shares at a premium (normally during boom periods when the company is said to be enjoying good business) as a consideration in cash or in kind which exceeds the nominal value of a share.[398] Today, once shares are issued at a premium, a sum equal to the aggregate amount or the value of the shares must be transferred to a premium account.[399]

3.5.6. Issuing Shares at a Discount in Zambia

I have pointed out that the standard articles of association found in schedule 1 of the Zambian Companies Act 1994 include articles governing the payment for shares.[400] However, the standard articles do not state that the shares issued to the allottee must be paid up when the allotment is made. Regulation 15 of the standard articles simply permits company directors to accept partial or full payment from an allottee before a call is made on the unpaid amount. This indicates that when shares are allotted, an allottee can decide to pay immediately or in the future. However, when a call is made on the unpaid-up share-capital, the allottee must pay up.[401]

If a member fails to pay up the amount that is called on his shares at the time and place mentioned in the notice, he could be charged interest on the principal amount.[402] There are also other consequences of failing to pay up for the shares. Under regulation 17, the company directors will be required to give what could be considered as the final notice, calling on the allottee to pay up the shares and to add interest to that amount. Failure to take heed of the notice could result in the shares being forfeited to the company.[403] The company could then reissue the shares to another person. In the standard articles, it is also provided that during a period when the call for payment has not been made, the allotting company has a first and paramount lien on every share that has not been fully paid up.[404] As long as part of the share-capital has not been paid up, the lien will extend to dividends that are payable in respect of the issued but unpaid-up share-capital.[405]

In Zambia, as I have already established,[406] the Companies Act 1994 does not prohibit the sale of shares at a discount.[407] The statute makes no specific reference to the issue of shares at a discount. In a leading Zambian case, *ZAMANGLO Industrial Corporation v. Zambia Privatisation Agency and The Attorney General*,[408] the granting of a declaratory order for the acquisition of additional shares at a discount in a privatised company followed the disclosure by the plaintiff (the disclosure was not contested by the state as the defendant) that another shareholder, with a similar standing to the plaintiff, had been issued additional shares at a discount.

3.5.7. Allotment of Shares at a Premium in Zambia

The Zambian Companies Act 1994, like the U.K. Companies Act 2006 and its predecessor statute, the English Companies Act 1985, has provisions permitting the allotment of shares at a premium.[409] Section 61(1) of the Zambian Companies Act 1994 provides as follows:

> Where a company issues shares at a premium, whether for cash or otherwise, a sum equal to the aggregate amount of value of the premiums on these shares shall be transferred to an account, to be called 'the share premium account'.

Thus, under the Zambian Companies Act 1994, as with the U.K. Companies Act 2006 and the English Companies Act 1985,[410] shares that are issued at a premium can be paid up in cash or otherwise.[411] I shall examine later what constitutes 'otherwise'. Here, suffice it to say that the allotting company must set aside a share premium account to which the aggregate amount or value of the premiums must be transferred.[412]

Neither the Zambian Companies Act 1994 nor the U.K. Companies Act 2006 (or the English Companies Act 1985) defines what constitutes the term *otherwise* as it applies to the share premium provision: 'if a company issues shares at a premium, whether for cash or *otherwise*' (italics added).[413] I can discern only one logical meaning—that is, that the term *otherwise* refers to non-cash considerations because these are something else other than cash.[414] However, it might also be that whereas in the United Kingdom non-cash considerations for shares in a public company require the valuation of the consideration,[415] in Zambia valuation is not necessary because the Zambian Companies Act 1994 says nothing about the valuation of non-cash considerations. An amendment to the Zambian Companies Act 1994 on this matter would help to improve the law so that one can determine the true value of a non-cash consideration.

I now turn to examine the concept of financial assistance in the acquisition of a company's shares.

3.6. FINANCIAL ASSISTANCE IN THE ACQUISITION OF A COMPANY'S SHARES

In Zambia, like the United Kingdom, it is a general rule that unlawful financial assistance that is rendered to an allottee of a company's shares by the company itself to enable the allottee to pay for and acquire the shares, constitutes a criminal offence.[416] The policy basis of prohibiting such financial assistance is somewhat unclear because the act of a company rendering financial assistance to an allottee of its shares does not alter or reduce the company's share-capital.[417] However, in the Australian case of *Darvall v. North Sydney Brick & Tile Co Ltd.*,[418] Kirby J. ruled that the purposes of the prohibition on financial assistance 'include the avoidance of the manipulation of the value of shares by companies and their officers dealing in such shares.'[419] In the English case of *Belmont Finance Corporation v. Williams Furniture Ltd (No. 2)*,[420] a company bought an asset for a price which, it later turned out, was grossly inflated, and the vendors of the asset used the proceeds of the sale to buy the company. The Court of Appeal held that this was unlawful financial assistance. The court was unanimous in ruling that it would have made no difference if the price which the company had paid had actually been a fair one because the company had acted without regard to its own commercial interests and with the sole purpose of providing the vendor of the assets with the funds to acquire the shares. According to Ferran, the court clearly did not consider that a reduction in net assets was a necessary prerequisite of unlawful financial assistance.[421]

In Zambia, the Companies Act 1994 provides the following examples of unlawful financial assistance:

a.   financial assistance given by way of gift:
b.   financial assistance given by way of guarantee, security or indemnity, other than an indemnity in respect of the indemnifier's own neglect or default, or by way of release or waiver;
c.   financial assistance given by way of—

    i.   a loan;

    ii.   any other agreement under which any of the obligations of any other party to the agreement remains unfulfilled; or

    iii. novation of, or the assignment of, any rights arising under any such loan or agreement; or

  d. any other financial assistance given by a company which has no net assets, or whereby the net assets of the company are reduced to a material extent.[422]

This statutory provision then goes on to define net assets and liabilities. However, in drafting the statutory provision, the draftsman simply reproduced verbatim the statutory provision on financial assistance that is in section 152(1) of the English Companies Act 1985.

A few observations merit mention here. First, the statutory provision on financial assistance in both the Zambian and English Companies Acts refers merely to examples of financial assistance and does not include definitions.[423] Nowhere in the Zambian and English Companies Acts is the term *financial assistance* defined. The same approach is carried through in section 677 of the U.K. Companies Act 2006, which provides as follows:

  1. In this Chapter 'financial assistance' means—

    a. financial assistance given by way of gift,

    b. financial assistance given—

       i.   by way of guarantee, security or indemnity (other than an indemnity in respect of the indemnifier's own neglect or default), or

       ii. by way of release or waiver,

    c. financial assistance given—

       i.   by way of a loan or any other agreement under which any of the obligations of the person giving the assistance are to be fulfilled at a time when in accordance with the agreement any obligation of another party to the agreement remains unfulfilled, or

ii. by way of the novation of, or the assignment (in Scotland, assignation) of rights arising under, a loan or such other agreement, or

d. any other financial assistance given by a company where—

i. the net assets of the company are reduced to a material extent by the giving of the assistance, or

ii. the company has no net assets.

2. 'Net assets' here means the aggregate amount of the company's assets less the aggregate amount of its liabilities.

3. For this purpose a company's liabilities include—

a. where the company draws up Companies Act individual accounts, any provision of a kind specified for the purposes of this subsection by regulations under section 396, and

b. where the company draws up IAS [International Accounting Standards] individual accounts, any provision made in those accounts.

Regarding the issue of financial assistance in the acquisition of company shares in the United Kingdom, an interesting departure from the English Companies Act 1985 in the U.K. Companies Act 2006 can be summed up as follows:

> The following sections replace Chapter 6 of Part 5 of the 1985 Act which contains a prohibition on the giving of financial assistance (broadly defined) by a company or any of its subsidiaries for the purpose of the acquisition of shares in itself. There are exceptions which apply to all companies, contained in section 153 of the 1985 Act, and a relaxation of the general rule for private companies in sections 155 to 158 of that Act ... As recommended by the CLR (Final Report, paragraph 10.6), the 2006 Act abolishes the prohibition on private companies giving financial assistance for a purchase of its own shares and, as a consequence,

the relaxation for private companies (sometimes referred to as the 'whitewash' procedure) is no longer required. The provisions in sections 155 to 158 have therefore been repealed and are not carried forward in the 2006 Act ... The key change is that the prohibition on private companies providing financial assistance for a purchase of own shares is not carried forward ... The general prohibition on the giving of financial assistance by a public company is required by the Second Company Law Directive (77/91/EEC) and this prohibition is retained in *subsection (1)*. As under the current law, the prohibition extends to post-acquisition assistance (see *subsection (3)*). The prohibition on the giving of post-acquisition assistance only applies if the company in which the shares were acquired is a public company at the time that the assistance is given (see *subsection (3)*. It follows that where a company has re-registered as a private company since the shares were acquired and is a private company at the time the post-acquisition assistance is given, the prohibition in this section will not apply. However, if at the time the shares were acquired the company was a private company, but at the time the post-acquisition assistance is given it has re-registered as a public company, the prohibition will apply.[424]

Second, what constitutes 'financial assistance by way of gift' under the Zambian Companies Act 1994 and/or under the U.K. Companies Act 2006? Both the Zambian and U.K. Companies Acts are silent on this matter. The same is true also for the English Companies Act 1985.[425] So, would financial assistance be unlawful if it was made by way of a small gift? Any gift, irrespective of its size, either in absolute terms or as a percentage of the donor company's total assets, can constitute this form of financial assistance.[426] Indeed, there is no de minimis exception.[427]

Would financial assistance by way of a gift include a situation where, for example, a company ends up allotting shares to an allottee who earlier extended a loan to the company so that the consideration of the allotment is a write-off of the debt that is owed by the company? Indeed, would such an arrangement constitute a legally permissible set-off of financial obligations? What about a situation in which shares are issued and allotted, as consideration, to an individual who has been providing contractual services to the company? Can such an arrangement be treated as a lawful transaction?

As a general rule, if a professional (e.g., an auditor or a lawyer) who performs services for a company buys shares in that company and the company agrees to pay for the shares in return for his or her professional services, such a payment consideration would not be treated as a gift because the payment is being made only to settle the debt that is owed by the company to the professional. However, if a professional who has already been paid by a company for his or her services then buys shares in that company and the company decides to pay for those shares, then that would constitute financial assistance. The same would be true if the company, having paid the professional already for his or her professional services, agrees to reimburse him or her for the amount he or she later spends to buy the shares.

When one analyses what constitutes a gift of financial assistance under Zambia's Companies Act 1994 or the U.K. Companies Act 2006, it is not easy to apply the 'net benefit' test that is spelt out in the English case of *Charterhouse Investment Trust Ltd. v. Tempest Diesel Ltd.*[428] In that case, Hoffmann J. pointed out that the term *financial assistance* had no technical meaning and that the term of reference would be to find out where the net benefit lay.[429] According to Hoffmann,

> There is no definition of giving financial assistance in the section [i.e., the English Companies Act 1985], although some examples are given. The words have no technical meaning and their frame of reference is in my judgement the language of ordinary commerce. One must examine the commercial realities of the transaction and decide whether it can properly be described as the giving of financial assistance by the company, bearing in mind that the section is a penal one and should not be strained to cover transactions which are not fairly within it … It does not matter that the company's balance sheet is undisturbed in the sense that the cash paid out is replaced by an asset of equivalent value. In the case of a loan by a company to a creditworthy purchaser of its shares, the balance sheet is equally undisturbed but the loan plainly constitutes giving financial assistance. It follows that if

the only or main purpose of such a transaction is to enable the purchaser to buy shares, the section is contravened ... This must involve a determination of where the net balance of the financial advantage lay.[430]

Going by Hoffmann's ruling in *Charterhouse Investment Trust Ltd v. Tempest Diesels Ltd*, it could be argued that if the company did not gain the net benefit of the transaction in giving financial assistance, then the transaction constituted unlawful financial assistance by way of a gift. Indeed, there are some illogical difficulties with this view. Consider the following example: X Company, a public company that runs a football club, has been experiencing financial difficulties lately. X Company has its shares listed on the International Stock Exchange. To improve its financial position, X Company decides to issue part of its authorised unissued share-capital to the public. Z Company, another football company, is interested in X Company shares. Z Company arranges with X Company that in return for the shares, Z Company will release one of its Brazilian players to join X Company football team. The deal is struck. In less than two seasons after joining X Company football club, the Brazilian turns out to be a great star who not only attracts large crowds but also leads X Company football club to the top of the premier league. The tabloids are now rating the Brazilian to be worth ten times more than the value of the shares received by Z Company.

In this example, could it be said that financial assistance was given at the time when X Company transferred its shares to Z Company? Would there be any need to value the non-cash consideration in this case, and if so, how would the consideration be valued? Is there any objective standard for valuing such a non-cash consideration? Would the case be different if the Brazilian player had turned out to be a bad player who could not increase X Company's income? In applying the net benefit test, how is one to determine the value of services in relation to the value of shares? There is definitely no objective standard.

In addition, is it not possible that there could be a situation in which a person who has often rendered services to a company at a cheap price in the past and has thus become a treasured business partner of the company is allotted shares and given financial assistance to pay for the shares? Where does the net benefit fall in this case? Is there an objective standard for determining the net benefit? The test is a dubious one. Would the allotment of shares at a discount also be treated as financial assistance because in a way the allottee is being assisted by the company to pay for the shares at a lower price?

The second feature that merits mention under the statutory provision relating to financial assistance in both the Zambian Companies Act 1994 and the U.K. Companies Act 2006 is that which requires that 'the net assets of the company are reduced to a material extent.'[431] Neither the Zambian Companies Act 1994 nor the U.K. Companies Act 2006 provides a definition of what constitutes a material reduction of net assets. The same can be said of the English Companies Act 1985. Again, this creates some confusion in the interpretation of the law. The author of *Gower's Principles of Modern Company Law* (6th edition) has asserted that material extent is a relationship between the value of the assistance and the value of the net assets.[432] By way of an example, the author argued that £50 would reduce the assets to a material extent if the net assets of the company were £100. But, the same amount of £50 would not materially reduce the net assets of the company if they were £10 million. He further argued that because what amounts to financial assistance is very broadly defined, even where the net assets may not be reduced materially, the courts are likely to declare that such financial assistance as unlawful.[433]

In Zambia, the Companies Act 1994 prohibits the rendering of financial assistance in the following manner: '(1) Subject to this Part, where a person is acquiring or is proposing to acquire any shares in a company, the company or any of its subsidiaries shall not give financial assistance directly for the purpose of that acquisition.'[434] In essence, what this means is that section 82(1) of the act allows for financial assistance in the acquisition of a company's shares as long as such assistance is not given directly for the purpose of that acquisition. Subparagraph (2) of section 82 of the Zambian Companies Act 1994 adds,

> Subject to this Part, where a person has acquired any shares in a company and any liability has been incurred (by that or any other person) for the purpose of that acquisition, the company and its subsidiaries shall not give any financial assistance directly or indirectly for the purpose of reducing or discharging the liability so incurred.[435]

In the English case of *Arab Bank plc v. Mercantile Holdings Ltd*,[436] the court held that the statutory prohibition on a company giving financial assistance for the purpose of acquiring its own shares or shares in its holding company does not apply to the giving of assistance by a subsidiary that is incorporated in an overseas jurisdiction. Millett J. considered the geographical scope of section 151 of the English Companies Act 1985 and concluded that this had inadvertently been altered during the consolidation of the United Kingdom's companies legislation in 1985. In particular, the English Companies Act 1985 appeared to have gone further than its predecessor, the English Companies Act 1980. In interpreting the statutory provision in the Companies Act 1985, Millett applied the presumption that in the absence of a contrary intention, section 151 could not have extraterritorial effect. The Department of Trade and Industry in the United Kingdom observed, however, that

> the difficulty with the 1985 Act provision arises as a result of how the prohibition is framed: in particular, the prohibition applies '*to the company or any of its subsidiaries*' and 'subsidiary', as defined in section 736 of the 1985 Act, includes foreign companies. The prohibition in the Act is restricted to UK public companies and their UK subsidiaries as a result of the definition of 'company' in section 1. Subsection (1) of that section makes it clear that, unless the context otherwise requires, 'company' means a company which is formed and registered under the Act or a former UK Companies Act.[437]

It would be interesting to see how the courts in Zambia will react to Millett's ruling in *Arab Bank plc v. Mercantile Holdings Ltd*[438] when they are faced with a similar situation under the Zambian Companies Act 1994. Section 82 of the Zambian Companies Act 1994, like the United Kingdom's counterpart statutory provisions,[439] restricts the granting of financial assistance in the acquisition of a company's shares. It covers financial assistance that is rendered to either an individual or a body corporate. It also draws a distinction between cases where shares are in the process of being acquired (subsection 1) and cases where shares have already been acquired (subsection 2). In the latter situation, there is an outstanding legal obligation to pay for the shares, whereas in the former situation, liability is just arising or is about to arise. The distinction is important because in the case of shares which are in the process of being acquired, liability crystallises on the happening of the acquisition event.

Further, as pointed out previously, section 82(1) of the Zambian Companies Act 1994 specifically deals with 'financial assistance *directly*' rendered, whereas section 82(2) deals with 'financial assistance *directly* or *indirectly*' (italics added) rendered. Again, the distinction is important because in cases where a person is acquiring or is proposing to acquire company shares indirectly, neither the company nor any of its subsidiaries can be considered to have rendered financial assistance to the allottee directly. The statutory provision hinders the rendering of direct financial assistance. The provision does not, however, hinder the rendering of indirect financial assistance.

All in all, section 82(2) of the Zambian Companies Act 1994 is a much wider provision in scope than section 82(1) is. Under section 82(2), companies are prohibited from rendering financial assistance either indirectly or directly to any party that has already acquired shares and has an outstanding obligation to pay for them. As has been noted already, the law prohibits indirect financial assistance as well. Examples of indirect financial assistance include financial assistance rendered to reduce or discharge liability.

In addition, whereas the law applying to situations where a person is acquiring or proposing to acquire shares focuses on that particular individual, the law on financial assistance relating to shares that have already been acquired covers not only the culpable individual but also any of his or her representatives or proxies. The policy bases underpinning the distinction regarding the types of parties that could be held liable in the case of shares that are in the process of being acquired compared to those that have already been acquired is somewhat vague. It is not clear why there should be this distinction.

As a general rule, section 82 of the Zambian Companies Act 1994 not only prohibits companies from rendering financial assistance, it also prohibits any of the company's subsidiaries from rendering such assistance. However, there are exceptions to the general rule, and I will examine them later.[440] Here, suffice it to say, in spelling out the prohibition on financial assistance relating to shares that are in the process of being acquired, the legislative draftsman did not ensure that the relevant words would be linked inseparably by using the word *and*. Instead, he drafted the Companies Act 1994 in such a way that it specifically says, 'the company *or* its subsidiaries' (italics added), which disconnects the words and allows for alternatives or options. This means that the parent company need not necessarily act together with the subsidiary in giving the assistance for liability to arise. Liability can arise even when the parent company or the subsidiary acted alone.

In contrast, in a situation where shares have already been acquired, the Companies Act 1994 uses a conjunction to indicate that the law is pointing to 'the company *and* its subsidiaries' (italics added). The consequences of using this conjunction—*and*—here must not be overlooked. It entails that both the company and the subsidiary must be involved in the transaction for liability to arise. If the parent or the subsidiary acts alone, liability will not arise. Again, the policy basis underpinning this distinction is not clear.

I now turn to look at the statutory provisions in the Zambian Companies Act 1994 permitting financial assistance in the acquisition of a company's shares.

3.6.1. Exceptions to the General Rule Regarding the Prohibition of Financial Assistance

Section 82(3) of the Zambian Companies Act 1994 provides as follows:

This section shall not prohibit a company from giving any financial assistance for the purpose of any acquisition of shares in the company or its holding company if—

a. the giving of the assistance is an incidental part of some larger purpose of the company, and the principal purpose of the company in giving that assistance is not to reduce or discharge any liability incurred by a person for the purpose of any such acquisition; and

b. the assistance is given in good faith in the interest of the company.

The two principal exceptions to the prohibition on rendering financial assistance, as spelt out earlier, can also be found in section 153(1) of the English Companies Act 1985 and section 678(2) of the U.K. Companies Act 2006.[441] In Zambia, as in England, a company giving financial assistance and relying on the first exception listed in section 82(3) of the Zambian Companies Act 1994[442] must be able to show two things.

First, it must be able to demonstrate that the assistance it provided was an incidental part of some larger purpose of the company. This larger purpose of the company can be found mainly in its objects clause or in a completed Form I, II, III, or IV, whichever is applicable (the model templates for Forms I, II, III, and IV can be found in the schedule to the Companies [Prescribed Forms] Regulations).[443] As discussed in chapter 2, it would appear that the rubric of the 'larger purpose of the company' in this case refers to the principal business of the company as spelt out in the completed Form I, II, III, or IV for those companies that are incorporated under the Companies Act 1994. For those companies that were incorporated prior to the repeal of the Companies Act 1921, the 'larger purpose of the company' can be inferred from the objects clause in the company's memorandum of association.[444]

The second condition to be met before a company can give financial assistance under the rule of the larger purpose of the company is that it must be able to show that the principal purpose of rendering that assistance was not to reduce or discharge any liability that had been incurred by the party that was acquiring or had acquired the shares. Viewed from a related angle, this position presupposes that the law permits a company to give financial assistance if the company can show that the secondary or subsidiary purpose of that assistance is actually to reduce or discharge liability incurred by the party that is acquiring the shares.

The second exception under section 82(3) of the Zambian Companies Act 1994 requires the assistance to have been given in good faith and in the interests of the company. Although the common law has dealt extensively with the aspects of company directors' duties when they can be said to be 'acting in the interests of the company',[445] it is not entirely clear what constitutes good faith. I have examined the concept of good faith in chapter 2.

3.6.2. Other Exceptions to the General Rule Prohibiting Financial Assistance

Section 82(4) of the Zambian Companies Act 1994 spells out more exceptions to the general rule prohibiting financial assistance in the acquisition of a company's shares. The statutory provision states as follows:

> This section shall not prohibit—
>
> a. any distribution of a company's assets by way of dividend lawfully made or any distribution made in the course of winding-up of the company;
> b. the allotment of any bonus shares;
> c. anything done in pursuance of an order of the court made under this Act;
> d. anything done under an arrangement made in pursuance of section two hundred and thirty-four;

e. anything done under an arrangement made between a company and its creditors which is binding on the creditors under section three hundred and twenty-five;
f. any reduction of capital confirmed by order of the court under this Part; or
g. a redemption of any share in accordance with this Part.

Section 82(5) and (6) continues,

(5) This section shall not prohibit—

a. the lending of money by the company in the ordinary course of its business, if the lending of the money is part of the ordinary business of the company;
b. the provision by a company, in accordance with an employee's share scheme, of money for acquisition of fully paid shares in the company to be held by or for the benefit of the company (including any director holding a salaried position in the company); or
c. the making by a company of loans to persons, other than directors, employed in good faith by the company, with a view to enabling those persons to acquire fully paid shares otherwise than as nominees of the company.

(6) In giving financial assistance to any person under subsection (5), a public company shall not reduce its net assets, other than *distributable profits*. (italics added)

A number of exceptions that are spelt out in section 82 of the Zambian Companies Act 1994 regarding the rendering of financial assistance replicate similar exceptions in section 153 of the English Companies Act 1985 (and the wording was arguably transplanted from that act as well). These exceptions are repeated somewhat in section 678 of the U.K. Companies Act 2006. Be that as it may, one important shortcoming of the law in Zambia is that the Zambian Companies Act 1994 does not define what constitutes distributable profits. In that act, a somewhat loosely drafted section 84 provides that 'no dividend shall be payable to the shareholders of a company except out of the profits arising or accumulated from the business of the company.' Even so, the statutory provision in the

Zambian act does not define the term *distributable profits*.[446] In contrast, the English Companies Act 1985 provides that

> 'distributable profits', in relation to the giving of any financial assistance—
>
> i. means those profits out of which the company could lawfully make a distribution equal in value to that assistance, and
> ii. includes, in a case where the financial assistance is or includes a non-cash asset, any profit which, if the company were to make a distribution of that asset, would under section 276 (distributions in kind) be available for that purpose,
>
> c. 'distribution' has the meaning given by section 263(2).[447]

Section 263 of the English Companies Act 1985, which is referred to in the previous statutory provision,[448] reads in part,

> For purposes of this Part, a company's profits available for distribution are its accumulated, realised profits, so far as not previously utilised by distribution or capitalisation, less its accumulated, realised losses, so far as not previously written off in a reduction or reorganisation of capital duly made.[449]

There is nothing in the Zambian Companies Act 1994 that is equivalent to the statutory provisions on distributable profits in the English Companies Act 1985—despite the fact that most of the provisions on financial assistance in the Zambian Companies Act 1994 seem to have been drawn from the English Companies Act 1985. A few similarities, however, appear between the English Companies Act 1985 and the Zambian Companies Act 1994 in the aspect of relaxing restrictions for private companies to give financial assistance, although these similarities are not carried forward in the U.K. Companies Act 2006.[450]

The provisions of the English Companies Act 1985 emphasized, among other things, that a private company could give financial assistance if the company had net assets which were not thereby reduced or, to the extent that they were reduced, if the assistance was provided out of distributable profits.[451] But, the Zambian Companies Act 1994 does not have such a provision for safeguarding against the depletion of the financial resources of the company when the financial assistance is not drawn from distributable profits.

3.6.3. Does Financial Assistance Render the Contract Void, and What Is the Nature of Liability for Financial Assistance?

I have argued earlier that the Zambian Companies Act 1994 prohibits generally the rendering of financial assistance by a company to an allottee of the company's shares to enable him or her to pay for the shares. Yet, the Zambian Companies Act 1994 is silent on whether the contract of buying these shares with the aid of finances from the allotting company would make the contract voidable or void *ab initio*. The same is true of the U.K. Companies Act 2006 and the English Companies Act 1985. Goulding observed, however,

> in *Victor Baterry Co. Ltd. v. Curry's Ltd.*,[452] it was held that, where the company had given a debenture as security for the money advanced to a person to enable him to purchase shares in a company, the debenture was not illegal and therefore was not void. The reasoning behind the decision was that if it were void, then the company which had contravened the provision would gain a benefit, the avoidance of the security, and the lender would lose. There was also a logical problem in that if the transaction itself was void, it was void *ab initio* and therefore technically no financial assistance could have been given.[453]

But, this approach was not followed in *Heald v. O'Connor*,[454] where it was held that a guarantee made in breach of the equivalent provision in section 151 (CA 1985) was illegal and void. According to Goulding,

> the problem with this approach is that if the company had actually advanced a sum of money by way of a loan to another person then it cannot sue on the loan because it was a party to the illegal

transaction itself and it was held in *Wallersteiner v. Moir*[455] that the prohibition was designed for the protection of the company. The solution for the company may be to sue the director and other persons who have participated in the infringement of section 151. In *Selanghor United Rubber Estates Ltd. v. Craddock (No. 3)*,[456] a company was caused by the majority of its directors to pay money to a third party, which was then used by Craddock to acquire the company's shares through an intermediary. Ungoed-Thomas J saw the case as an unlawful loan. Where the directors act for the company in the illegal transaction with a third party the company is itself a party to the transaction and cannot, because of the illegality, claim any rights from the transaction. But if instead the company alleges a breach of trust it is not relying on the transaction at all. The action is against the directors and constructive trustees for perpetrating the transaction and for making the company a party to it in breach of trust owed to the company by the directors and thereby causing the company loss.[457]

In a number of jurisdictions, including countries that have a common law or Roman Dutch law system, unlawful financial assistance per se does not invalidate a contract of sale relating to the allotment of shares. In countries such as Australia, the law treats unlawful financial assistance as not affecting the validity of any resulting contractual rights.[458] In Zimbabwe, the law provides that such a contract would be voidable and can thus be set aside by the court at the suit of the company or its members, its liquidator, its creditors, or any party to the transaction.[459] In Zambia and the United Kingdom, no such equivalent statutory provision exists. Company legislation in these two countries is silent on the matter, and indeed, the case law on the subject is not conclusive either. It would be helpful to bring the law in Zambia in line with the Australian position, thereby giving legislative weight to the holding in *Victor Battery Co. Ltd. v. Curry's Ltd.*[460]

I now turn to look at the liability of culpable parties under Zambia's Companies Act 1994 when a company provides financial assistance to a purchaser of the company's shares.

3.6.4. Liability for Engaging in Financial Assistance

Section 82(3) of the Zambian Companies Act 1994 provides as follows:

> If a company fails to comply with subsection (1) or (2), the company, and each officer in default, shall be guilty of an offence, and shall be liable on conviction to a fine ... or to imprisonment..., or to both.

It is clear from this statutory provision that the Companies Act 1994 of Zambia provides for criminal sanctions against the company and its directors only. The issue of criminal liability to be faced by a recipient of unlawful financial assistance is not addressed. Another shortcoming of the Zambian Companies Act 1994 is that it does not provide for civil remedies against the offending parties. In any event, it is not easy to establish which party would bring a civil claim against the company, the company's directors, or any third party given that under the Companies Act 1994, it is the company and its directors that are seen to be the defaulting parties. It could be argued, however, that the shareholders (on behalf of the company) might wish to bring a derivative suit to restrain the company's directors from providing any unlawful financial assistance where such assistance would amount to 'fraud on the minority' and the wrongdoers are themselves in control of the company.[461] Equally, where such financial assistance has already occurred, the shareholders could bring a derivative suit to recover the loss that was incurred by the company.[462] A notable civil remedy for the shareholders in this situation would be to seek restitution from the directors (and any third party who, with knowledge, comingled in the assets and was not a bona fide purchaser for value) which would require them to restore the value that the company lost to the extent that they either jointly or severally caused the company loss through their unlawful financial assistance.[463] Indeed, both in Zambia and in England, as shown earlier, the directors of a company have statutory duties to act in good faith in the interests of the company when they give financial assistance under the exceptions that were spelt out earlier. It must be observed that the statutory duty to act in good faith and in the interests of the company codifies the common law fiduciary duty of directors to act in the interests of the company.[464]

3.7. CONCLUSION

This chapter opened up with an examination of the relevance of the concept of par value in the modern world of commerce. Following that was an examination of the legal aspects of share watering and financial assistance in the acquisition of a company's shares. The chapter drew some analogies from the United Kingdom, especially because Zambia's legal system is based on the English common law.[465] It was argued, among other things, that the concept of par value has little relevance to company law in Zambia and many other common law jurisdictions and that shares of no-par-value often reflect the true value of the shares. Whereas Zambian and English company law still recognize the concept of par value when it comes to the allotment of shares, the law in the United States, Ghana, New Zealand, and Canada shows that in many respects, the concept of par value is now obsolete and redundant.

In examining the law in Zambia on share watering and the prohibition of financial assistance in the acquisition of a company's shares, I observed that a number of weaknesses relating to the Zambian Companies Act 1994 were due mainly to the draftsman paying insufficient attention to parallel legislation in other jurisdictions. For example, matters such as share watering and non-cash considerations should not have been left to the standard articles of association. It was shown in chapter 2 that under the Zambian Companies Act 1994, there is no mandatory requirement, strictly speaking, for a company to have articles of association. So, what happens when a company decides not to have any articles of association? How is one to treat such a company if its directors commit the company to acts of share watering and accepting non-cash considerations? Besides, not every company in Zambia has adopted the standard articles that are found in schedule 1 to the Companies Act 1994.

Against this background, it would not be far-fetched to argue that problems which often arise with what is commonly known as legal technical assistance explain some of the shortcomings of the law in a developing country such as Zambia. Legal technical assistance[466] often entails the donors themselves sending some so-called experts to developing countries to draft the laws of these countries. No doubt, this form of technical support has often brought along with it some form of mediocrity and some unsuitable legislative models.[467]

CHAPTER 4

WRONGFUL TRADING AND FRAUDULENT TRADING

4.0. INTRODUCTION

This chapter examines the efficacy of the legal framework that deals with the liability of company directors for fraudulent trading and wrong-ful trading, including the salient and pertinent aspects of fraud commit-ted by the officers of companies that have gone into liquidation.

> Where a company is insolvent in the sense that its liabilities exceed its assets, its shareholders (and directors) have an incentive to con-tinue trading as they have everything to gain and nothing to lose. Should the company trade out of its difficulties this will benefit the shareholders whereas if it continues to decline they will, because of the principle of limited liability, suffer no additional losses and these will be borne by the company's creditors. Where an insolvent company continues to trade the persons who make the decision that it should do so are not the persons who will 'lose' if the company is unsuccessful. Thus the principle of limited liability creates a per-verse incentive for an insolvent company to continue to trade.[468]

Closely related to the central theme of the chapter, the absence of a legal framework in Zambia for licensing and regulating insolvency practitioners—a practice that provides a means of protecting consumers and the market from malpractices of unlicensed and unauthorized persons who serve as insolvency practitioners—poses a great challenge to the development of the country's corporate insolvency law. As a corollary, some insolvency practitioners, including some company directors, are also known to engage in malpractices that range from unethical professional conduct to utter disregard of the fundamental principles of corporate insolvency law.[469] A report in the *Post* newspaper in Zambia helps to demonstrate this point.[470]

> THE liquidation of Zambia National Oil Company (ZNOC) must be stayed in public interest, former ZNOC chief executive Dennis Mumba has said. Mumba, in his affidavit filed in the Lusaka High Court on October 25, 2002, stated that the liquidation of ZNOC was initiated in order to perpetuate fraud against the creditors and public who have the ultimate beneficial interest in ZNOC as a public company. Mumba said if the court could not stay the liquidation then it should appoint an independent liquidator to manage the liquidation process as a court supervised liquidation. He said the liquidation of ZNOC was not done in good faith and in the interest of the public as the liquidation process was approached with 'a lackadaisical attitude and lacked transparency'.[471]

However, it is recognized that too-strict regulation of insolvency practitioners or company directors could be detrimental to the development of a sound legal framework for corporate insolvency. This is especially the case if the market, profession, or person that is being regulated is relatively unsophisticated and the degree of financial misconduct does not warrant such excessive regulation.

But, in Zambia, the case is rather different. Various state-owned enterprises have been privatized, and such privatizations have at times involved liquidations or some insolvency workouts to restructure financially distressed companies.[472] Yet, the proceeds of these winding-ups and workouts have not been fully accounted for.[473] As one report shows,

GOVERNMENT must account for over US$90 million of privatisation proceeds, Zambia Union of Financial Institutions and Allied Workers (ZUFIAW) general secretary Joyce Nonde demanded ... Nonde said Zambians needed to be told what had happened to US$90 million privatisation proceeds and whether a social safety net mechanism had been established to mitigate the impact of the privatisation process in Zambia. 'Before we embark on more borrowing, we need to ask ourselves as a country how we have utilised the little resources that came with privatisation of our assets. This government made some noise over the US$90 million but they have gone quiet just as they have remained silent over the cobalt report,' she said ... funds from the privatisation proceeds were supposed to be used on victims of liquidations or redundancies apart from recapitalising[474]

Furthermore, as I pointed out earlier,[475] there are no professionally regulated insolvency practitioners in Zambia. In many cases, chartered accountants and certified accountants serve as liquidators.[476] These individuals and their firms rarely obtain any meaningful legal counsel from qualified lawyers.[477] Also, given that these accountants sometimes wear the hat of an insolvency practitioner, a number of them have enriched themselves selfishly by amassing huge assets from the estates of the insolvent companies that are under their control.[478] It is common practice in Zambia today for such accountant-insolvency practitioners to undervalue the assets of the debtor company for which they are acting and then proceed to sell themselves these assets before disposing of the remaining assets to various creditors.[479] Because there is no formal body to regulate insolvency practitioners, these accountants often pay themselves hefty bills from the estate of the insolvent company, leaving the bulk of the unsecured creditors with nothing to claim.[480] The situation is exacerbated by the increasing levels of misfeasance concerning some company directors in Zambia.[481] The case of *Access Finance Services et al v. Bank of Zambia*,[482] discussed in chapter 2 and also reiterated later, illustrates this point very well.

Here, as noted in the epigraph of this chapter, I will focus on the legal liability of company directors for fraudulent trading and wrongful trading,[483] including the salient aspects of the law relating to fraud committed by an officer of a company that has gone into liquidation. The focus of the chapter is underscored by views such as those expressed by the then-president of the Republic of Zambia, Levy Patrick Mwanawasa, when he called on the business community in Zambia 'to help in the anti-corruption crusade by engaging in good corporate practices and to place themselves above dubious dealings'.[484] Mwanawasa was quoted as having said that

> good corporate governance was one of the tenets of his adminis-tration and the corporate sector should join hands to help eradi-cate corruption ... since most corrupt practices involved people from the economic and business sector, the corporate community should take a leading role in fighting corruption. In his address on the theme: 'Corporate Governance and Corruption', Dr Mwana-wasa said: 'Government officials cannot corrupt themselves, but are assisted by business people. The Government alone cannot, therefore, fight and win the war against corruption in our country. The Institute of Directors (IOD) and its members must join hands with the Government in combating the vice.[485]

According to Mwanawasa, the Zambian government takes the issue of good corporate practices seriously, as is evidenced by its fight against corruption.[486] Mwanawasa observed that bad corporate practices or an absence of good corporate practices tends to undermine economic pros-perity because investors often shun corruption-plagued countries.[487] The former Zambian president argued that if corrupt practices were to be rife in Zambia, it would be difficult to create efficient businesses and demand improved performance and accountability from investors.[488]

In contrast, although jurisdictions such as Australia have parallel legislative developments regarding insolvent trading,[489] it is beyond the scope of this chapter to delve into the intricacies of Australian jurispru-dence. Here, suffice it to say, although fraudulent trading and wrongful trading, generally speaking, are topics that are often treated as separate and stand-alone discussions in some academic literature,[490] these topics pose relatively similar risks in corporate governance and compliance.

Where compliance is weak, there is a higher likelihood that valuable and useful information will not flow in time to senior management to enable them to make timely and less costly decisions. Shortcomings of this nature can lead to business or corporate failure.[491] Such risks are often associated with weaknesses in the company's compliance and risk management systems, especially in its internal controls, accounts, and audits.[492]

Commenting on the importance of good corporate governance, the World Bank observed that

> for emerging countries, improving corporate governance can serve a number of important public policy objectives. Good corporate governance reduces emerging market vulnerability to financial crises, reinforces property rights, reduces transaction costs and the cost of capital, and leads to capital market development ... Studies have shown that good corporate governance practices have led to significant increases in economic value added (EVA) of firms, high productivity, and lower risk of systemic financial failures for countries.[493]

In this chapter, analogies are drawn from English common law and English jurisprudence on corporate insolvency.[494] For example, whereas the coming into force of the English Companies Act 2006 introduced the statutory duty in the United Kingdom of a company director to act in good faith and promote the success of the company,[495] the Zambian Companies Act 1994 does not have the equivalent of such a provision. Yet, the Zambian case of *Access Finance Services et al v. Bank of Zambia*,[496] highlighted later, helps to shed light on how reckless some company directors in Zambia have been. From a public policy point of view, there is much depth to the argument that in order to strengthen the legal framework for corporate governance in Zambia, the Zambian government should strongly consider introducing legislation for the disqualification of recalcitrant company directors. Indeed, Zambia should enact a statute that disqualifies company directors who have been convicted of offences such as fraudulent trading, wrongful trading, and fraud by officers of companies that have gone into liquidation from serving as company directors.

Where such persons have been disqualified by a court order but are seen to be acting in disregard of that court order, the convicts should be held personally responsible for all of the relevant debts of the company if, at any time,

1. in contravention of a disqualification order, the convict was involved in the management of the company, or
2. as a person who was involved in the management of the company, the convict was or was willing to act on instructions that were given without the leave of the court by a person whom he or she knew at that time to be the subject of a disqualification order or to be an undischarged bankrupt.[497]

Although the Institute of Directors has now been set up in Zambia,[498] the country continues to experience a weak compliance culture in the area of corporate governance. There are not many mechanisms that deal with the enforcement of directors' liability other than relying on the judicial process to sound out the liability of culpable directors. Zambia should consider the introduction of legislation that deals with the disqualification of recalcitrant directors who act in breach of the law. Currently, in Zambia, even the role of external auditors is downplayed for the most part. Many companies rarely file their annual returns. Incentive for company directors to act responsibly, professionally, and diligently often lies in the power of the shareholders to appoint and dismiss directors. Also, shareholders may bring a derivative suit against culpable directors for injury they have caused to the company.[499] But, the problem is that without adequate and reliable information coming from the directors themselves, shareholders, external auditors, and other stakeholders such as creditors may have difficulties monitoring the directors' compliance with the law.

In the famous English case of *Foss v. Harbottle*,[500] two minority shareholders initiated legal proceedings against, among others, the directors of the company. They claimed that the directors had misapplied the company's assets. The court dismissed their claim and held that when a company is wronged by its directors, it is only the company that has standing to sue. In effect, the court established two rules. The first rule is known as the 'proper plaintiff rule':

> First, the proper plaintiff in an action in respect of a wrong alleged done to a company … is *prima facie* the company itself. Secondly, where the alleged wrong is a transaction which might be made binding on the company … on all its members by a simple majority of the members, no individual member of the company is allowed to maintain an action in respect of that matter for the simple reason that if a mere majority of the members of the company … is in favour of what has been done then *cadit quaestio*— the matter admits of no further argument.[501]

The second rule derived from this case was the 'majority rule principle.' This rule states that if the alleged wrong can be confirmed or ratified by a simple majority of the company's members in a general meeting, then the court will not interfere.

The first part of this chapter addresses liability for fraudulent trading. The second part deals with liability for wrongful trading, and the third and fourth parts examine, respectively, the power of a court of law to assess damages against delinquent officers and the financial crime of fraud committed by officers of companies that have gone into liquidation.

4.1. FRAUDULENT TRADING

In Zambia, fraudulent trading constitutes both a criminal offence and a civil wrong.[502] I will examine both of these aspects of fraudulent trading. Section 384 of Zambia's Companies Act 1994, covering the criminal offence of fraudulent trading, provides that

> a person who is *knowingly* a party to the carrying on of any business of the company for a fraudulent purpose shall be guilty of an offence, and shall be liable on conviction to a fine not exceeding one thousand monetary units or to imprisonment for a period not exceeding twelve months, or to both. (italics added)

But then, how does one define the terms *knowingly* and *knowledge* when seeking to determine whether a person was '*knowingly* a party to the carrying on of any business of the company for a fraudulent purpose' (italics added)?[503] Should one apply a criminal law standard or a civil law standard in defining this term? Where the Companies Act 1994 provides that fraudulent trading is a criminal offence,[504] then the criminal law standard applies. In contrast, where the Companies Act 1994 provides that fraudulent trading should be treated as a civil wrong,[505] the term *knowingly* should be construed in the civil law context.

Although no statute can be readily cited as an example of a foreign piece of legislation in which the term *knowledge* or *knowingly* has been fully defined, that point alone does not defeat the view that clarity in the law regarding the meaning of terms such as *knowledge* would facilitate a smooth interpretation of the statute. In Zambia, the term *knowledge* is not defined anywhere in the Companies Act 1994. However, in *Selanghor v. Craddock (No. 3)*,[506] Ungoed-Thomas J., defining the term *knowledge* in a civil law case, was of the view that it meant 'circumstances which would indicate to an honest and reasonable man that such design was being committed, or would put him on inquiry'. The test applied by Ungoed-Thomas is an objective test of a 'reasonable' man. In *Re Montagu's Settlements*,[507] another civil law case, it was held that knowledge is not confined to actual knowledge, but includes actual knowledge that would have been acquired but for shutting one's eyes to the obvious or wilfully and recklessly failing to make such inquiries as a reasonable man would make. Again, the objective test of a 'reasonable' man is applied here.

In *Baden Delvaux and Lecuit v. Societe Generale*,[508] another civil law case, it was pointed out that

> knowledge can comprise any one of five different mental states…:
>
> i.   actual knowledge;
> ii. wilfully shutting one's eye to the obvious;
> iii. wilfully and recklessly failing to make such inquiries as an honest and reasonable man would make;

> iv. knowledge of circumstances which would indicate the facts to an honest and reasonable man;
> v. knowledge of circumstances which would put an honest and reasonable man on inquiry.[509]

The ruling in *Baden Delvaux and Lecuit v. Societe Generale* imports both an objective test and a subjective test of knowledge. To satisfy the subjective test, unlike in the objective test, the intention of the accused to engage in the relevant misconduct must be proved.[510] Paragraphs (i) and (ii) relate to the subjective test which requires the prosecution to show that the accused had 'actual knowledge' or that he 'willfully shut his eyes to the obvious'. In contrast, paragraphs (iii), (iv), and (v) relate to the objective test of how a reasonable person, when placed under similar circumstances, would have reacted. It could be argued, however, that financial misconduct containing objective elements of mens rea imputes a civil negligence-based test into the determination of criminal offences.[511]

In contrast to the civil law position, the criminal law position was spelt out in *Nelson v. Larholt*,[512] where it was held that knowledge meant more than constructive knowledge in the sense of shutting one's eyes to the obvious. In *Warner v. DPP*,[513] Lord Reid held that knowledge could include 'willfully shutting one's eyes to the truth.' The term *willful*, however, could indicate deliberate or reckless acts or omissions.[514] In the American case of *U.S. v. Jewell*,[515] Jewell drove a car containing a substantial cargo of marijuana into the United States. The court's reasoning was that if the circumstances suggested the probability of the presence of marijuana and Jewell purposely refrained from investigating in order not to know, then he was guilty of knowingly importing and possessing a controlled substance with the intent to distribute it. However, the mere fact that the circumstances suggested the presence of marijuana in the car was not enough. Jewell could not be convicted of knowingly importing the marijuana on the basis that he should have known it was in the car because a reasonable person would have known. But, if the circumstances had made Jewell aware of the probability of the presence of marijuana and he had deliberately shut his eyes, so to speak, in order not to see what was there to be seen, then Jewell had the mens rea concept,[516] which falls under the category of knowledge. The English may have a 'corner' on the label *willful blindness*, but the underlying doctrine is as firmly established in the United States as it is in England.[517] Indeed,

> a doubtful suggestion ... is this: 'One problem with the willful blindness doctrine is its bias towards visual means of acquiring knowledge.' Such phrases as 'deliberately shutting his eyes' and 'willful blindness' have always been employed as metaphors to indicate a conscious effort to avoid learning the truth, by whatever means knowledge is to be obtained. In a case that illustrates this point, *State v. Farnes*, 171 Mont. 368, 558 P.2d 472 (1976), the Defendant was convicted of theft of a horse for having 'knowingly' sold it for the purpose of depriving the owner of his property. The state statute provides that 'when knowledge of the existence of a particular fact is an element of an offence, such knowledge is established if a person is aware of a high probability of its existence.' There was evidence to the effect that the defendant was aware of a high probability that the horse was stolen. This was held sufficient to support the conviction.[518]

The relevant statutory provision in Zambia's Companies Act 1994 prohibiting fraudulent trading refers to situations where a company is either solvent or insolvent.[519] In essence, criminal liability for fraudulent trading can be triggered even when a company is solvent. However, the culpable director, even when he or she is convicted, cannot be disqualified from serving as a director of any company. There is a need to amend the law in this regard or to introduce legislation to disqualify recalcitrant directors from serving as the directors of companies. As an incentive to promote compliance with best practices in corporate governance, Zambia should consider introducing legislation that deals with the disqualification of recalcitrant directors.

Second, and as shall be seen when I examine wrongful trading, a notable difference between fraudulent trading and wrongful trading is that the statutory provision against fraudulent trading imposes criminal liability on any person who is knowingly a party to the carrying on of any business of the company for a fraudulent purpose. In this case, liability is not restricted to an officer of the company.[520] It can fall on company directors, employees of the company, agents of the company, business partners of the company, or any other third party that has been contracted by the company to carry on its business.

To illustrate, X and Y, the directors of Company Z, decide to commit Company Z to a business transaction to smuggle marijuana from Zambia to the Netherlands, purporting that Company Z is exporting flowers. The subject matter of the alleged transaction—or the description of the goods, as it were—is concealed, and the directors offer misleading information fraudulently that Company Z is exporting flowers to the Netherlands. Also, the directors, both X and Y, have partnered with an employee of the Zambia Revenue Authority so that Company Z can benefit from the law's provisions for tax exemptions on certain agriculture-related exports.

In the meantime, one of the shareholders of Company Z, who is an uncle to director X and a resident in Zambia, has a private business enterprise in the Netherlands. This foreign-based business enterprise purports to be importing the 'flowers' from Company Z, and Company Z prepares an invoice reflecting an exorbitant contract price for the alleged flowers. In reality, no such flowers are being sold and no contract payment is being made by the foreign-based firm to Company Z. If anything, the business enterprise in the Netherlands is being used merely as conduit and shield to conceal the illegal transactions that are being orchestrated by X and Y. The monetary gains from the sales of marijuana are then remitted to Company Z in Zambia, purporting to be contractual payments by the Netherlands-based firm for the 'flowers' it allegedly bought from Company Z.

Apart from attracting criminal liability in Zambia for tax evasion,[521] drug trafficking,[522] and money laundering,[523] the business activities that are being pursued by directors X and Y will bring further liability (i.e., both criminal and civil liability) on them for fraudulent trading under

Zambia's Companies Act 1994. The shareholder who is participating in the scheme, as well as the employee of the Zambia Revenue Authority and any other accomplices or abettors, will also be held criminally liable for fraudulent trading, tax evasion, and money laundering.

Third, under the statutory provision in Zambia's Companies Act 1994 dealing with fraudulent trading, the culpable party must have acted fraudulently. The nature and scope of the business could be anything; it will be admissible in evidence as long as the business was conducted fraudulently. However, it is not the purpose of this chapter to delve into the intricacies of what constitutes fraud in criminal law. There is an abundance of literature on this subject.[524] Dine argued, for example, that it is necessary to establish that there was trading with the 'intent to defraud'.[525] According to Dine,

> This requires the court to find that the directors were acting *dishonestly*, not just that they were acting unreasonably. The difficulty of establishing *dishonesty* has made this action of little use. It is wider than wrongful trading, however, in that it is available against 'any persons who were knowingly parties to the carrying on of the business' of the company.[526]

On the same issue of criminal fraud, Podgor observed,

> The focus of many white collar criminal offenses is fraud. Yet, fraud is not a crime with prescribed elements. In the federal system, there is no indictment or conviction for fraud. Rather, as in English law, the term 'fraud' is a 'concept' at the core of a variety of criminal statutes. Although fraud is not a crime in itself, fraud is an integral aspect of several criminal statutes. For example, one finds generic statutes such as mail fraud and conspiracy to defraud being applied to an ever-increasing spectrum of fraudulent conduct. In contrast, other fraud statutes, such as computer fraud and bank fraud, present limited applications that permit their use only with specified conduct. In recent years, criminal fraud statutes have multiplied, offering new laws that often match legislative or executive priorities.[527]

The concept of fraud, according to Podgor,[528] appears in varying roles within criminal statutes. In addition to fraud being conduct that is subject to punishment, it can also present itself as the level of mens rea that is required for certain criminal activity.[529] For example, section 384 of Zambia's Companies Act 1994, dealing with the criminal offence of fraudulent trading, uses the term *fraudulent purpose* to describe the intent that is required of the actor. Podgor observed that other statutes may use terms such as *obtains by fraud* to describe both the method of conduct as well as the mental element.[530]

4.1.1. Civil Liability for Fraudulent Trading

Although section 384 of Zambia's Companies Act 1994, dealing with the criminal offence of fraudulent trading, does not require a company to be insolvent for liability to be triggered, section 383(1) provides as follows:

> In the course of the winding-up of a company or any proceedings against a company, the court may, on the application of the liquidator or any creditor or member of the company, if it is satisfied that a person was knowingly a party to the carrying on of any business of the company for a fraudulent purpose, make an order that the person shall be personally responsible, without any limitation of liability, for the debts or other liabilities of the company or for such of those debts or other liabilities as the court directs.

This statutory provision is complemented by subsection 383(4), which provides that the entire section 383

> shall apply whether or not the person concerned has been convicted of an offence against section *three hundred and eighty-four* (i.e. the criminal offence of fraudulent trading) or of any other offence in respect of the matters on the ground of which the order is made.

I will take a more reasoned look at section 383 of the Companies Act 1994.

First, the triggering of civil liability under section 383 is not dependent on whether or not a criminal conviction has been secured under section 384. This means that the court can give a ruling for civil liability even if there is no conviction for a predicate criminal offence of fraudulent trading. Second, section 383, on civil liability, can be invoked only in the course of a winding-up or any other proceedings against the company. What does this mean? It means that no action for civil liability can be brought before a court of law if the company is not in winding-up or facing any other proceedings.

Third, although any person can have civil liability relating to fraudulent trading, it is a liquidator, member, or creditor of the company that can bring an action for such liability. It does not matter whether the creditor is a secured or unsecured creditor; both are eligible to bring an action for civil liability. Fourth, the court is likely to apply the civil law standards of *knowingly* and *fraudulent purpose* if no criminal conviction has been secured. I have already examined the term *knowingly* in the civil law context and distinguished its use from that in the criminal law context.[531] It is important to stress that the criminal law context and the civil law context of fraud differ in the level of proof that is required.[532] For civil cases, the standard of proof is based on a 'preponderance of probabilities.'[533] In criminal fraud, the standard is 'beyond reasonable doubt.'[534] Commenting on the civil law context of fraud, Goode argued,

> A representation, it will be recalled, is a statement of fact, express or implied, anterior to the contract, which is intended to and does induce the person to whom it was made to enter into the contract but is not at the time of making intended as a promise, though it may later become incorporated as a term of the contract. Since a representation is not as such a promise, its falsity cannot constitute a breach of contract or give rise to an action for damages for breach of contract. If there is any remedy at all, it must lie in tort or statute. Hence a fraudulent misrepresentation is actionable not because of the character of the statement as a representation inducing a contract but because the law of tort gives a general remedy in deceit for fraudulent statements.[535]

Fifth, under section 383 of Zambia's Companies Act 1994, the veil of incorporation of the company can be lifted and the concept of limited liability suspended until the debts or other liabilities of the company (or such other debts and liabilities as the court may direct) have been made good by the culpable individuals. The court has powers to order measures that are expected to give effect to the liabilities of culpable persons, in particular providing that those liabilities should be a charge on any debt or obligation that is due from the company to these persons or on any interest in the company of which the culpable persons have a direct or indirect benefit.[536] The court can make further orders to enforce any charge that has been imposed by it, as it thinks necessary.[537]

4.2. WRONGFUL TRADING

In Zambia, wrongful trading constitutes both a criminal offence and a civil wrong.[538] As a general rule, if an officer of a company who is knowingly a party to the contracting of a debt by the company has, at the time the debt is contracted, no reasonable or probable ground of expectation (after taking into consideration any other liabilities of the company at the time) of the company's being able to pay the debt, the officer will be guilty of an offence and will be liable, on conviction, to a fine, imprisonment, or both.[539] This rule covers criminal liability for wrongful trading and applies only to officers of the company.[540] Under this rule, it must be proven beyond reasonable doubt that the officer of the company, acting with knowledge when he or she committed the company to further debts, had no probable ground of expectation that the company would pay back its debts. Yet, again, the Companies Act 1994 does not spell out a requirement to disqualify directors who act in breach of the law.

It should be borne in mind that section 2 of the Companies Act 1994 provides that the term *officer* includes the following:

a.   a director, secretary or executive officer of a body corporate;
b.   a local director of a foreign company;
c.   a receiver of any part of the undertaking of a body corporate appointed under a power contained in any instrument; and,
d.   a liquidator of a body corporate appointed by members in a voluntary winding-up.

The term *director* includes not only de facto and de jure directors but also shadow directors.[541] Overall, the term *officer* does not include (a) a receiver of any part of the undertaking of a body corporate appointed by the court, (b) a liquidator of a body corporate appointed by the court or by the creditors of the body corporate, or (c) an auditor of a body corporate.[542]

Another term that needs to be understood properly is *knowingly*. I have already examined the criminal law context in which the term should be understood. What does 'no reasonable or probable ground of expectation of the company's being able to pay the debt' mean? This phrase points to the solvency state of the company. When can it be said that a company is insolvent? I will take a more reasoned look at the concept of there being no reasonable or probable ground of expectation of the company's being able to pay the debt.

4.2.1. The Concept of Corporate Insolvency and that of 'No Reasonable Ground of Expectation'

The use of the word *reasonable* in the phrase *no reasonable ground of expectation* imports an objective test of determining whether the wrong-doer expected the company to be in a position to pay the debt. If the test were to state simply that the wrongdoer should expect or should have expected the company to pay the debt, that would import a subjective test. Indeed, there would be no room to consider what a reasonable third party would have done had he or she been in the wrongdoer's position. Rather, the test would focus primarily on the intention of the wrongdoer without inferring comparisons of reasonableness. For an expectation to arise in this situation, the wrongdoer would have to show that he or she relied on some factual representation and not just a mere hunch. There is a causal relationship between the costs of reliance, on the one hand, and expectancy costs, on the other.

Generally, the concept of corporate insolvency in Zambia can be addressed from two different but related angles. The first viewpoint falls under company law, and the second falls under banking law. I shall look at both.

Under the Banking and Financial Services Act 1994, a bank or financial institution is said to be insolvent when

a. it ceases to be able to meet its obligations as they fall due; or
b. its assets are insufficient to meet its liabilities; or
c. the amount of its regulatory capital requirement prescribed by the Bank of Zambia is nil or lower.[543]

In essence, the banking law in Zambia provides for three tests of insolvency for banks and financial institutions:

a. the cash flow test of insolvency;
b. the balance sheet test of insolvency; and
c. the capital requirement test of insolvency.

The cash flow test relates to a bank or financial institution that is licensed by the Bank of Zambia under the Banking and Financial Services Act 1994 being able or unable to meet its debt obligations when they fall due.[544] This is the same test that is reflected in section 357(1) of the Companies Act 1994, which refers to there being 'no reasonable or probable ground of expectation of the company's being able to pay the debt'.[545] In contrast, the balance sheet test deals with situations where a bank or financial institution may be able to meet the demands of the creditors, but its liabilities, in the balance sheet, exceed its assets.[546] This test is not covered by section 357(1) of the Companies Act 1994. What this means is that if a company can pay its debts when they fall due, even if its liabilities far exceed its assets, then criminal liability for wrongful trading will not arise. Yet, one knows that a company, bank, or financial institution can be insolvent even if it is able to pay its debts.[547] Indeed, under the balance sheet test of insolvency, it should matter that the liabilities of a bank or financial institution have exceeded its assets, because that means that the institution is technically insolvent.[548] The policy basis underpinning this view is that both the cash flow test and the balance sheet test of insolvency serve the same corporate governance and internal-risk-control purposes of ensuring that the management of a company, bank, or financial institution does not commit the business entity to further debt obligations when it is reasonably clear that the books of account are in the red.

The third test of insolvency, the capital requirement test, unlike the first two tests that have been discussed, is peculiarly limited to banks and financial institutions. Whereas in common law and under the Companies Act 1994, the concepts of cash flow and balance sheet tests of insolvency can be applied to almost all of the companies and bodies corporate in Zambia,[549] the capital requirement test cannot be applied to any Zambian company or body corporate that exists and operates outside the framework of the Banking and Financial Services Act 1994. This distinction is an important departure from the framework for insolvency law under the Companies Act 1994. As far as offences of fraudulent trading and wrongful trading are concerned, banks and financial institutions that are licensed by the Bank of Zambia may also be subject to the statutory provisions of the Banking and Financial Services Act 1994 relating to unsafe and unsound practices. Although I have already examined in chapter 2 the Zambian case of *Access Finance Services et al v. Bank of Zambia,*[550] it would be helpful here to revisit that case because it deals with a pertinent issue relating to bank insolvency in Zambia. To recapitulate, in the case, the central bank, the Bank of Zambia (BoZ), took over possession of both Access Finance Services Limited and Access Leasing Limited in early 2003.[551] The two companies were alleged to have been involved in criminal activities that included unsafe and unsound practices.[552] Contesting the decision of the central bank, the applicants—Aaron Chungu, Access Finance Services Limited (AFSL), and Access Leasing Limited (ALL)—applied for judicial review to the High Court of Zambia.

The applicants challenged the decision of the BoZ to place them into compulsory winding-up. The BoZ argued that both AFSL and ALL had not only breached the law but had also operated their businesses recklessly, prompting the BoZ to place them under liquidation. According to the BoZ, the two institutions were closed down on the grounds that they had violated the Banking and Financial Services Act 1994 as well as other written laws and because they were insolvent.[553] The BoZ submitted before High Court Judge Japhet Banda that the wording of sections 81, 84(B), and 101 of Zambia's Banking and Financial Services Act 1994 made it clear that parliament left it to the BoZ to determine the facts that might compel the bank to take its supervisory actions against any bank or financial institution.[554] The BoZ contended that parliament had entrusted it to determine the insolvency or solvency of any financial institution as well as what action was necessary to enable the BoZ to carry out its functions under Zambia's Banking and Financial Services Act 1994.[555] The BoZ was of the view that as a supervisory agency, it had exercised its powers properly upon examining the business activities and financial books of AFSL and ALL. According to BoZ, 'It's not open to the applicants under judicial review application to challenge the merits of BoZ's decision. All they could do is to call into question the decision making process that BoZ followed.'[556]

Indeed, section 77(1) of Zambia's Banking and Financial Services Act 1994 provides as follows:

> Where, in the opinion of the Bank of Zambia, a bank or financial institution is *committing* or *pursuing* or *is about to commit* or *pursue* on behalf of the bank or financial institution *any act* or *course of conduct* that is *considered by the Bank of Zambia as unsafe or unsound practice*, the Bank of Zambia may enter into one or more written agreements with the bank or financial institution or its board of directors to establish a programme of action to counteract the unsafe or unsound practice and to establish or maintain safe and sound practices in the conduct of the business of the bank or financial institution.[557] (italics added)

Section 77(1) does not provide a definition of 'unsafe and unsound practice' but merely refers to the term and highlights the steps that the BoZ should take whenever, at its discretion, it determines that an act or course of conduct of a particular bank or financial institution constitutes 'unsafe and unsound practice.'[558]

Notwithstanding the submissions that were made by the parties to the case,[559] not much thought was accorded by the court to the concept of unsafe and unsound practice under Zambia's Banking and Financial Services Act 1994. Judge Banda merely alluded to section 77 of the act on pages J13 and J19 of his ruling, without explaining, obiter dictum, what constitutes unsafe and unsound practice. Although an order for certiorari was granted on the grounds that the BoZ had misdirected itself in determining that AFSL and ALL were insolvent and that the two companies should be placed under compulsory liquidation, the court did not address fully the issue of whether AFSL and ALL had engaged in unsafe and unsound practices that would have entitled the BoZ to take punitive or corrective measures against the two companies. However, in making the ruling, Judge Banda should have taken cognizance of the High Court's unlimited jurisdiction and should have spelt out a judicial interpretation of unsafe and unsound practice.

4.2.2. A Critical Analysis of the Ruling in Access Finance Services et al v. Bank of Zambia

Given the facts and the ruling in *Access Finance Services Limited and Access Leasing Limited v. Bank of Zambia*,[560] what would happen if, for example, although AFSL and ALL had engaged in unsafe and unsound practices, they then ceased to do so? Would this fact alone exonerate them from liability? Section 77(1) of Zambia's Banking and Financial Services Act 1994 is written only in the present and future tenses:

> Where, in the opinion of the Bank of Zambia, a bank or financial institution is *committing* or *pursuing* or *is about to commit* or *pursue* on behalf of the bank or financial institution *any act* or *course of conduct* that is *considered by the Bank of Zambia as unsafe or unsound practice*. (italics added)

Indeed, these are some of the issues that should have been resolved by an obiter dictum of the court.

What would happen if AFSL and ALL, for example, were to engage in unsafe and unsound practices solely for corrective purposes and in order to prevent future abuses? Could they still be held liable under section 77 of Zambia's Banking and Financial Services Act 1994? The court, with the assistance of the legal counsel of either party and through an obiter dictum, should have given thoughtful consideration to such matters because the High Court of Zambia does enjoy unlimited jurisdiction.

4.2.3. Other Relevant Incidents Covered by the Banking and Financial Services Act 1994

As a general rule, when banks and financial institutions in Zambia are insolvent, they are prohibited from receiving deposits, entering into any new business, and continuing to conduct existing banking or financial services business.[561] They may do so only if undertaking such an action would point to the orderly realisation, conservation, or preservation of the bank's or financial institution's assets.[562] A transaction with a depositor or a creditor and a settlement in a netting or gross settlement arrangement under the system of settlement approved by Bank of Zambia or provided for in or under any written law will not be treated as a part of the prohibition only because of the insolvency of the bank or financial institution if the transaction or settlement took place prior to a resolution to liquidate the bank or financial institution or prior to the appointment of a receiver or the taking possession of the bank or financial institution by Bank of Zambia.[563] It is a criminal offence for any director, chief executive, chief financial officer, manager, or employee of a bank or financial institution who knows or who could, in the proper performance of his duties, reasonably be expected to know about the insolvency of the bank or financial institution to cause or permit an act in contravention of the rule prohibiting the receipt of deposits or the entering into new or the continued conduct of banking or financial services business.[564] The question, then, is, When can it be said that the concerned officer of the bank or financial institution knew that the bank or financial institution was insolvent? What constitutes knowledge? Although the Banking and Financial Services Act 1994 is silent on this matter, I have already examined the criminal law context in which the term *knowingly* should be understood.[565]

4.2.4. Civil Liability for Wrongful Trading

Unlike the statutory provisions prohibiting fraudulent trading, which are drafted in a manner that clearly distinguishes the provision on civil liability from that on criminal liability, the statutory provisions covering civil liability and criminal liability for wrongful trading are both placed in one section of the statute. As a general rule, if a person has been convicted of an offence of wrongful trading, a court of law, on the application of the liquidator or any creditor or member of the company, can make an order that the culpable person be held personally responsible, without any limitation to liability, for the debts or other liabilities of the company.[566] But, the court order does not disqualify the culpable director from holding a directorship in the company or any other company. The court's order can provide for measures to give effect to the liabilities of the person under the order. In particular, it can provide that those liabilities will be a charge on any debt or obligation that is due from the company to him or her or on any interest in the company of which he or she has, directly or indirectly, the benefit.[567] As in the case of civil liability for fraudulent trading, the court can make such further orders as it thinks are necessary to enforce any charge that is imposed for civil liability relating to wrongful trading.[568] But, I will take a more reasoned look at the statutory provision for civil liability for wrongful trading.

First, to trigger the statutory provisions for civil liability for wrongful trading, there should be an underlying criminal conviction of wrongful trading. This requirement entails that if there is no underlying criminal conviction for wrongful trading, then there can be no civil liability for wrongful trading. The commencement of an action for civil liability for wrongful trading depends on whether or not there is a conviction for criminal liability. The shortcoming of this approach is that because the standard of proof required in criminal law cases is much higher than that in civil law cases, and given the length of time that it normally takes for the state to conduct some criminal trials in Zambia, the statutory provision on civil liability may be of little use and value.

Second, only a liquidator, creditor, or member of the company can bring an action for civil liability for wrongful trading. It does not matter whether the creditor is secured or unsecured; both can bring an action for civil liability for wrongful trading. Third, for such civil liability to ensue, the company must be insolvent in the sense that it has failed the cash flow test. Fourth, under civil liability proceedings for wrongful trading, as in the case of civil liability for fraudulent trading, the concept of limited liability is suspended and the corporate veil of the company can be pierced so that the culpable individuals are made to account personally and without any limitation of liability. But, is the policy objective underpinning the wrongful trading legislation meant to be penal, or is it meant to focus on compensation?

Commenting on parallel and comparable legislation in the United Kingdom, Dine argued as follows:

> The approach of the courts in these circumstances has been much more akin to the approach of a criminal court undertaking a sentencing exercise than to a civil court assessing compensation. In *Re a company* (No. 001418 of 1988) Judge Bromley QC held that the civil action for fraudulent trading 'was in the nature of a punitive provision.' It followed that a director could be ordered to pay an amount which 'may be or contain a punitive element as well as a compensatory element,' ... This legislation apparently has dual purposes. One is the provision of compensation for the victims of fraudulent, reckless and negligent directors. It is nevertheless clear that, perhaps because there are victims who have suffered as a result of the behaviour of such people, the courts have introduced a punitive element in assessing the extent of the liability of directors. The relationship 'indicator' which requires the imposition of a sentence which results in the severe deprivation of an individual's liberty may be satisfied with regard to wrongful trading. It is to this element and the jurisprudence which surrounds it that reference was made by *Knox J. in Re Produce Marketing Consortium (No. 2)* ... He was concerned to impose a 'just' penalty in all the circumstances of the case, rather than assess an amount of compensation.[569]

Dine added that where the courts have the legal authority to impose a severe penalty, they should formulate rules that will assist them in arriving at severe penalties.[570] According to Dine,

> The Cork proposals themselves contain an extraordinary ambivalence. On the one hand the emphasis is put on the establishment of a new method of compensation for victims:
>
> 'It is right that it should be an offence to carry on a business dishonestly; and right that, in the absence of dishonesty, no offence should be committed. Where, however, what is in question is not the punishment of an offender, but the provision of a civil remedy for those who have suffered financial loss, a requirement that dishonesty be proved is inappropriate…'
>
> On the other hand deterrence and retribution appear to be foremost in the paragraph entitled 'The justification for the new concept' which argues:
>
> '…a new climate should exist in which downright irresponsibility is discouraged and in which those who abuse the privilege of limited liability can be made personally responsible for the consequences of their conduct.'[571]

4.3. THE POWER OF THE COURT TO ASSESS DAMAGES AGAINST DELINQUENT OFFICERS AND FRAUD BY OFFICERS OF COMPANIES THAT HAVE GONE INTO LIQUIDATION

As a general rule, if in the course of a winding-up it appears that any person who has taken part in the formation or promotion of the company, or any past or present liquidator or officer has misapplied or retained, or become liable or accountable for, any money or property of the company, the court can, on the application of the liquidator or of any creditor or member, inquire into the conduct of that person, liquidator or officer and compel him to repay or restore the money or property, or any part thereof, with interest at such a rate as the court thinks just, or to contribute such sum to the assets of the company by way of compensation in respect of the misapplication or retainer as the court thinks just.[572] Further, the court can pass a ruling where a person is found guilty of misfeasance or breach of trust or duty in relation to the company.[573] Such a person can be compelled by the court to contribute a sum to the assets of the company by way of compensation in respect to the breach of trust or duty.[574]

The general rule regarding the power of the court to assess damages against delinquent officers applies to the receipt of any money or property by an officer of the company during the two years preceding the commencement of the winding-up, whether by way of salary or otherwise, that appears to the court to have been unfair or unjust.[575] This rule applies to the conduct of a person even if that person is also criminally liable for the same conduct.[576] Section 359 of the Companies Act 1994 spells out the aspects of criminal law that are applicable to the prosecution of delinquent officers and members of the company. Section 360, the provision covering frauds committed by the officers of companies that have gone into liquidation, adds as follows:

> A person who while an officer of a company which is subsequently ordered to be wound-up by the court or which subsequently passes a resolution for voluntary winding-up—
>
> a. induced any person to give credit to the company by false pretences or by means of any other fraud;
> b. with intent to defraud creditors of the company, made or caused to be made any gift or transfer of charges on, or caused or connived at the levying of any execution against, the property of the company; or
> c. with intent to defraud creditors of the company, concealed or removed any part of the property of the company within two months before the date of any unsatisfied judgement or order for payment of money obtained against the company; shall be guilty of an offence, and shall be liable on conviction to a fine not exceeding two thousand monetary units or to imprisonment for a period not exceeding two years, or to both.

Like the statutory offence that is outlined in section 359 of the Companies Act 1994, the offence of fraud committed by the officers of companies that have gone into liquidation covers both compulsory winding-up situations and those frauds that occur during a voluntary winding-up.

4.4. CONCLUSION

This chapter has examined the law in Zambia regarding the legal liability of company directors for fraudulent trading and wrongful trading, including the salient and pertinent aspects of fraud that is committed by the officers of companies that have gone into liquidation. In addition to highlighting the need to regulate and license insolvency practitioners in Zambia, the chapter argued that Zambia should consider enacting a statute that provides for the disqualification of persons who have been convicted of certain offences—wrongful trading, fraudulent trading, and fraud by officers of companies that have gone into liquidation—from serving as company directors.

The chapter argued further that Zambia continues to experience a weak compliance culture in the area of corporate governance, and that there are not many mechanisms to deal with the enforcement of directors' liability other than to rely on the judicial process. As an incentive to promote more efficient compliance with best practices in corporate governance and to deter misfeasance and misconduct by company directors, the introduction of legal rules for the disqualification of recalcitrant directors will strengthen the legal framework for corporate insolvency in Zambia. Currently, even the role of external auditors is downplayed for the most part, and many companies rarely file their annual returns. The poor culture of filing annual returns in Zambia deprives many creditors of reliable information on which to base their judgments for monitoring the directors of debtor companies. But, legislative intervention, through the introduction of legal rules to disqualify recalcitrant directors, together with a strong compliance and law enforcement culture, could help to mitigate the risks in this regard.

CHAPTER 5

CONCLUSION AND POLICY RECOMMENDATIONS

This book has examined the pertinent aspects of company law in Zambia arising from the enactment of the Zambian Companies Act 1994. However, not every single aspect of the Zambian Companies Act 1994 was examined because the book focuses mainly on contemporary legal issues that are not fully addressed or settled by Zambian jurisprudence. These issues include the legal status of the *ultra vires* doctrine in company law, the liability of company directors for wrongful or fraudulent trading, and the concepts of issuing shares of par value and no-par-value, which includes share watering, allotting shares at a discount, and providing financial assistance in the acquisition of a company's shares.

The book highlighted prominent areas of Zambian company law, arguing, for example, that in spite of the enactment of the Zambian Companies Act 1994, the *ultra vires* doctrine has not been abolished in Zambia. It was also observed that the intention of the legislative draftsman to abolish the *ultra vires* doctrine in Zambia's company law did not succeed for a number of reasons. Chief among them, as I have argued, is that the legislative draftsman did not pay sufficient attention to parallel legislative developments in other jurisdictions. In addition, there was limited participation by indigenous professionals and stakeholders in the preparation of the Zambian Companies Act 1994.

In examining the concept of issuing shares of par value, including the related aspects of paying up for shares, the book questioned the relevance of the par value concept in the modern world and, by parity of reasoning, its relevance to Zambian company law. Analogies were drawn from parallel legislative developments in various jurisdictions.

In the area of corporate insolvency law, which also forms a pillar of company law, the book examined the efficacy of the legal framework dealing with the liability of company directors for fraudulent or wrongful trading, including the salient and pertinent aspects of fraud committed by the officers of companies that have gone into liquidation. A comparative study of the law in Zambia and the United Kingdom was provided.

The preceding chapters did not delve into the intricacies of cross-border insolvency as a prominent aspect of company law that should have been addressed during the preparation and enactment of the Zambian Companies Act 1994. Instead, I purposely reserved that discussion for this chapter. It is submitted here that the Zambian government should strongly consider introducing legislation or a robust regulatory framework to address cross-border insolvency. Not much thought was accorded to this issue during the enactment of the Zambian Companies Act 1994. Indeed, the act does not have statutory provisions on cross-border insolvency. Yet, one does not have to go far to find a model law on cross-border insolvency.

The United Nations Commission on International Trade Law (UNCITRAL) in Vienna, Austria, was adopted on 30 May 1997. It is a model law designed to assist countries to equip their insolvency laws with a modern, harmonized, and fair framework to address more effectively instances of cross-border insolvency.[577] Those instances include cases where the insolvent debtor has assets in more than one country and those where some of the creditors of the debtor are not from the country where the insolvency proceeding is taking place.[578] The model law respects the differences among national procedural laws and does not attempt a substantive unification of insolvency law.[579] Instead, it offers several solutions, including providing foreign assistance for an insolvency proceeding that is taking place in the enacting state, supporting a foreign representative's access to the courts of the enacting state, recognising foreign proceedings, encouraging cross-border cooperation, and coordinating concurrent proceedings.[580] To that end, in adopting the model law, a country can enjoin or adapt it to its own country-specific conditions.

Goode argued, however, that countries differ in their approach to addressing problems of cross-border insolvency.[581] According to Goode,

> Two opposing pairs of principles are of particular significance. They relate respectively to jurisdiction over a company and jurisdiction over assets ... The principle of unity ascribes exclusive jurisdiction over winding-up to the courts of the state of the company's incorporation,[582] to which all other courts defer. If strictly applied such a principle would route winding-up to a single forum and avoid the problems of cocurrent liquidations, but would also expose local creditors in other states to risk of loss of the assets within their jurisdiction. The principle of unity is a theoretical model, not a reality, for in no jurisdiction are courts willing to give up all control over local assets where there are local creditors.[583]

Goode argued further that the principle that is adopted almost everywhere is that of plurality, which admits of concurrent proceedings in different jurisdictions.[584] According to Goode, in most states the plurality arises through the adoption of the principle of territoriality. Some states, however, recognise the concept of a main liquidation in one jurisdiction and one or more ancillary liquidations in other jurisdictions which are confined to local assets and, in some countries, to local creditors.[585] Referring to the principles of territoriality and universality in cross-border insolvency, Goode observed,

Under the principle of universality, to which English law subscribes, a winding-up proceeding covers not only the company's local assets but assets situated anywhere in the world, though it is recognised that the ability of the liquidator to have resort to those assets is dependent on local law and recognition by local courts.[586] However, the majority of jurisdictions adopt the principle of territoriality, by which the winding-up process is confined to assets (and sometimes to creditors) within the jurisdiction. The principle of universality would, of course, be a necessary concomitant of the principle of unity, but can also apply in jurisdictions (of which England is one) which recognise plurality of jurisdiction. This creates potential conflict where there are concurrent liquidation proceedings in two different jurisdictions and both rights over the debtor company's assets on a world-wide basis reclaimed in both jurisdictions.[587]

Closely related to the concepts of unity and universality is the notion of nondiscrimination against foreign creditors.[588] Indeed, 'if all the company's assets, in whatever part of the world, are to be subsumed within a single liquidation, then claims of foreign creditors must be admitted on the same basis as those of local creditors.'[589] This principle was ably articulated in an opinion on U.S. bankruptcy law for the assistance of the English court in *Felixstowe Dock and Railway co. v. US Lines Inc*[590] by Judge Howard C. Buschman of the U.S. District Court for the Southern District of New York.[591] Buschman observed,

> The intended scope of bankruptcy and reorganisation jurisdiction extends beyond the border of the United States … The nature of the jurisdiction is in rem. The res, the estate of the debtor created by the commencement of a bankruptcy or reorganisation case, is viewed as a single entity to be dealt with in a single proceeding. The broad scope of bankruptcy jurisdiction under United States law is intended to permit similarly situated creditors, regardless of where they are located, to be treated equally in a bankruptcy or reorganisation case. Discrimination on the basis of citizenship is not permitted. All creditors are given the opportunity to file claims against the state and their recovery is not limited to the assets in their own country.[592]

According to Goode, the position is the same under English insolvency law.[593] Likewise, the position is no different under Zambia's insolvency law. The jurisdiction of the Zambian courts in insolvency proceedings is governed generally by the Zambian Companies Act 1994 and by the English common law rules pertaining to the conflicts of laws. In the case of banks and financial institutions, Zambia's Banking and Financial Services Act 1994 provides an additional legal regime for determining the jurisdiction of the Zambian courts.

Generally, it is a widely accepted principle that the law of the place where the liquidation is opened (*lex fori concursus*) governs all matters relating to the winding-up, whether they are substantive or procedural, including the assets comprising the estate, the proof and ranking of claims, the admissibility of set-off, and the avoidance of preferences and other transactions.[594]

Against this background, and in addition to the recommendations that were articulated in the preceding chapters on the various ways in which to strengthen the legal and institutional framework for company law, the following are some additional recommendations.

1. Many law reform specialists tend to preoccupy themselves with introducing new legislation when they are attempting to strengthen the legal and institutional framework for doing business. However, practical experience in many developing countries, Zambia included, tends to show that quite often, lax compliance and enforcement are the major issues. To that end, the proposals that have been outlined in this book can succeed only with effective and efficient compliance and enforcement. Therefore, promoting public awareness through training, seminars, workshops, and research is one of the efforts that can help to develop a robust culture of compliance and enforcement. Building the institutional capacity of regulatory bodies, in addition to making available adequate resources, can also strengthen the regulatory and enforcement arm of the government. This is particularly the case when a regulatory body enjoys autonomy even when it is

accountable to an overarching supervisory authority such as the parliament.

2. Closely tied to the issue in the first point, Zambia should consider introducing legislation or a sound regulatory framework for disqualifying people who have been convicted of certain offences—wrongful trading, fraudulent trading, and fraud committed by the officers of companies that have gone into liquidation—from serving as company directors. Such a piece of legislation or regulatory framework should be distinct from the Companies Act 1994, although if it were presented as a statutory instrument, it could be a part of the broader legislative code of corporate insolvency law in Zambia. However, if it were to be enacted as a separate and freestanding piece of legislation, the enactment would not be dependent on any enabling principal legislation.

3. To strengthen the regime of corporate insolvency law in Zambia, the Zambian government should actively consider enacting an insolvency act. The legislature would have to take an audit of all of the statutory provisions in the Zambian Companies Act 1994 and any other piece of legislation that deals with corporate insolvency law in Zambia. Then, it could amend such pieces of legislation and thoughtfully reenact the relevant statutory provisions, together with any new or additional statutory provisions, as the Insolvency Act.

4. Further, Zambia should consider introducing legislation or a sound regulatory framework for regulating insolvency practitioners. Again, such a piece of legislation or regulatory framework should be distinct from the Companies Act 1994, although if it were presented as a statutory instrument, it could be a part of the broader legislative code of corporate insolvency law in Zambia. However, if it were enacted as a separate and freestanding piece of legislation, the enactment would not be dependent on any enabling principal legislation.

Overall, the absence of a legal framework for licensing and regulating insolvency practitioners as a means of protecting consumers and the market from the malpractices of unlicensed and unauthorized persons who serve as insolvency practitioners poses a great challenge to the development of corporate insolvency law in Zambia.

5. Zambia should also consider introducing the concept of shares of no-par-value to enable small- and medium-sized enterprises to raise capital more easily. This would be helpful because some of these entities are family-owned, with few or no institutional investors.

6. Zambia should reconsider the reasons that were put forth for the attempt to abolish the *ultra vires* doctrine in the Companies Act 1994. If, indeed, the goal of the Zambian government was to abolish the *ultra vires* doctrine so as to enable small- and medium-sized enterprises to adapt quickly (for their own survival and growth) to different or multiple business objects, then that goal should be spelt out clearly through elegantly drafted statutory provisions.

7. Closely related to the fifth recommendation, Zambia should reconsider the approach in the Companies Act 1994 to abolish the common law doctrine of constructive notice.

8. Finally, Zambia should consider strengthening the law on share watering. It should not leave much of the regulation of share watering to the standard articles of association for a company because different companies often adopt different articles.

NOTES

PREFACE

1. [1956] 1QB 1 at pp. 16–17, cited also in Okuk v. Fallscheer [1980] PNGLR 274 at 286.
2. Per Denning, LJ in *Nyali Ltd v. Attorney General* [1956] 1QB 1 at pp. 16–17.
3. [1956] 1QB 1 at pp. 16–17, cited also in *Okuk v. Fallscheer* [1980] PNGLR 274 at 286.
4. See J. C. Care and L. Haller, 'In Harmony or Out of Tune: Is Advocates' Immunity an Appropriate Principle in Common Law Countries?' *Journal of South Pacific Law* 8, no. 2 (2004), accessed 8 October 2009, http://www.paclii.org/journals/fJSPL/vol08no2/5.shtml.
5. Ibid.
6. Ibid.

ACKNOWLEDGMENTS

7. See O. Mailatia, 'Nigeria: In Praise of the Judiciary', *Daily Trust*, 7 July 2008, accessed 10 June 2009, http://allafrica.com/stories/200807071608.html.

CHAPTER 1

8. See I. Shivji, 'The Life and Time of Babu: The Age of Revolution and Liberation', *Law, Social Justice and Global Development (LGD)* 2 (2001), accessed 25 June 2009, http://www2.warwick.ac.uk/fac/soc/law/elj/lgd/2001_2/shivji/.
9. See, for example, J. M. Mulwila, 'Parastatal Companies and the Law in Zambia' (PhD diss., University of London, 1980). See also, generally, J. M. Chulu, 'Corporate Governance in Zambia' (PhD diss., University of Essex, 2008); A. A. K. Mwape, 'Bank Governance and Regulation in East and Southern African Countries' (PhD diss., SOAS, University of London, 2006); and T. M. Liswaniso-Kampata, 'The Challenges of Corporate Governance in Banking Supervision: An Evaluation of Some Financial Sector Development Plan Recommendations' (LLM diss., University of Warwick, 2008).

10. See generally K. K. Mwenda, *Zambia's Stock Exchange and Privatisation Programme: Corporate Finance Law in Emerging Markets* (Lewiston, NY: The Edwin Mellen Press, 2001).
11. Ibid.
12. Ibid.
13. See generally K. K. Mwenda, 'Can Insider Trading Predicate the Offence of Money Laundering?' *Michigan State University Journal of Business and Securities Law* 6, no. 2 (Spring 2006).
14. See generally, for example, Mwenda, *Zambia's Stock Exchange and Privatisation Programme: Corporate Finance Law in Emerging Markets*, and Mwenda, 'Can Insider Trading Predicate the Offence of Money Laundering?'.
15. See Zambia's Companies Act 1994, secs. 162, 163, and 164.
16. Pursuant to the Accountants Act 2008, the relevant regulatory body (i.e., ZICA), acting in consultation with other industry and sector stakeholders, can then pass secondary legislation or other codes of conduct to provide for the application of IFRS.
17. See Caparo Industries plc v. Dickman & Others [1990] 1 All ER HL 568 and Al-Saudi Banque v. Clark Pixley [1990] 1 Ch. 313, showing that in general, auditors owe a duty of care only to the company (as a legal entity) rather than to any individual shareholder or creditor. Cf. JEB Fasteners Ltd v. Marks Bloom & Co. [1983] 1 All ER 583 and Twomax Ltd v. Dickson, McFarlane and Robinson [1983] SLT 98, which tended to show the possibility that under some highly restrictive circumstances, auditors may be held liable to third parties. See also Candler v. Crane Christmas & Co [1951] 1 All ER 426; McNaughton (James) Paper Group Limited v. Hicks Anderson & Co. [1991] 1 All ER 134 and [1990] BCC 891; and Berg Sons & Co. Limited & Others v. Adams & Others [1992] BCC 661. Following the case of *Barings plc and another v. Coopers & Lybrand* ([1997] BCLC 427), auditors of subsidiary companies could owe a duty of care to the parent company (as a legal person) but not to any human stakeholder.
18. [1896] 1 Ch. 6, 11.
19. Ibid.
20. E. Woolf, 'A Return to Rational Concepts', *Accountancy* (Institute of Chartered Accountants in England and Wales), 1993, accessed 8 May 2009, http://www.faqs.org/abstracts/Business/A-return-to-rational-concepts-Whose-fault-is-it-anyway.html.
21. Ibid.
22. Ibid.

23. Ibid.
24. [1896] 2 Ch. 279.
25. Ibid., 288–289. See also D. Singh, *Banking Regulation of UK and US Financial Markets* (Aldershot, UK: Ashgate Publishing Limited, 2007), 163; Re London and General Bank [1895] 2 Ch. 166; and Re D'Jan of London Ltd Copp v. D'Jan [1994] BCLC 561.
26. See Singh, *Banking Regulation of UK and US Financial Markets*, 163.
27. Ibid. and Kraji v. McGrath [1986] 1 All ER 54, 61.
28. [1957] 2 All ER 118, 122.
29. See Singh, *Banking Regulation of UK and US Financial Markets*, 163.
30. R. Curd and K. Hare, 'United Kingdom: Auditors' Negligence: Liability to Company and Shareholders', 2 June 2008, accessed 3 May 2009, http://www.mondaq.com/article.asp?articleid=61268. See *Cook and Another v. Green and Others Chancery Division District Registry (Manchester)*, 2 May 2008, and the English Companies Act 1985, secs. 151, 155, and 156. Note that the restrictions on financial assistance in relation to most acquisitions of shares in private companies (including the whitewash procedure) were scheduled to be repealed on 1 October 2008.

CHAPTER 2

31. See section 2 of Zambia's Banking and Financial Services Act 1994 (as amended in 2000) on the statutory definition of the terms 'bank' and 'financial institution'.
32. See generally the Companies Act 1921 of Zambia, which was repealed and replaced by the Zambian Companies Act 1994. See also Guinness v. Land Corporation of Ireland (1882) 22 Ch. D 349.
33. See *Infra.* (n. 34).
34. A telephone interview on 9 December 2008 between Lusaka, Zambia, and Washington, DC, in which this author, calling from Washington DC, held an interview discussion with Michael Musonda, the former chairman of the Law Association of Zambia and current lecturer in company law and procedure at the Zambia Institute for Advanced Legal Education as well as a senior practicing lawyer in Zambia. Also, Tony Bwembya, the assistant registrar at the Zambia Patents and Companies Registration Office (PACRO), responded in an e-mail dated 11 December 2008 to Noyoo Noyoo, a senior corporate lawyer in the banking sector in Zambia, answering queries that I had raised through Noyoo, 'My view is that the removal of the Memo was merely intended to reduce on the requirements for incorporating a

company. The requirements for the objects clause has actually been retained in that Companies Form 2 still requires that the applicants specify the principal business and any other business. Furthermore, section 7(2) provides that *"the articles may contain restrictions on the business that a company may carry on"*, thus departing from the traditional role of covering mainly issues to do with the internal management of the company for which articles of association are often known for. Additionally, section 22(3) prohibits the company from carrying on any business that it is restricted by the articles. To this extent, I opine that the *ultra vires* doctrine is pretty much alive.'

35. This is evident from a seminar paper that was presented in Lusaka, Zambia, by James Graham, a foreign consultant and the legislative draftsman who was recruited by the Zambian government to provide leadership in drafting the Zambian Companies Act 1994. See J. Graham, 'The New Companies Act: (A) An Introduction to the New Act; and (B) Forming a Company' (seminar paper, Companies Act Seminar, Pamodzi Hotel, Lusaka, 12 October 1994), 3. Cf. Freshint Ltd and Others v. Kawambwa Tea Company [2008] ZMSC 26; [1996] Ltd. (130/2005) [2008] ZMSC 22; SCZ No. 33 of 2008 (8 May 2008), accessed 2 January 2009, http://www.saflii.org/zm/cases/ZMSC/2008/26.html.

36. See Graham, 'New Companies Act', 3.

37. That is, when I examine in this chapter the statutory requirement for a summary statement regarding the principal and other business of a company, which is supposed to be included in the completed Forms I, II, III, or IV of the Companies (Prescribed Forms) Regulations (i.e., Statutory Instrument No. 17 of 1995, issued pursuant to sec. 400 of the Companies Act 1994).

38. See *Infra.* (n.39–42).

39. See the Companies Act 1994, secs. 2 and 7.

40. Ibid., sec. 22(3).

41. See Statutory Instrument No. 17 of 1995, issued pursuant to sec. 400 of the Zambian Companies Act 1994.

42. See the text of this book supported by the following endnotes: *Infra.* (n.168–179).

43. Graham, 'New Companies Act', 3.

44. (1843) 2 Hare 461 (Court of Chancery (Vice-Chancellor)).

45. See *Supra.* (n.44).

46. See *Infra.* (n.47).

47. See K. K. Mwenda, *Combating Financial Crime: The Legal, Regulatory and Institutional Frameworks* (Lewiston, NY: The Edwin Mellen Press,

2006), 20–24. See also generally K. K. Mwenda, 'Zambia's Securities Act 1993 on Trial: The Case of Insider Dealing', *Statute Law Review* 18, no. 2 (1997); K. K. Mwenda, 'Insider Dealing Law in Zambia: A Flawed Concept', *University of Ghana Law Journal* 19 (1996–1999); K. K. Mwenda, 'Redefining Insider Dealing Law for Emerging Markets: A Comparative Legal Study', *University of Zimbabwe Law Review* 14 (1997); and K. K. Mwenda, 'The Securities Act 1993 of Zambia: A Comment on the Defective Provisions for Controlling Insider Dealing In Zambia', *University of Stellenbosch Law Review 8, no. 2 (1997).*

48. See *Infra.* (n.236).
49. E-mail to this author from Michael Musonda, the former chairman of the Law Association of Zambia and current lecturer in company law and procedure at the Zambia Institute for Advanced Legal Education as well as a senior practicing lawyer in Zambia, 23 January 2009.
50. In Canada, the Canadian Supreme Court in the case of *Communities Economic Development Fund v. Canadian Pickles Corp.*—[1991] 3 S.C.R. 388, accessed 11 January 2009, http://scc.lexum.umontreal.ca/en/1991/1991rcs3-388/1991rcs3-388.html—observed that 'the doctrine of *ultra vires* has been abolished by statute for corporations incorporated under the business corporations legislation in most Canadian jurisdictions. The following jurisdictions have statutory provisions reversing the presumption that corporations have limited capacity: Canada (*Canada Business Corporations Act*, R.S.C., 1985, c. C-44, s. 15(1)), Alberta (*Business Corporations Act*, S.A. 1981, c. B-15, s. 15(1)), British Columbia (*Company Act*, R.S.B.C. 1979, c. 59, s. 21(1)), Manitoba (*The Corporations Act*, R.S.M. 1987, c. C-225, s. 15(1)), New Brunswick (*Business Corporations Act*, S.N.B. 1981, c. B-9.1, s. 13(1)), Newfoundland (*The Corporations Act*, S.N. 1986, c. 12, s. 30(1)), Ontario (*Business Corporations Act, 1982*, S.O. 1982, c. 4, s. 15), Saskatchewan (*The Business Corporations Act*, R.S.S. 1978, c. B-10, s. 15(1)), and the Yukon (*Business Corporations Act*, R.S.Y. 1986, c. 15, s. 18(1)). The doctrine of *ultra vires* may still apply in the Northwest Territories, and in Nova Scotia. Prince Edward Island is a letters patent jurisdiction.' The Canadian Supreme Court continued, 'the general abolition of the doctrine of *ultra vires* is in accordance with sound policy and common sense. The original purposes of the doctrine, which were, in the words of the *1967 Interim Report of the Select Committee on Company Law* (tabled before the Ontario Legislative Assembly, at p. 25) "to protect creditors by ensuring that the company's funds to which creditors must look for payment were not dissipated in unauthorized activities

and to protect investors by allowing them to know the objects for which their money was to be used", have been largely frustrated. Subsequent statutory and case law developments have made the doctrine a protection to no one and a trap for the unwary. No less an authority than L. C. B. Gower has recommended, in *Gower's Principles of Modern Company Law* (4th ed. 1979), at p. 179, "total abolition of the *ultra vires* rule in so far as it affects the capacity of companies" and indeed referred favourably to the approach taken by the *Canada Business Corporations Act* in this respect ... However, in spite of the general trend towards abolition of the doctrine of *ultra vires*, the limited aspects of the doctrine ... may be present with respect to corporations created by special act for public purposes. Not only is there a long line of cases supporting the principle, but one may argue that this protects the public interest because a company created for a specific purpose by an act of a legislature ought not to have the power to do things not in furtherance of that purpose. Of course, it is open to the legislature to rebut this presumption because, for example, the legislature may provide for other remedies short of invalidity for acts contrary to the statute.'

51. See generally Jamaica's Companies Act 2004, No. 10 of 2004, accessed 11 January 2009, http://www.mct.gov.jm/Companies%20Act%20b.pdf.

52. See sec. 28 of Mauritius' Companies Act 2001, accessed 11 January 2009, http://www.gov.mu/portal/sites/ncb/fsc/download/compact2001.doc.

53. Sec. 169 of Mauritius' Companies Act 2001 deals with applications to a court of law by a company or any of its directors or shareholders for an injunction to restrain the company or any of its directors from engaging in conduct that would contravene the constitution of the company. Further, section 170 of Mauritius' Companies Act 2001 codifies the common law position for a derivative action by a shareholder or director of a company on behalf of the company. Finally, section 174 of that statute empowers a shareholder or a former shareholder to bring a personal action against a culpable director for breach of duty owed to that shareholder in the latter's capacity as a shareholder.

54. Section 42 of the English Companies Act 2006 provides as follows:

'1. Sections 39 and 40 (company's capacity and power of directors to bind company) do not apply to the acts of a company that is a charity except in favour of a person who—

a. does not know at the time the act is done that the company is a charity, or

   b. gives full consideration in money or money's worth in relation to
       the act in question and does not know (as the case may be)—
       i.   that the act is not permitted by the company's constitution, or
       ii. that the act is beyond the powers of the directors.

2. Where a company that is a charity purports to transfer or grant an inter-
    est in property, the fact that (as the case may be)—
    a. the act was not permitted by the company's constitution, or
    b. the directors in connection with the act exceeded any limitation on
        their powers under the company's constitution,
does not affect the title of a person who subsequently acquires the property
or any interest in it for full consideration without actual notice of any such
circumstances affecting the validity of the company's act.

3. In any proceedings arising out of subsection (1) or (2) the burden of
    proving—
    a. that a person knew that the company was a charity, or
    b. that a person knew that an act was not permitted by the company's
        constitution or was beyond the powers of the directors,
lies on the person asserting that fact.

4. In the case of a company that is a charity the affirmation of a transac-
    tion to which section 41 applies (transactions with directors or their
    associates) is ineffective without the prior written consent of—
    a. in England and Wales, the Charity Commission;
    b. in Northern Ireland, the Department for Social Development.

5. This section does not extend to Scotland (but see section 112 of the
    Companies Act 1989 (c. 40)).'

55. Section 41 of the English Companies Act reinforces the provisions of sec-
    tion 40 of the statute in the following manner:

'1. This section applies to a transaction if or to the extent that its validity
     depends on section 40 (power of directors deemed to be free of limita-
     tions under company's constitution in favour of person dealing with
     company in good faith).
Nothing in this section shall be read as excluding the operation of any other
enactment or rule of law by virtue of which the transaction may be called in
question or any liability to the company may arise.

2. Where—
    a. a company enters into such a transaction, and

b. the parties to the transaction include—
   i.   a director of the company or of its holding company, or
   ii. a person connected with any such director,
the transaction is voidable at the instance of the company.

3. Whether or not it is avoided, any such party to the transaction as is mentioned in subsection (2)(b)(i) or (ii), and any director of the company who authorised the transaction, is liable—
   a. to account to the company for any gain he has made directly or indirectly by the transaction, and
   b. to indemnify the company for any loss or damage resulting from the transaction.

4. The transaction ceases to be voidable if—
   a. restitution of any money or other asset which was the subject matter of the transaction is no longer possible, or
   b. the company is indemnified for any loss or damage resulting from the transaction, or
   c. rights acquired bona fide for value and without actual notice of the directors' exceeding their powers by a person who is not party to the transaction would be affected by the avoidance, or
   d. the transaction is affirmed by the company.

5. A person other than a director of the company is not liable under subsection (3) if he shows that at the time the transaction was entered into he did not know that the directors were exceeding their powers.

6. Nothing in the preceding provisions of this section affects the rights of any party to the transaction not within subsection (2)(b)(i) or (ii).
But the court may, on the application of the company or any such party, make an order affirming, severing or setting aside the transaction on such terms as appear to the court to be just.

7. In this section—
   a. "transaction" includes any act; and
   b. the reference to a person connected with a director has the same meaning as in Part 10 (company directors).'

56. E-mail to this author from Annie Senkwe Nsenduluka, senior state advocate in the Attorney-General's Chambers of the Republic of Zambia, dated 2 January 2009.

57. I held several discussions with many prominent legal scholars and legal practitioners in Lusaka, Zambia, between 15 November 2008 and 15

December 2008. The views expressed on this particular issue were relatively consistent.

58. See explanation in note 58.

59. P. Davies, examining the position in the United Kingdom, observed that at some point, 'the courts sought to narrow the scope of the resulting *vires* by distinguishing between "objects" (in the sense of types of business) and "powers" and, applying the *ejusdem generis* rule of construction, ruling that the powers could be used only in relation to the objects. But that too was circumvented by the device of ending the "objects" clause by stating that each of the specified objects or powers should be treated as independent and in no way ancillary or subordinate one to another, and, at a later date, by also inserting a power "to carry on any other trade or business whatsoever which can, in the opinion of the board of directors, be advantageously carried on by the company in connection with or as ancillary to any of the above businesses or the general business of the company...".' Davies, *Gower's Principles of Modern Company Law*, 6th ed. (London: Sweet and Maxwell, 1997), 204. See Cotman v. Brougham [1918] A.C. 514. See also Introductions Ltd. v. National Provincial Bank [1970] Ch. 199, C.A.; Bell Houses Ltd v. City Wall Properties Ltd [1966] 2 Q.B. 656, C.A.; Newstead v. Frost [1980] 1 W.L.R. 135, H.L.; Charterbridge Corporation Ltd. v. Lloyds Bank [1970] Ch. 62; Re Halt Garage Ltd [1982] 3 All E.R. 1016; Rolled Steel Products (Holdings) Ltd v. British Steel Corp. [1986] Ch. 246, [1985] 3 All ER 1, [1985] 2 WLR 908; and Brady v. Brady [1988] BCLC 20, C.A., revd. [1989] A.C. 755, H.L.

60. Section 2 of the English Law (Extent of Application) Act 1963 of Zambia—the Zambian statute which provides for the applicability of certain aspects of English law to Zambia—provides that subject to provisions of the Zambia Independence Order 1964 and to any other written law, the common law and doctrines of equity apply to Zambia.

61. E-mail from Michael Musonda (see note 49).

62. Ibid. Musonda continued, 'If you examine any typical memorandum of Association, you will confirm that it essentially embodies what I have summarised earlier. The key difference between the different variants of the Incorporation Form and the Memorandum of Association is that the bulk of the latter was devoted to describing the "*objects*" for which the company had been incorporated ... "*objects clauses*" were being drafted in such a manner as to entitle a company to virtually engage in any type of business. What the Incorporation Form does is to move away from that needless piling of words upon other words in order to have the company undertake any

business by simply making a requirement to have prospective incorporators indicate the "*principal business*" for which their company had been formed and any other business which may be incidental to the carrying on of the principal business or which, in the opinion of the company's directors, may be beneficial or advantageous to the carrying on of the company's principal business. Having regard to the foregoing, my humble view would be that the document which was known as a Memorandum of Association under the repealed Act has assumed a different *form* (as opposed to changing its *substance*) under the new statute. In short, although the Incorporation Form (via its different variants) is distinguishable in *form* from the memorandum of association, the *substance* of the two documents is substantially the same. Needless to say, the Incorporation Form under the current Act serves the same constitutive function which the memorandum of association served under the repealed Act. (I must confess that the drafter of the Act may not have pondered over the issues I have canvassed above).'

63. See, for example, Musonda's explanation in note 63.

64. See Statutory Instrument No. 17 of 1995, issued pursuant to sec. 400 of the Zambian Companies Act 1994.

65. See the schedule to the Companies (Prescribed Forms) Regulations for templates of Forms I, II, III, and IV.

66. Ibid.

67. See K. K. Mwenda, *Banking Supervision and Systemic Bank Restructuring: An International and Comparative Legal Perspective* (London: Cavendish Publishing, 2000), 2–7, and K. K. Mwenda, 'Legal Construction of the Term "Bank": A Comparative Study', *Tilburg Foreign Law Review* 8, no. 2 (2000): 113–120.

68. Ibid.

69. See the Banking and Financial Services Act 1994, sec. 2 (as amended in 2000). Examples of unincorporated associations in Zambia include partnerships. Under the English Partnership Act 1890, the statute that governs partnership law in Zambia, section 1 of that statute defines a partnership as: '(1)... the relation which subsists between persons carrying on a business in common with a view of profit. (2) But the relation between members of any company or association which is (a) Registered as a company under the Companies Act 1862, or any other Act of Parliament for the time being in force and relating to the registration of joint stock companies, or (b) Formed or incorporated by or in pursuance of any other Act of Parliament or letters patent, or Royal Charter, or (c) A company engaged in working mines within and subject to the jurisdiction of the Stannaries: is not a partnership within the meaning of this Act.' By parity of reasoning, the relationship among the

members of a company that is incorporated under Zambia's Companies Act 1994 or its predecessor, the Zambian Companies Act 1921, does not constitute a partnership. However, a group of companies can, as separate legal persons acting jointly or with individuals, form a partnership.

70. See the explanation in note 70.
71. See generally note 70.
72. See section 2(1) of the Banking and Financial Services Act 1994.
73. See the Banking and Financial Services Act 1994, sec. 2(1) (prior to the enactment of the 2000 Amendment Act).
74. The statutory definition of financial services is distinguishable from that of financial services *business* in section 2 of the Banking and Financial Services Act 1994 (as amended in 2000).
75. See the text in this book supported by the following endnotes: Infra. (n.78–81).
76. See the text in the book supported by *Infra.* (n.80–82).
77. See sec. 2 of the Banking and Financial Services Act 1994 prior to the enactment of the Banking and Financial Services (Amendment) Act 2000.
78. As amended in 2000.
79. As amended in 2000.
80. See also generally K. K. Mwenda, 'Legal Aspects of Banking and Financial Services Supervision in Zambia', *International Business Law Journal* 2, no. 35 (October 2001).
81. See the first paragraph of chapter 1 in this book. See also generally the following two Zambian statutes: (a) the English Law (Extent of Application) Act 1963 (as amended in 1973, 1991 and 2002); and, (b) the Interpretation and General Provisions Act 1964 (as amended through and up to 1994).
82. See Re Port Canning and Land Investment Co. (1871) 7 Begal LR 583, at pp. 598–611; Eastern Counties Railway v. Hawk (1855) 10 ER 928, at p. 934; K. Greenfield, 'Ultra Vires Lives? A Stakeholder Analysis of Corporate Illegality', *Virginia Law Review* 87 (2001): 1279, 1302–1323; and S.Budylin, 'Going Beyond: The Ultra Vires Problem in Russian Corporate Law', *Columbia Journal of East European Law* 2, no. 1 (2008): 128–141. See also generally Hammersmith and Fulham London Borough Council v. Hazell [1992] 2 AC 1; L. Wolff, 'The Disappearance of the *Ultra Vires* Doctrine in Greater China: Harmonized Legislative Action or (Simply) an Accident of History?' *Northwestern Journal of International Law and Business* 23 (2003): 633–657. See also generally W. W. C. Ming, 'Ultra Vires and Corporate Capacity in Singapore', *Singapore Academy Law Journal* 1, (1989); L. H. Leigh, 'Objects, Powers and Ultra Vires', *Modern Law Review* 33 (1970); Charterbridge

Corporation v. Lloyds Bank Ltd. (1969) 2 All ER 1185; A. Baxt, 'Companies, Powers, Objects in Memorandum and the Doctrine of Ultra Vires', *Australian Law Journal* (1969); R. C. Beuthin, 'The Ultra Vires Doctrine—An Obituary Notice', *South African Law Journal* 83 (1966); Lovering v. Seabrook Island Property Owners Assoc., 289 S.C. 77, 344 S.E. 2d 862 (Ct. Appls. 1986), aff'd. & mod. 291 S.C. 201, 352 S.E.2d 707 (1987); and Gilbert v. McLeod Infirmary (1951) 219 S.C. 174, 64 S.E.2d 524.

83. (1612) 10 Co. Rep. 1a. 23a.

84. Davies, *Gower's Principles of Modern Company Law*, 202. Cf. *Ashbury Rly Carriage & Iron Co Ltd v. Riche* (1875) L.R. 7 H.L. 653. Also, Davies observed that 'it was not until the latter part of the nineteen century that it was clearly established that the strict type of *ultra vires* applied to companies. Until 1844 the most common type of company—the deed of settlement company—had no corporate personality; that was enjoyed only by chartered companies (to which the strict doctrine did not apply) and by companies directly incorporated by statute (a rare breed until the railway boom). After the Joint Stock Companies Act 1856, deed of settlement companies became superseded by registered incorporated companies with limited liability and memorandum of association which had to specify their objects. Only then were the courts forced to decide whether or not the *ultra vires* doctrine applied. And in the landmark decision in *Ashbury Carriage Company v. Riche* the House of Lords finally decided that it did. If a company, incorporated by or under a statute, acted beyond the scope of the objects stated in the statute or in its memorandum of association, such acts were void as beyond the company's capacity even if ratified by all the members' (203).

85. See Davies, *Gower's Principles of Modern Company Law*, 202–203. See also S. Goulding, *Principles of Company Law* (London: Cavendish Publishing, 1996), 123–138, and J. H. Farrar and B. M. Hannigan, *Farrar's Company Law*, 4th ed. (London: Butterworths, 1998), 99–114.

86. F. Rose, *Nutshells: Company Law* (London: Sweet & Maxwell, 1998), 45.

87. Ibid.

88. Ibid.

89. L. S. Sealy, *Cases and Materials in Company Law* (London: Butterworths, 1996), 147.

90. Ibid.

91. (1875) L.R. 7 H.L. 653 (House of Lords). See also Sealy, *Cases and Materials in Company Law*, 151, for a summary of the facts and the holding.

92. See Enerst v. Nicholls (1875) 6 HL Cas 401.

93. [1953] Ch. 131.

94. See Goulding, *Principles of Company Law*, 123.
95. [1953] Ch. 131.
96. See Goulding, *Principles of Company Law*, 123. Cf. *Rolled Steel* [1986] Ch. 246 per Browne-Wilkinson LJ.
97. Goulding, *Principles of Company Law*, 123.
98. Ibid.
99. *Cotman v. Brougham* [1918] AC 514.
100. Bell Houses Ltd. v. City Wall Properties Ltd [1966] 1 WLR 1323.
101. Goulding, *Principles of Company Law*, 123.
102. Sealy, *Cases and Materials in Company Law*, 147.
103. Ibid.
104. Ibid.
105. Ibid., 148.
106. (1880) 5 App Cas 473 (House of Lords).
107. See Goulding, *Principles of Company Law*, 124.
108. [1918] AC 514.
109. See General Auction Estate and Monetary Company v. Smith [1891] 3 Ch. 342. In Zambia, section 15(1) of the Companies Act 1994 limits the incidental or ancillary power of public companies to borrow as follows: 'A public company shall not transact any business, exercise any borrowing powers or incur any indebtedness, except for a purpose incidental to its incorporation or to the obtaining of subscription to, or payment for, its shares, unless the Registrar has issued it with a certificate under this section.'
110. See Attorney General and Ephraim Hutchings v. Great Eastern Railway Co. (1880) 5 App Cas 473.
111. Re Introductions Ltd [1970] Ch. 199.
112. See also *Charterbridge Corp Ltd v. Lloyds Bank Plc* [1970] Ch. 62.
113. *Rolled Steel Products (Holdings) Ltd v. British Steel Corp* [1986] Ch. 246. The Court of Appeal stated that the ratification should be by all shareholders, but the basis for such a stringent requirement is not clear.
114. Goulding, *Principles of Company Law*, 124.
115. See the Cohen Committee 1945, Cmnd. 6659. In the United Kingdom, there have been a number of law reform commissions that have been set up to examine, inter alia, the prospects for abolishing, retaining, or refining the *ultra vires* doctrine. See, for example, the Cohen Committee 1945, Cmnd. 6659, para. 12; the Jenkins Committee 1962, Cmnd 1749, paras. 35–42; and D. D. Prentice, *Reform of the* Ultra Vires *Rules: A Consultative Document* (London: Department of Trade and Industry, 1986).

116. 1945, Cmnd 6659, para 12.

117. 1962, Cmnd 1749, para 42.

118. 'Reform of the *Ultra Vires* Rule: A Consultative Document' (DTI, 1986).

119. Goulding, *Principles of Company Law*, 124–125.

120. Section 35(1) of the English Companies Act 1985, as amended by the 1989 Companies Act—which introduced and imported section 35A and section 35B into the Companies Act 1985—provides as follows: '(1) The validity of an act done by a company shall not be called into question on the ground of lack of capacity by reason of anything in the company's memorandum.' Davies observed that subsection (1) of section 35A of the English Companies Act 1985 retains the expressions 'dealing with the company' and 'in good faith', both of which caused some difficulty in the earlier version of section 35.120. He argued, thus, 'But happily subsection (2) gives help in their interpretation. It provides:

    "(2) For this purpose—

    a person 'deals with' a company if he is a party to any transaction or other act to which the company is a party;

    a person shall not be regarded as acting in bad faith by reason only of his knowing that an act is beyond the powers of the directors under the company's constitution; and

    a person shall be deemed to have acted in good faith unless the contrary is proved."

    Subsection (2)(a) provides a straightforward test of whether a person is "dealing with the company". He will be, so long as he is a party to a transaction (e.g., a contract) or an act (e.g., a payment of money) to which the company is also a party. It no longer matters whether the person is an insider or an outsider, as it did under the *Turquand* rule.' Davies, *Gower's Principles of Modern Company Law*, 215. On the rule in the *Turquand* case, see Royal British Bank v. Turquand (1856) 6 E. & B. 327, Exch. Ch.

121. Rose, *Nutshells: Company Law*, 45.

122. Ibid. Cf. the Zambian case of *Bank of Zambia v. Chibote Meat Corporation Limited* (SCZ Judgement No. 14 of 1999).

123. See Rose, *Nutshells: Company Law*, 45.

124. That is, the Companies Act 2006.

125. Department of Trade and Industry, 'Companies Act 2006: Explanatory Notes', p. 1, accessed 20 December 2008, http://www.opsi.gov.uk/acts/acts2006/en/ukpgaen_20060046_en.pdf.

126. See the U.K. Companies Act 2006 (Commencement No. 5, Transitional Provisions and Savings) Order 2007 (Statutory Instrument No. 3495

(C. 150) of 2007). Significant portions of the U.K. Companies Act 2006 were implemented on 1 October 2007 and 6 April 2008, with the remainder expected to come into force on 1 October 2008 and 1 October 2009. It was intended that the U.K. Companies Act 2006 should be implemented in stages, with full implementation by October 2008, but an announcement from the Department for Business, Enterprise and Regulatory Reform (BERR) delayed this process by a year. The commencement date for most of the provisions that were due to be in force on 1 October 2008 was therefore postponed until 1 October 2009.

127. See *Supra*. (n.55–56).
128. See the U.K. Companies Act 2006, sec. 42. See also the U.K. Charities Act 1993, sec. 65.
129. See generally the U.K. Charities Act 1993.
130. A. Sulkowski and K. Greenfield, 'A Bridle, a Pod and a Big Stick: An Evaluation of Class Actions, Shareholder Proposals and the Ultra Vires Doctrine as Methods for Controlling Corporate Behavior', *Boston College of Law Faculty Papers*, Paper No. 92 (Boston: Boston College of Law, 2005). The abstract is available at http://lsr.nellco.org/cgi/viewcontent.cgi?article=1092&context=bc/bclsfp.
131. (1843) 2 Hare 461 (Court of Chancery [Vice-Chancellor]). This case was brought by two shareholders in the Victoria Park Company (incorporated by statute) against the company's five directors and others. The shareholders alleged that the property of the company had been misapplied and wasted and certain mortgages had been improperly given over the company's property. The case asked that the defendants should be held accountable to the company, and it also sought the appointment of a receiver. The vice-chancellor ruled, however, that it was incompetent for the plaintiffs to bring such proceedings, the sole right to do so belonging to the company in its corporate character. Against this background, the exceptions to the rule in *Foss v. Harbottle* are usually grouped under four heads: (1) when the act that is complained of is *ultra vires* or illegal, (2) when the matter is one which could validly be done or sanctioned only by some special majority of members, (3) when the personal and individual rights of the plaintiff as a member have been invaded, and (4) when what has been done amounts to a 'fraud on the minority', and the wrongdoers are themselves in control of the company. For further details on the four exceptions to the rule in *Foss v. Harbottle*, see K. Wedderburn, 'Shareholders' Rights and the Rule in *Foss v. Harbottle*', *Cambridge Law Journal* (1957): 203.

132. See the explanation in note 132.
133. See also the U.K. Department of Trade and Industry, 'Companies Act 2006: Explanatory Notes', p. 15, accessed 20 December 2008, http://www.opsi.gov.uk/acts/acts2006/en/ukpgaen_20060046_en.pdf.
134. Ibid.
135. In March 1998, the U.K. Department of Trade and Industry commissioned a fundamental review of company law in the United Kingdom. An independent steering group led the Company Law Review (CLR), whose terms of reference required them to consider how core company law could be modernized in order to provide a simple, efficient, and cost-effective framework for British business in the twenty-first century.
136. The U.K. Department of Trade and Industry, 'Companies Act', 15.
137. Ibid.
138. Ibid., 18.
139. Ibid.
140. Ibid.
141. Ibid.
142. Ibid.
143. Ibid.
144. Ibid.
145. Ibid.
146. See Vallejo v. Wheeler 98 Eng. Rep. 1012; Banque Financiere de la Cité S.A. v. Westgate Insurance Co. Ltd (unreported, Court of Appeal of England, 28 July 1988); Allen v. Flood 1898 App. Cas. 1, at 46 (P.C. 1897); and the ICC Arbitration Case No. 8611 of 1997.
147. T. Keily, 'Good Faith and the Vienna Convention on Contracts for the International Sale of Goods (CISG)', *Vindobona Journal of International Commercial Law and Arbitration* 3, no. 1 (1999): 15–40, accessed 28 July 2008, http://www.cisg.law.pace.edu/cisg/biblio/keily.html#faith.
148. See E. A. Farnsworth, 'The Eason-Weinmann Colloquium on International and Comparative Law: Duties of Good Faith and Fair Dealing under the UNIDROIT Principles, Relevant International Conventions, and National Laws', *Tulane Journal of International and Comparative Law* 3, no. 47 (1995): 59–61.
149. See H. K. Lücke, 'Good Faith and Contractual Performance', in *Essays on Contract*, ed. P. Finn (Sydney: The Law Book Company Limited, 1987), 160.
150. See generally T. Keily, 'Good Faith'.
151. Ibid.

152. *Supra.* (n. 123).
153. See the text of this book supported by endnotes, *Supra.* (n.125-130).
154. See generally the U.K. Charities Act 1993.
155. *Freshint Ltd and Others v. Kawambwa Tea Company* [2008] ZMSC 26; [1996] Ltd. (130/2005) [2008] ZMSC 22; and SCZ No. 33 of 2008 (8 May 2008), accessed 2 January 2009, http://www.saflii.org/zm/cases/ZMSC/2008/26.html.
156. Ibid.
157. Ibid.
158. [1994] Z.R. 136, cited in the Zambian case of *Freshint* [2008] ZMSC 26; [1996] Ltd. (130/2005) [2008] ZMSC 22; and SCZ No. 33 of 2008 (8 May 2008), accessed 2 January 2009, http://www.saflii.org/zm/cases/ZMSC/2008/26.html. See also the following Zambian cases: Avolon Motors v. Gadsden and another [1998] ZR 41; BP Zambia Plc v. Interland Motors Ltd [2001] ZR 37; Magnum v. Quadri and another [1981] ZR 141; and *Bank of Zambia v. Chibote*, SCZ Judgement No. 14 of 1999.
159. See *Freshint* [2008] ZMSC 26; [1996] Ltd. (130/2005) [2008] ZMSC 22; and SCZ No. 33 of 2008 (8 May 2008), accessed 2 January 2009, http://www.saflii.org/zm/cases/ZMSC/2008/26.html.
160. Ibid.
161. See Barclays Bank Ltd v. Quistclose Investments Ltd [1970] AC 567. In this English case, Rolls Razor was deeply indebted to Barclays Bank. It needed further additional sums to be able to pay a dividend which it had declared. Rolls Razor borrowed funds from Quistclose Investments in order to satisfy the dividend declared. The terms of the loan were such that the funds would be used only for the sole purpose of paying the dividend. The loan was paid into an account with Barclays Bank, and Barclays Bank was given notice of the arrangement. However, between the time that the loan was advanced and the dividend was paid, Rolls Razor went into liquidation. Barclays Bank claimed that they were entitled to exercise a set-off of the money in the account against the debts that Rolls Razor owed. Quistclose Investments claimed that the moneys had to be returned to them, as the purpose for which they had been lent had now failed and was incapable of being fulfilled (as Rolls Razor was now in liquidation). The House of Lords (with the leading judgment being given by Lord Wilberforce) unanimously held that the money was held by Rolls Razor on trust for the payment of the dividends; that purpose having failed, the money was held on trust for Quistclose Investments. The fact that the transaction was a loan did not exclude the implication of a trust.

Barclays Bank, having notice of the trust, could not retain the money as against Quistclose Investments. Similarly, the liquidator of Rolls Razor could not claim title to the money because the assets did not form a part the beneficial estate of Rolls Razor. See also Carreras Rothmans v. Freeman Mathews Treasure [1985] Ch. 207; Twinsectra v. Yardley [2002] UKHL 12; Re Kayford (in liquidation) [1975] 1 WLR 279; and Re EVTR Ltd. [1987] BCLC 647.

162. Telephone interview with Michael Musonda, the former chairman of the Law Association of Zambia (see note 34).

163. Ibid. See also the e-mail response from Tony Bwembya in note 34.

164. [2008] ZMSC 26; [1996] Ltd. (130/2005) [2008] ZMSC 22; and SCZ No. 33 of 2008 (8 May 2008), accessed 2 January 2009, http://www.saflii.org/zm/cases/ZMSC/2008/26.html.

165. See Graham, 'New Companies Act: (A) An Introduction to the New Act; and (B) Forming a Company', 3.

166. See the email response from Tony Bwembya in note 34.

167. These regulations are contained in Statutory Instrument No. 17 of 1995, issued pursuant to section 400 of the Zambian Companies Act 1994.

168. However, in his e-mail to this author (see note 49), Musonda argued, 'The Companies Act 1994 has somewhat demystified company formations. While it is an obvious advantage for one to posses some "competence" and "skill" when filling out an Incorporation Form, not much "*skill*" or "*competence*" may be required for one to indicate the "*General business*" of the company as "*trading*", or "*farming*" or "*transportation*" or "*manufacturing*" or "*banking*" and other business as "*any other business incidental to the foregoing or which may be advantageous or beneficial to the carrying on of the principal business*".' But, even this seemingly easy task of entering information on Forms I, II, III, or IV may not be that easy to someone who is not literate or who is semiliterate.

169. E-mail from Annie Senkwe Nsenduluka (see note 57).

170. That is, Statutory Instrument No. 17 of 1995, issued pursuant to section 400 of the Zambian Companies Act 1994.

171. [1994] Z.R. 136, cited in the Zambian case of *Freshint Ltd and Others v. Kawambwa Tea Company* [2008] ZMSC 26; [1996] Ltd. (130/2005) [2008] ZMSC 22; and SCZ No. 33 of 2008 (8 May 2008), accessed 2 January 2009, http://www.saflii.org/zm/cases/ZMSC/2008/26.html.

172. Ibid. See also *Bank of Zambia v. Chibote Meat Corporation Limited*, SCZ Judgement No. 14 of 1999.

173. As noted earlier, these regulations are contained in Statutory Instrument No. 17 of 1995, issued pursuant to section 400 of the Zambian Companies Act 1994.

174. See the e-mail response from Tony Bwembya in note 34.

175. See the e-mail from Michael Musonda in note 49. The United Kingdom, as noted earlier, provides a leading example of a common law jurisdiction with such legislative requirements. Also, in Zambia prior to the repeal of the Companies Act 1921, there was a statutory requirement in that act placing an obligation on the incorporators of a company to furnish the registrar of companies with a memorandum of association that would contain, inter alia, an objects clause.

176. Statutory Instrument No. 17 of 1995, issued pursuant to section 400 of the Zambian Companies Act 1994.

177. Companies Act 1994, sec. 20(1).

178. See also the telephone interview with Michael Musonda in note 34.

179. Sealy, *Cases and Materials in Company Law*, 147.

180. However, section 22(1) of the Zambian Companies Act 1994 does not apply to a statutory body corporate that is created under a separate piece of legislation from the Companies Act 1994. Unless provided for explicitly in that separate piece of legislation, such a statutory body corporate does not have the capacity, rights, powers, and privileges that an individual enjoys.

181. *Supra.* (n.178).

182. See *Supra.* (n.178).

183. [1978] ZLR 197.

184. See also the following English cases referred in the judgement pertaining to the Zambian case of J. P. Karnezos v. Hermes Safaris Limited [1978] ZLR 197; Re German Date Coffee Company (1882) 20 Ch. D. 169; and Simpson v. Westminster Palace Hotel Company (1860) 8 HLC 712.

185. *J. P. Karnezos v. Hermes Safaris Limited* [1978] ZLR 197, p. 200.

186. On the concept of a company being a 'legal person' under Zambia's Companies Act 1994, see *Associated Chemicals Limited v. Hill and Delamain Zambia Limited and Ellis and Company (Third Party)* (Supreme Court of Zambia [SCZ] Judgment No. 2 of 1998).

187. Further, sections 390 through 401 of the Zambian Companies Act 1994 contain 'transition provisions' for companies that were incorporated prior to the repeal of the Companies Act 1921 but which now exist under the Companies Act 1994.

188. The term *former Act* is defined in section 2 of the Zambian Companies Act 1994 as 'the Companies Act repealed by section four hundred and two; Cap. 686 of the 1971 Edition.'

189. Companies Act 1994, sec. 391.

190. Ibid.

191. See the Development Bank of Zambia Act (CAP 363) (as amended in 2001 and 2005, respectively).

192. See *Supra.* (n.70). It is, however, not clear why the legislative drafts-man had to include in the Zambian Companies Act 1994 a provision for partnerships of less than twenty individuals without cross-referencing or acknowledging legislation on partnership law in Zambia. What would happen in the event that the relevant statutory provisions of the Companies Act 1994 and the Partnership Act 1890 conflict? Which of the two statutes would prevail? We are left to look to the Interpretation and General Provisions Act 1964 (as amended through and up to 1994) for inspiration. But even then, there is no clear-cut guidance in the Interpretation and General Provisions Act 1964.

193. See the Banking and Financial Services Act 1994, sec. 4(1) (as amended in 2000). See also the statutory definition of *bank* in section 2 of the Banking and Financial Services Act 1994 (as amended in 2000), which stipulates that '*bank* means a company conducting banking business.' I have already examined the term *banking business*.

194. See generally the Companies Act 1994.

195. See generally the Companies Act 1921.

196. It is unlikely that the registrar of banks would register a foreign company that is not lawfully constituted or recognised as a company under the Zambian Companies Act 1994. Section 2 of the Banking and Financial Services Act 1994 (as amended in 2000) clearly stipulates that the word *company* under the Banking and Financial Services Act 1994 has the same meaning as that in the Companies Act 1994.

197. See the Banking and Financial Services Act 1994, sec. 10(1) (as amended in 2000).

198. Ibid.

199. See Mwenda, *Banking Supervision and Systemic Bank Restructuring: An International and Comparative Legal Perspective*, 35.

200. As amended in 2005.

201. See Mwenda, *Banking Supervision and Systemic Bank Restructuring: An International and Comparative Legal Perspective*, 35.

202. See the text in this book supported by the following endnotes: *Supra.* (n.187–197).
203. Ibid.
204. The registrar is appointed by the minister of finance pursuant to provisions of the Banking and Financial Services Act 1994, sec. 20: 'The Minister, on the recommendation of the Bank of Zambia, shall appoint a Registrar of Banks and Financial Institutions to administer the Register and to exercise and perform such other functions as are conferred or imposed upon him by or under this or any other Act or by the Governor of the Bank of Zambia, and may designate an employee of the Bank of Zambia as the Deputy Registrar of Banks and Financial Institutions who shall be subject to the control and directions of the Registrar and be competent to exercise and perform any of the powers and functions of the Registrar ... The Registrar and Deputy Registrar shall each hold office for a term of five years unless removed for negligence of duty or misconduct, and shall be eligible for reappointment.'
205. See the Banking and Financial Services Act 1994, sec. 4(1): 'Upon application by a company, the Registrar, in consultation with the Minister, may grant a licence authorising the company to conduct banking business.' Further, section 10(1) of that statute provides, 'Upon application by any person, the Registrar, in consultation with the Minister, may grant a licence authorising the applicant to conduct any regulated financial service business.' Cf. chapter 6 of the Banking and Financial Services Act 1994 (as amended in 2000).
206. See generally chapter 6 of the Banking and Financial Services Act 1994 (as amended in 2000).
207. Bank of Zambia, 'Requirements for Setting up a Bank in Zambia', accessed 23 December 2008, http://www.boz.zm/banksupervision_requirements.htm.
208. Ibid.
209. Ibid.
210. Banking and Financial Services Act 1994, sec. 17(1).
211. Ibid., sec. 17(2).
212. Ibid., sec. 17(3). Under section 8 of the Banking and Financial Services Act 1994, the authorised activities of a bank, in addition to the taking of deposits, include the following (Cf. the definition of financial services in section 2 of the same act, which replicates most of these provisions): 'Except where the conditions attached to a particular licence otherwise

provide, a banking licence shall be taken to authorise its holder to engage in any of the following activities in addition to banking business: (a) making loans and extending credit to any person on the security of property of any kind or unsecured; (b) dealing as a principal or as an agent in—

i.   bills of exchange, promissory notes, cheques, travellers' cheques and like instruments;

ii.   the currency of Zambia and, subject to the regulations made under this Act, in the currency of any other country and foreign exchange transactions; and

iii.   gold, silver or platinum bullion or coins;

(c) providing money transfer services and facilities; (d) the issue and administration of payment, credit or debit cards and, in co-operation with others, the operation of payment, credit card and debit card systems; (e) providing guarantees, letters of credit and other assurances of payment; (f) finance leasing; (g) factoring, with or without recourse; (h) acting as a trustee of any trust, executor or administrator of any estate or in any fiduciary capacity for any person; (i) acting as a financial agent for any person; (j) providing safekeeping and custodial services for financial assets and securities; (k) providing merchant banking services including the arrangement and underwriting of shares, trade financing, corporate financing and the provision of financial advice; and (l) dealing as a principal or as an agent for its customers in financial futures and options and in exchange, currency and interest rate swap agreements. (2) The Minister, on the recommendation of the Bank of Zambia, may by regulation prescribe the meaning to be given to any expression used in this section and not otherwise defined for the purposes of this Act.'

213.   On the concept of unsafe and unsound practice of a bank or financial institution in Zambia, see the Banking and Financial Services Act 1994, sec. 77(1).

214.   See the Banking and Financial Services Act 1994, sec. 2.

215.   See *Infra*. (n.217).

216.   2003/HP/359, an unreported case in the High Court of Zambia (judgement delivered on 1 September 2004). See also the appeal to the Supreme Court of Zambia, Bank of Zambia v. Chungu and Others (163/2005) [2008] ZMSC 12; SCZ No. 15 of 2008 (24 April 2008), which also did not fully or critically address the concept of unsafe and unsound practice under Zambia's Banking and Financial Services Act 1994. It dealt instead with the issue of whether a solvent bank or financial institution can be

placed under compulsory liquidation by the Bank of Zambia under the statutory provision relating to unsafe and sound practice even when the bank or financial institution is not insolvent.

217. See Bank of Zambia, 'Press Statement, January 14, 2003: BOZ Takes Possession of Access Financial Services and Access Leasing', accessed 17 April 2005, http://www.boz.zm/Media/Access_%20Financial_Services.htm. See also Access Finance Services Limited and Access Leasing Limited v. Bank of Zambia 2003/HP/359, an unreported case in the High Court of Zambia (judgement delivered on 1 September 2004).

218. See Bank of Zambia, 'Press Statement, January 14, 2003: BOZ Takes Possession of Access Financial Services and Access Leasing'.

219. Access Finance Services Limited and Access Leasing Limited v. Bank of Zambia 2003/HP/359, an unreported case in the High Court of Zambia (judgement delivered on 1 September 2004).

220. See *Zambezi Times Online*, 'Access Finance Engaged in Crime', accessed 17 April 2005, http://www.zambezitimes.com/fulltxt.php?id_news=1879.

221. Ibid.

222. Ibid.

223. Ibid.

224. Ibid.

225. Ibid.

226. Ibid.

227. Banking and Financial Services Act 1994, sec. 77(1) (as amended in 2000).

228. Section 77(2) of Zambia's Banking and Financial Services Act 1994 reads as follows: 'Where the Bank of Zambia is unable to obtain an agreement under subsection (1) within a time, and in a form and content, satisfactory to the Bank of Zambia, or where the Bank of Zambia considers that the need for prompt action makes the negotiating of such an agreement impractical, the Bank of Zambia may direct the bank or financial institution or any director, manager or other person concerned in its management to do either or both of the following: (a) cease or refrain from doing the act or pursuing the course of conduct; (b) perform such acts as, in the opinion of the Bank of Zambia, are necessary to rectify the situation.' In particular, but without limiting the generality of subsection (2), the Bank of Zambia can, in accordance with section 77(3) of Zambia's Banking and Financial Services Act 1994, (a) direct the culpable bank or financial institution to refrain from adopting or pursuing a particular course of action or to restrict the scope of its business in a particular way; (b) impose any limitation on

the bank's acceptance of deposits or the payment of interest thereon, the granting of credit, the making of investments or the payment of dividends; (c) prohibit the bank or financial institution from soliciting deposits or the payment of the interest thereon either generally or from specified persons or classes of persons; (d) prohibit the bank or financial institution from entering into any other transaction or class of transactions, or from commencing or continuing any activity which it is permitted under Zambia's Banking and Financial Services Act 1994 to carry on; or (e) require the suspension or removal from office of any director, officer, or other person.

229. Constant reference was made in the judgement to sections 81, 84, 86, and 101 of the Banking and Financial Services Act 1994.

230. See for example, Eden, 568 F.2d at 611; Groos Nat'l Bank v. Comptroller of the Currency, 573 F.2d 889, 897 (5th Cir. 1978); and La Marque, 610 F.2d at 1264. See also In re Franklin Nat'l Bank Securities Litigation, 478 F. Supp. 210, 221 (E.D.N.Y. 1979); First Nat'l Bank of Eden v. Department of the Treasury, 568 F.2d 610, 611 n.2 (8th Cir. 1978) (per curiam); First Nat'l Bank of La Marque v. Smith, 610 F.2d 1258, 1265 (5th Cir. 1980); and Briggs v. Spaulding (1891) 141 U.S. 132, 165–166.

231. 2003/HP/359, an unreported case in the High Court of Zambia (judgement delivered on 1 September 2004).

232. *Supra.* (n.168–184).

233. See the Banking and Financial Services Act 1994, sec. 4(2) (as amended in 2000).

234. *Cf.* the statutory requirements set forth in section 4 of the Banking and Financial Services Act 1994.

235. In many common law jurisdictions, including the United Kingdom, the memorandum and articles of association are public documents and thus, they give rise to the doctrine of constructive notice. In Zambia, in contrast, section 24 of the Companies Act 1994 has abolished the common law doctrine of constructive notice. On the doctrine of constructive notice generally, see Re Jon Beauforte (London) Ltd [1953] Ch 131. See also Re Airdale Co-op. Worsted Society [1933] 1 Ch. 639; Sinclair v. Brougham [1914] A.C. 398, H.L.; Re Diplock [1948] Ch. 465, C.A.; and Agip (Africa) Ltd v. Jackson [1991] Ch. 547, C.A.

236. Although the statutory requirement for a company applying for a banking licence to provide a memorandum of association to the registrar of banks and financial institutions has now been done away with, does that mean the *ultra vires* doctrine has also been done away with?

237. See the Banking and Financial Services Act 1994, sec. 4(2) (as amended in 2000).
238. See K. K. Mwenda, *Legal Aspects of Corporate Capital and Finance* (Washington, DC: Penn Press, 1999), 30–34.
239. See generally K. K. Mwenda, 'A Company without A Memorandum Of Association: Policy Implications', *Southern Africa Journal of Comparative and International Law* 32, no. 1 (March 1999).
240. See section 399 of Zambia's Companies Act 1994, which provides that 'nothing in this Act shall abrogate or affect any special legislation relating to companies carrying on the business of banking, insurance or any other business', indicating that the statutory provisions of the Companies Act 1994 cannot override the provisions of such pieces of legislation as the Banking and Financial Services Act 1994.
241. See the Banking and Financial Services Act 1994 (as amended in 2000), sec. 4.
242. See the Companies Act 1994, sec. 399.
243. See the relevant text in the book that is supported by the following endnotes: *Supra.* (n.178, 179, 182–184).
244. Ibid.
245. The said Section 4(2) provides that: "(2) The application shall be in such form and accompanied by such fees as may be prescribed by regulation, and the form of application shall require at least the following particulars to be supplied: (a) the articles of association of the company; (b) the physical and postal addresses of its head office and the permanent residential addresses of its directors, chief executive officer, managers and shareholders; (c) the name and permanent residential address of every subscriber for any class or series of shares issued by the company in a number that will exceed one per centum of all the shares of that class or series, whether such shares carry the right to vote in all circumstances or not; (d) the addresses of each branch proposed to be opened by the company and, in the case of a mobile office, the area proposed to be served; (e) full particulars of the business it proposes to conduct under the authority of the licence; (f) the amount of its capital; and (g) such assurances and evidence of the foregoing as the Registrar may require to be given by the applicant."
246. See the text in this book supported by the following endnotes: *Supra.* (n.168–184).
247. See sections 7 and 8 of Zambia's Companies Act 1994.

248. (1882) 22 Ch. D 349 (Court of Appeal).
249. See also Welton v. Saffery (1897) A.C. 299.
250. *Guinness v. Land Corporation of Ireland* (1882) 22 Ch. D 349 (Court of Appeal).
251. [1952] 2 All ER 871.
252. See Re Duncan Gilmour & Co. Ltd. [1952] 2 All ER 871.
253. See the text in this book supported by the following endnotes: *Supra.* (n.168–184).
254. Cf. Davies, who argued that 'Professor Prentice had recommended that companies should be afforded the capacity to do any act whatsoever and should have the option of not stating their objects in their memoranda. Unfortunately, this straightforward solution was not adopted, notwithstanding the precedents for it in some other common law countries. Some of those countries, however, were not subject to two complications which arose here. First, our companies, as we have seen, are not necessarily "business corporations"; on the contrary most of these limited by guarantee are formed to enable the advantages of corporate personality and limited liability to be obtained by those undertaking activities which are not the carrying on of business with a view for a profit ... The second complication (from which non-E.C. countries are free) was that the Second Company Law Directive requires that, in the case of public companies, the statutes or instruments of incorporation shall state the objects of the company. But total abolition of limitations on capacity was in no way dependent on abolition of objects clauses and, if the Directive precluded the latter, it certainly did not preclude the former' (*Gower's Principles of Modern Company Law*, 208).
255. Davies, examining the position in the United Kingdom, observed that at some point, 'the courts sought to narrow the scope of the resulting *vires* by distinguishing between "objects" (in the sense of types of business) and "powers" and, applying the *ejusdem generis* rule of construction, ruling that the powers could be used only in relation to the objects. But that too was circumvented by the device of ending the "objects" clause by stating that each of the specified objects or powers should be treated as independent and in no way ancillary or subordinate one to another, and, at a later date, by also inserting a power "to carry on any other trade or business whatsoever which can, in the opinion of the board of directors, be advantageously carried on by the company in connection with or as ancillary to any of the above businesses or the general business of the company..."' (*Gower's Principles of Modern Company Law*, 204).

See *Cotman v. Brougham* [1918] A.C. 514. See also *Introductions Ltd.*
[1970] Ch. 199, C.A.; *Bell Houses Ltd v. City Wall Properties Ltd* [1966]
2 Q.B. 656, C.A.; *Newstead v. Frost* [1980] 1 W.L.R. 135, H.L.; *Charter-bridge Corporation Ltd. v. Lloyds Bank* [1970] Ch. 62; *Re Halt Garage Ltd* [1982] 3 All E.R. 1016; *Rolled Steel Ltd v. British Steel Corp* [1986]
Ch. 246; and *Brady v. Brady* [1988] BCLC 20, C.A., revd. [1989] A.C.
755, H.L.

256. See the text of this book supported by the following endnotes: *Supra.*
(n.33–36).

CHAPTER 3

257. See *Infra.* (n.355) See also *Infra.* (n.273–276).

258. Creditors could fall under different categories. For example, an ordinary
bank depositor who holds a client's account at the bank will be treated
as an unsecured creditor. However, it is possible that the bank will have
obtained some finance from secured creditors. Such secured creditors
often hold floating and/or fixed charges as a form of collateral for the
finance they are advancing the bank. But, admittedly, the ranking of priorities and claims relating to the debts that the bank owes can be altered
through debt subordination agreements. I have examined this aspect of the
law elsewhere; see generally K. K. Mwenda and A. Laszczynska, 'Legal
Problems of Debt Subordination: A Comparative Study', *African Journal
of Comparative and International Law* 10, pt. 4 (December 1998). On the
ranking of priorities and claims, see also generally R. M. Goode, *Legal
Problems of Credit and Security* (London: Sweet and Maxwell, 1988);
R. M. Goode, *Principles of Corporate Insolvency Law*, 2nd ed. (London:
Sweet and Maxwell, 1997); P. R. Wood, *Project Finance, Subordinated
Debt and State Loans* (London: Sweet and Maxwell, 1995); R. M. Goode,
Commercial Law, 2nd ed. (London: Penguin Books, 1995); F. Oditah,
Legal Aspects of Receivables Financing (London: Sweet and Maxwell,
1991); and W. J. Gough, *Company Charges*, 2nd ed. (London: Butter-
worths, 1996).

259. (1891) 139 U.S. 417, 11 S.Ct. 530.

260. R. W. Hamilton, *Corporation Finance: Cases and Materials* (St. Paul,
MN: West Publishing, 1989), 73–75.

261. See Mwenda, 'Zambia's Securities Act 1993 On Trial: The Cases of
Insider Dealing', 159.

262. See generally also K. K. Mwenda, 'Legal Problems of Financial Assistance: A Comparative Legal Study', *The African Journal of International and Comparative Law* 9, pt. 4 (1997): 919–933; Mwenda, *Legal Aspects of Corporate Capital and Finance*, 70–94; K. K. Mwenda and D. Ailola, 'Legal Aspects of Corporate Finance: A Comparative Study of the Law on Financial Assistance', *Southern Africa Journal of Comparative and International Law* 31, no. 2 (July 1998); K. K. Mwenda and S. S. Silomba, 'Corporate Law Developments Relating to Payment for Shares in Zambia', in *Frontiers of Legal Knowledge: Business and Economic Law in Context*, edited by K. K. Mwenda and D. A. Ailola (Durham, NC: Carolina Academic Press, 2003); and K. K. Mwenda and S. S Silomba, 'Legal Aspects of Share Watering: A Comparative Study', *Stellenbosch Law Review* (University of Stellenbosch, South Africa) 1 (2000).

263. (1892) 48 Minn. 174, 50 N.W. 1117.

264. B. Manning and J. J. Hanks, *Legal Capital* (Westbury NY: Foundation Press, 1990), 50.

265. Ibid., 51–52.

266. 30 F. Cas 435 (No. 17, 944) (C.C.D. Me. 1824).

267. See Manning and Hanks, *Legal Capital*, 50.

268. For a definition of share watering, see Hamilton, *Corporation Finance: Cases and Materials*, 75.

269. See Manning and Hanks, *Legal Capital*, 49.

270. Mwenda, *Legal Aspects of Corporate Capital and Finance*, 60.

271. Ibid.

272. (1897) 1 Ch. 796.

273. Ibid.

274. (1898) 6 S.L.T.

275. (1898) 6 S.L.T. at p. 251.

276. 30 F. Cas 435 (No. 17, 944) (C.C.D. Me. 1824).

277. See, for example, Manning and Hanks, *Legal Capital*, 51.

278. R. W. Hamilton, *Corporations*, 4th ed. (St. Paul, MN: West Publishing Co., 1997), 2.

279. See Mwenda, *Legal Aspects of Corporate Capital and Finance*, 48–68.

280. Ibid.

281. Hamilton, *Corporation Finance: Cases and Materials*, 75. The reason for giving shares a par value is mainly historical. At a time when it was envisaged that the nominal value of shares would be so large that a substantial proportion would be left uncalled, the introduction of the par value concept was a convenient yardstick to measure the extent of

liability of shareholders. For an elaborate discussion about this view, see, for example, Committee of Inquiry into the Working and Administration of the Present Company Law of Ghana, *Final Report of the Committee of Inquiry into the Working and Administration of the Present Company Law of Ghana* ('Gower's Report') (Accra: Government Printers, 1961), 53.

282. See Orregun Gold Mining Co. Of India v. Ropley (1892) A.C. 125.
283. B. Manning and J. J. Hanks Jr., *Legal Capital* (Westbury, NY: Foundation Press, 1990), 25–26.
284. Ibid.
285. See generally chapter 2.
286. The lack of statutory obligations in the Companies Act 1994 for companies to have a memorandum of association entails that a company can, if it so wishes, have a memorandum of association and an objects clause.
287. Cf. the English Companies Act 1985, sec. 2(5)(a).
288. See *Orregun Gold Mining Co of India Ltd. v. Roper* [1892] AC 125.
289. Hamilton, *Corporations*, 598–599.
290. E. Ferran, *Company Law and Corporate Finance* (Oxford: Oxford University Press, 1999), 282.
291. Ibid.
292. [1987] 2 All ER 70; [1987] BCC 93.
293. This view was also confirmed in a discussion with G. K. Lipimile, the executive director of the Zambia Competition Commission in Lusaka on 22 December 1998. Lipimile was involved in the drafting of the Companies Act 1994.
294. See the Zambian Companies Act 1994, secs. 6(2)(e) and 10(2).
295. Ibid., secs. 19, 17, 31, 32, 33, 34, and 35.
296. Ibid., sec. 14.
297. Ferran, *Company Law and Corporate Finance*, 284.
298. J. C. BonBright, 'The Dangers of Shares Without Par Value', *Columbia Law Review* 24 (1924): 449.
299. Ibid., 448–450.
300. [1892] AC 125, 133–134, HL.
301. Ferran, *Company Law and Corporate Finance*, 284.
302. R. Pennington, *Pennington's Company Law* (London: Butterworths, 1990), 21.
303. Manning and Hanks, *Legal Capital*, 30.
304. For example, BonBright, 'Dangers', 3.
305. See D. Frederick, 'The Par Value Of Stock', *Yale Law Journal* 16 (1906–1907): 249.

306. 129 Pennsylvania St. 405.

307. 139 (1891) US. 417, 11 Sup. Ct. 530 (1891).

308. Ibid.

309. See Manning and Hanks, *Legal Capital*, 27.

310. See C. Allen, 'Non Par Value Stock', *Central Law Journal* 90 (1920): 170.

311. Hamilton, *Corporations*, 207.

312. See generally C. Allen, 'Non Par Value Stock'. See also generally V. Morawetz, 'Shares Without Nominal or Par Value', *Harvard Law Review* 26 (1913) and J. E. Goodbar, 'No Par Value Stock—Its Nature And Use', *Miami Law Quarterly* 3, no. 1 (1948).

313. M. C. Harmen, 'Memorandum to Gedge Committee, in the Board of Trade, Report of the Committee on Shares of No Par Value', Cmd 9112 of 1954 (the Gedge report).

314. Ibid. See also A. A. Berle, 'Problems of Non Par Stock', *Columbia Law Review* 25 (1925): 44, where he observed that the first authorisation for the issuance of shares of no-par-value was made under chapter 351 of the Laws of the Sate of New York in 1912. Since then, other American states have enacted legislation to permit the issuance of no-par-value shares.

315. See Manning and Hanks, *Legal Capital*, 29.

316. See Harmen, 'Memorandum from the Council of the Chartered Institutes of Secretaries of Joint Stock Companies and Other Public Bodies to the Gedge Committee', 11.

317. See Ferran, *Company Law and Corporate Finance*, 285.

318. Ibid.

319. Ibid.

320. See the New Zealand Companies Act 1990, sec. 28.

321. See the Canadian Companies Act 1934, sec. 12(7).

322. See generally the *Final Report of Commission of Enquiry into Working and Administration of Company Law of Ghana*.

323. See Ghana's Companies Code 1963, sec. 40(1), and New Zealand's Companies Act 1990, sec. 28.

324. See Australia's Company Law Review Act 1998, sec. 254C, Sch. 5.

325. See *Final Report of Commission of Enquiry into Working and Administration of Company Law of Ghana*, 53.

326. See also H. E. Boschma, M. L. Lennarts, and J. N. Schulte-Veenstra, *Alternative Systems for Capital Protection* (Alphen aan den Rijn, Netherlands: Kluwer Law International, 2006), examining the position of the Netherlands, an EU member state as well. In that book, the authors considered,

inter alia, whether the concept of nominal value of shares in the Nether-lands should be abolished and replaced with that of no-par-value shares (NPV shares).

327. Freshfields, Bruckhaus and Deringer, *Consultation Study Concerning the Implications of Adopting a No-par Value Share Regime in Hong Kong: Final Report*, 29 November 2004, 7–11, accessed 8 February 2009, http://www.fstb.gov.hk/fsb/co_rewrite/eng/pub-press/doc/no-par_e.pdf. This study cites Austria, Belgium, British Columbia, British Virgin Islands, Cayman Islands, Germany, Guernsey, Jersey, and South Africa as some of the jurisdictions in which it is optional to issue shares of no-par-value.

328. See Harmen, 'Memorandum from the Council of the Chartered Insti-tute of Secretaries of Joint Stock Companies and Other Public Bodies to Gedge Committee', 7.

329. See Pennington, *Pennington's Company Law*, 21.

330. See Ferran, *Company Law and Corporate Finance*, 285.

331. See Hamilton, *Corporations*, 206.

332. See generally Berle, 'Problems'.

333. Ibid.

334. BonBright, 'Dangers', 449.

335. Ibid.

336. 1924 Tex. Civ. App. 260. S.W. 614.

337. Hamilton, *Corporations*, 207.

338. Ibid.

339. Borland Trustees v. Steel Brothers and Co. (1901) 1 Ch. 279. See also Re Paulin [1935] 1 K.B. 26 and IRC v. Crossman [1937] A.C. 26.

340. See *Sutton's Hospital* (1612) 10 Co Rep. 1; Tillard v. Brown (1668) 1 Lev 237; and Salmon v. Hamborough Company (1671) 1 Ch. Cas 204, HL.

341. London Sack & Bag Co. v. Dixon & Lugton [1943] 2 All ER 763, CA.

342. See *Infra.* (n.353) at 897.

343. [1915] 1 Ch. 881 at 897.

344. In most common law legal systems, such a procedure is found in the Companies Act.

345. See *Orregun Gold Mining Co of India Ltd. v. Roper* [1892] AC 125; Re White Star Line [1938] Ch. 458; Tintin Exploration Syndicate v. Sandys (1947) 177 L.T. 412; Re Bradford Investments plc (No. 2) [1991] BCLC 688; Pro-Image Studios v. Commonwealth Bank of Australia (1990–1991) 4 ACSR 586; and System Controls plc v. Munro Corporation plc [1990] BCC 386.

346. See *Infra.* (n. 357).

347. On dividend yields, see generally R. A. Brealey and S. C. Myers, *Principles of Corporate Finance* (New York: McGraw-Hill, 1991) and E. W. Davis and J. Pointon, *Finance and the Firm: An Introduction To Corporate Finance* (Oxford: Oxford University Press, 1994).
348. Including the English Companies (Amendment) Act 1989.
349. Elsewhere, I have examined this aspect in great detail. See Mwenda, 'Legal Problems of Financial Assistance: A Comparative Legal Study', 919–933.
350. English Companies Act 1985, sec. 100.
351. See Hamilton, *Corporation Finance Cases and Materials*, 75.
352. See, for example, Andrews v. Gas Meter Co. [1897] 1 Ch. 361 (Court of Appeal) and Peter's American Delicacy Co. Ltd. v. Heath (1939) 61 CLR 457 (High Court of Australia).
353. English Companies Act 1985, sec. 2(5)(a).
354. Ibid., sec. 99(1).
355. Ibid.
356. Ibid., sec. 738(2).
357. Ibid., sec. 738.
358. U.K. Companies Act 2006, sec. 581.
359. Ibid., sec. 582(1).
360. Ibid., sec. 582(2).
361. See the U.K. Companies Act 2006, sec. 580(2). See also the English Companies Act 1985, sec. 100(2).
362. See the U.K. Companies Act 2006, sec. 588(1). See also the English Companies Act 1985, sec. 112.
363. See the U.K. Companies Act 2006, sec. 588(2). See also the English Companies Act 1985, secs. 112(1) and (3).
364. See the U.K. Companies Act 2006, sec. 590. See also the English Companies Act 1985, sec. 114.
365. U.K. Companies Act 2006, sec. 580(1) is also found in the previous statute, the English Companies Act 1985, sec. 100, as 'A company's shares should not be allotted at a discount.'
366. See J. C. Shepperd, *Law of Fiduciaries* (Toronto: Carswell, 1981), 362. See also Regal (Hastings) Ltd v. Gulliver [1942] 1 All E.R. 378 and cf. Phipps v. Boardman [1966] 3 All E.R. 721.
367. Ibid. See also generally P. Loose, J. Yelland, and D. Impey, *The Company Director: Powers and Duties* (Bristol: Jordan Publishing, 1993).
368. English Companies Act 1985, sec. 103.
369. Ibid., sec. 103(1)

370. See *Infra*. (n. 382 and 383).
371. English Companies Act 1985, sec. 99(2). See also *Pro-Image Studios v. Commonwealth Bank* (1991) 4 ACSR 586 and *Re White Star Line* [1938] Ch 458.
372. English Companies Act 1985, sec. 102(1).
373. Ibid., secs. 100 and 114.
374. Ibid.
375. See the U.K. Companies Act 2006, secs. 580(2) and 590.
376. English Companies Act 1985, secs. 103(1) and 108.
377. U.K. Companies Act 2006, sec. 593.
378. See the U.K. Companies Act 2006, sec. 595. See also the English Companies Act 1985, sec 103(5).
379. See Viscount Dilhorne in Scott v. Metropolitan Police Commissioner [1975] A.C. at 819: 'In my opinion it is clear the law that an agreement by two or more by dishonesty to deprive a person of something which is his or to which he is or would be, or, might be entitled and an agreement by two or more by dishonesty to injure the proprietary right of his, suffices to constitute the offence of conspiracy to defraud.' J. Dine also observed, 'The common law crime of conspiracy to defraud is very wide. It will usually take one of the three forms: (a) where loss is suffered; (b) where the victim is deceived into taking an economic risk; and (c) where a public official is induced by deception to act contrary to his public duty'. Dine, *Criminal Law in the Company Context* (Aldershot: Dartmouth Publishing, 1995), 141.
380. See the standard texts on criminal law with regard to what constitutes fraud. See also R v. Allsop (1976) 64 Cr. App. R 29; Attorney General's Reference (No. 1 of 1982) [1983] Q.B. 751; and R. v. Cooke [1986] A.C. 909.
381. See *Supra*. (n.383 and n. 384).
382. See the U.K. Companies Act 2006, sec. 593.
383. See *Supra*. (n.395 and n.396).
384. (1897) 1 Ch. 796.
385. (1898) 6 S.L.T.
386. (1898) 6 S.L.T. at p. 251.
387. See Haigh v. Brooks (1840) 10 A.&E. 309, 320; Westlake v. Adams (1858) 5 C.B (N.S) 248, 265; Wild v. Tucker [1914] 3 K.B. 36, 39; cf. Langdale v. Danby [1982] 1 W.L.R. 1123; C.C.C. Films (London) Ltd. v. Impact Quadrant Films Ltd. [1985] Q.B. 16, 27; Brady v. Brady [1989] A.C. 755, 775; Normid Housing Association Ltd. v. R. John Ralphs [1989] 1 Lloyd's

Rep. 265, 272; Gaumont-British Pictures Corp. v. Alexander [1936] 2 All E.R. 1686; and Midland Bank & Trust Co. Ltd v. Green [1981] A.C. 513, 532.

388. See the text of this book supported by the following endnotes, *Supra.* (n.392–398).

389. Particularly on the incorporation of a partnership. See, for example, *Re Wragg* (1897) 1 Ch. 796.

390. See Re Keith Bray pty Ltd. (1991) 5 ACSR 450–452; Flitcroft's Case (1882) 21 Ch. D. 519; Hong Kong Gas Co. v. Glen [1914] 1 Ch. 527; and Famatima Development Corp. Ltd v. Bury [1910] A.C. 439.

391. See Davies, *Gower's Principles of Modern Company Law*, 282–294.

392. [1952] Ch. 124, [1951] 2 All E.R. 994 (Chancery Division).

393. Ferran, *Company Law and Corporate Finance*, 307–308.

394. [1980] 3 All ER 295.

395. Following Lord Wright in Lowry (Inspect of Taxes) v. Consolidated African Selection Trust Ltd. [1940] AC 648, HL.

396. Ferran, *Company Law and Corporate Finance*, 308.

397. See *Henry Head & Co. Ltd. v. Ropner Holdings Ltd* [1952] Ch. 124, [1951] 2 All E.R. 994 (Chancery Division).

398. See the repealed English Companies Act 1948, sec. 56. Cf. the English Companies Act 1985, sec. 130. See also *Shearer (Inspector of Taxes) v. Bercain Ltd* [1980] 3 All E.R. 295; Drown v. Gaumont British Corp. [1937] Ch. 402; Re Ratners Group plc. [1989] BCLC 612; and Re Ossory Estates plc [1988] BCLC 213.

399. See the U.K. Companies Act 2006, sec. 610. See also the English Companies Act 1985, sec. 130.

400. See the text of this book supported by the following endnotes: *Supra.* (n. 401–410).

401. Regulation 9 of schedule 1 of the Zambian Companies Act 1994. Schedule 1 contains the standard articles of association. There is no mandatory obligation to adopt the standard articles. These articles can be modified or replaced altogether by other contractual rules.

402. Ibid., reg. 12.

403. Ibid., regs. 16 and 17.

404. Ibid., reg. 16.

405. Ibid.

406. See the text of this book supported by the following endnotes, *Supra.* (n.412–417).

407. See Ibid.

408. 1996/HP/706, an unreported Zambia High Court case.
409. Zambian Companies Act 1994, sec. 61. Cf. the position in the United Kingdom, as discussed earlier.
410. The English Companies Act 1985, sec. 130(1) provided in part that 'if a company issues shares at a premium, whether for cash or *otherwise*, a sum equal to the aggregate amount or value of the premiums on those shares shall be transferred to an account called "the share premium account"' (italics added). This statutory provision is now repeated in section 610(1) of the U.K. Companies Act 2006.
411. Zambian Companies Act 1994, sec. 61.
412. Ibid.
413. Ibid., sec. 61(1).
414. On what constitutes cash, see Clealand's Case (1872) LR 14 Eq 387; Kent's Case (1888) 39 Ch. D 259; Re Hiram Maxim Lamp [1903] 1 Ch. A 70; and Re Jones, Llyod & Co. Ltd. (1889) 41 Ch. 159. Cf. the English Companies Act 1985, sec 739(1).
415. See *Supra*. (n.387–388).
416. See the Zambian Companies Act 1994, sec. 82(3). Cf. the U.K. Companies Act 2006, sec. 678. See also the English Companies Act 1985, sec. 151. See also Barclays Bank plc v. British & Commercial Holdings plc [1995] BCC 1059, CA, where the Court of Appeal held that the assistance has to be financial in nature and that it has to amount to help as opposed to mere cooperation. For Australian cases, see Burton v. Palmer (1980) 5 ACLR 481, NSW SC, 489 per Mahoney J, and Industrial Equity Ltd v. Tocpar Pty Ltd [1972] 2 NNSWLR 505, NSW EqD, 514 per Helsham J.
417. However, Ferran argued that 'the giving of financial assistance is banned in order to ensure that those who buy shares in companies do so from their resources and not from those of the company. In *Wallersteiner v. Moir*, Lord Denning MR summed up the abuse succinctly, describing it simply as a "cheat" ... In some circumstances, the effect of giving financial assistance may be to boost the price of the shares of the company giving the assistance. An obvious example of this is a takeover situation where the consideration for the offer to the shareholders of the target takes the form of shares in the bidder and, to ensure that the price of those shares remains attractive, the bidder organises a share-support operation in which purchasers of its shares are indemnified against any losses they may suffer as a result of their purchase. Looked at from this angle, the ban on the giving of financial assistance is closely connected to the rule whereby companies are prohibited from trading in their own shares. The Greene Committee

referred to the practice of "share trafficking" when recommending that financial assistance should be prohibited ... Another reason for banning financial assistance is to prevent the management of the company from interfering with the normal market in the company's shares by providing support from the company's resources to selected purchasers. In this respect, the ban on financial assistance again complements the ban on a company purchasing its own shares, one purpose of which is to prevent the management of a company from seeking to influence the outcome of a takeover bid by purchasing its own shares' (Ferran, *Company Law and Corporate Finance*, 372–373).

418. (1989) 15 ACLR 230, NSW CA, 256 per Kirby J.

419. Ibid. See also Trevor v. Whitworth (1887) 12 App Cas 409, HL.

420. [1980] 1 All ER 393 CA.

421. Ferran, *Company Law and Corporate Finance*, 375.

422. Zambian Companies Act 1994, sec. 82(9).

423. Similarly, in his analysis of financial assistance in Wallersteiner v. Moir [1974] 3 All ER 217, CA, 239, Lord Denning MR observed, 'You look to the company's money and see what has become of it. You look to the company's shares and see into whose hands they have got. You will then soon see if the company's money has been used to finance the purchase'. This points merely to an example of financial assistance.

424. Department of Trade and Industry, 'Companies Act 2006: Explanatory Notes', p. 153, accessed 1 February 2009, http://www.opsi.gov.uk/acts/acts2006/en/ukpgaen_20060046_en.pdf.

425. Cf. Milburn v. Pivot Ltd (1997) 25 ACSR 237 Fed Ct of Aust-Cen Div.

426. See Ferran, *Company Law and Corporate Finance*, 387.

427. Ibid.

428. [1986] BCLC 1. See also Carney v. Herbert [1985] 1 All ER 438; *Brady* [1988] 2 WLR 1308; Plaut v. Steiner [1989] BCC 352; and *Belmont Finance Ltd. v. Williams (No. 2)* [1980] 1 All ER 393 in the United Kingdom, now reversed by provisions of the English Companies Act 1985 (see sections 97, 98, and 151–158) and making the company (and not just the directors) criminally liable. See also Heald v. O'Connor [1971] 1 WLR 497.

429. See *Infra*. (n. 443).

430. Per Hoffmann J in *Charterhouse Investment Trust Ltd. v. Tempest Diesels Ltd.* [1986] BCLC 1, as in Sealy, *Cases and Materials in Company Law*, 390–391.

431. See the text of this book supported b the following endnotes: *Supra*. (n. 436-440, and n. 443).

432. See Davies, *Gower's Principles of Modern Company Law*, 266.

433. Ibid.

434. Companies Act 1994, sec. 82(1).

435. Ibid., sec. 82(2).

436. [1994] 2 All ER 74.

437. Department of Trade and Industry, 'Companies Act 2006: Explanatory Notes', p. 154, accessed 1 February 2009, http://www.opsi.gov.uk/acts/acts2006/en/ukpgaen_20060046_en.pdf.

438. [1994] 2 All ER 74.

439. See the U.K. Companies Act 2006, secs. 678, 679, 680, and 681.

440. See the text of this book under the following subheading in Chapter 3: '3.6.1. Exceptions to the General Rule Regarding the Prohibition of Financial Assistance'.

441. Cf. British and Commonwealth Holdings plc v. Barclays Bank plc [1996] 1 WLR 1.

442. See the text of this book supported by the following endnotes: *Infra.* (n.456–458).

443. That is, Statutory Instrument No. 17 of 1995, issued pursuant to sec. 400 of the Companies Act 1994.

444. See *Ashbury Rly Carriage and Iron Co. Ltd v. Riche* (1875) LR 7HL 653 (House of Lords); Attorney-General and Ephraim Hutchings v. Great Eastern Railway Co. (1880) 5 App. Cas 473 (House of Lords); *Cotman v. Brougham* [1918] A.C. 514 (House of Lords); H. A. Stephenson & Son Ltd. v. Gillanders Aruthnot & Co (1931) 45 CLR 476 (High Court of Australia); *Bell Houses Ltd. v. City Wall Properties Ltd* [1966] 2 QB 656, [1966] 2 All E.R. 674 (Court of Appeal); *Re Introductions Ltd.* [1970] Ch. 199, [1969] 1 All E.R. 887 (Court of Appeal); *Rolled Steel Products (Holdings)Ltd v. British Steel Corp.* [1986] Ch 246, [1985] 3 All E.R. 52 (Court of Appeal); and English Companies Act 1985 sec. 2(1)(c). Note that all previous English Companies Acts since 1856 required a company to include in its memorandum a statement of its objects. In comparison, as discussed in chapter 2, the Zambian Companies Act 1994 has done away with the requirement that a company should have a memorandum of association, replacing this requirement with Forms I, II, III, and IV in the Schedule to the Companies (Prescribed Forms) Regulations. I have already established in chapter 2 that the Zambian Companies Act 1994 has not abolished the *ultra vires* doctrine. In essence, English case law on the *ultra vires* doctrine, such as the *Rolled Steel* case (cited earlier), still applies to Zambia.

445. See, for example, D. D. Prentice, 'Creditors' Interests and Directors' Duties', *Oxford Journal of Legal Studies* 10, no. 2 (1990): 265–277.

446. Cf. Aveling Barford Ltd v. Perion Ltd [1989] BCLC 626. The decision in *Aveling Barford* concerned the sale of a property by a company (which had no distributable profits) at a considerable undervalue to another company that was controlled by the company's ultimate sole beneficial shareholder. The transaction was held to be void as an unauthorised return of capital. The U.K. Department of Trade and Industry—'Companies Act 2006', 176, accessed 1 February 2009, http://www.opsi.gov.uk/acts/acts2006/en/ukpgaen_20060046_en.pdf—observed that 'whilst this case decided nothing about the situation where a company that has distributable profits makes an intra-group transfer of assets at book value, there was a concern that, as such a transfer of an asset at book value may have an element of undervalue, the transaction would constitute a distribution thereby requiring the company to have distributable profits sufficient to cover the difference in value. The result has been that companies are often required either to abandon a transfer or to structure it in a more complex way, for example, having the assets revalued and then sold (or distributed under sec. 276 of the 1985 Act) so that the distributable reserves are increased by the "realised profit" arising on the sale/distribution followed by a capital contribution of the asset to the relevant group member.'

447. English Companies Act 1985, sec. 152(1).

448. Ibid.

449. Ibid., sec. 263(3).

450. See the text of this book supported by the following endnote, *Infra.* (n.464).

451. English Companies Act 1985, sec. 155(2).

452. [1946] Ch. 242.

453. Goulding, *Principles of Company Law*, 156.

454. [1971] 1 WLR 497.

455. [1974] 1 WLR 991.

456. [1968] 1 WLR 1555. See also *Belmont Finance Corporation Ltd. v. Williams Furniture Ltd.*[1979] Ch. 250.

457. Goulding, *Principles of Company Law*, 156.

458. See Mwenda, 'Legal Problems of Financial Assistance: A Comparative Legal Study', 931.

459. Ibid.

460. [1946] 2 Ch. 242. The case is discussed earlier.

461. See *Foss v. Harbottle* (1843) 2 Hare 461 (Court of Chancery [Vice-Chancellor]). See also chapter 2 on a discussion regarding the exceptions to the rule in *Foss v. Harbottle*.

462. Ibid.

463. See Goulding, *Principles of Company Law*, 156. See also *Belmont Finance* [1979] Ch 250, in Sealy, *Cases and Materials in Company Law*, 339. In the *Belmont Finance* case, a company referred to as 'City' owned all of the shares in Belmont. The directors of Belmont and others agreed to a complex transaction under which, inter alia, a property was sold to Belmont for £500,000 and all of the shares in Belmont were sold by City to the vendors of that property for £489,000. The transaction was illegal for breach of the statutory provision which is now section 151 of the English Companies Act 1985. Buckley LJ ruled as follows: 'I now come to the constructive trust point. If a stranger to a trust (a) receives and becomes chargeable with some part of the trust fund or (b) assists the trustees of a trust with knowledge of the facts in a dishonest design on the part of the trustees to misapply some part of a trust fund, he is liable as a constructive trustee (*Barnes v. Addy* per Lord Selborne LC) ...

    A limited company is of course not a trustee of its own funds: it is their beneficial owner; but in consequence of the fiduciary character of their duties the directors of a limited company are treated as if they were trustees of those funds of the company which are in their hands or under their control, and if they misapply them they commit a breach of trust ... So, if the directors of a company in breach of their fiduciary duties misapply the funds of their company so that they come into the hands of some stranger to the trust who receives them with knowledge (actual or constructive) of the breach, he cannot conscientiously retain those funds against the company unless he has some better equity. He becomes a constructive trustee for the company of the misapplied funds.'

464. See Loose, Yelland, and Impey, *The Company Director: Powers and Duties*, 171.

465. See chapter 2.

466. See generally J. Faundez, 'Legal Technical Assistance', in *Good Government and Law: Legal and Institutional Reform in Developing Countries*, ed. J. Faundez, 1–24 (London: MacMillan, 1996).

467. See, for example, the analysis in Mwenda, 'Zambia's Securities Act 1993 on Trial: The Case of Insider Dealing', 159.

CHAPTER 4

468. Prentice, 'Creditors' Interests and Directors'[Per earlier text citations, author's response, and bibliography] Duties', 265.
469. See *Infra*. (n.484).
470. Ibid.
471. A. Malupenga, 'Ex-Chief Executive Challenges ZNOC's Liquidation in Court', *The Post*, 6 November 2002, accessed 28 November 2007, http://www.accessmylibrary.com/comsite5/bin/pdinventory.pl?pdlanding=1&referid=2930&purchase_type=ITM&item_id=0286-27009281.
472. See Trade Compliance Center, 'Zambia: Trade Policy Review Summaries—1996 (Zambia's Trade and Economic Reforms, 23 August 1996)', accessed 15 December 2007, http://tcc.export.gov/Country_Market_Research/All_Research_Reports/exp_005844.asp.
473. See *Infra*. (n.488).
474. L. Moonze, "Account for $90m, Nonde Tells Government," *Post newspaper*, (December 15, 2003), available Online at: http://www.accessmylibrary.com/comsite5/bin/pdinventory.pl?pdlanding=1&referid=2930&purchase_type=ITM&item_id=0286-19713310>>, website visited on November 30, 2007.
475. See the text of this book between *Supra*. (n. 481) and *Supra*. (n.482).
476. This view was evident from the responses of more than ten interviewees—out of a total of fifteen professional persons who I interviewed in a field study in Lusaka, Zambia, between 15 July 2007 and 30 August 2007.
477. Ibid.
478. Ibid.
479. Ibid.
480. Ibid.
481. See *Supra*. (n.484).
482. 2003/HP/359, an unreported case in the High Court of Zambia (judgement delivered on 1 September 2004).
483. See also generally L. Sameta, 'Directors' Liability for Insolvent Trading in Zambia' (LLM diss., University of Warwick, 1996).
484. *Times of Zambia*, 'Zambia: Mwanawasa Prescribes Corruption Panacea', 18 October 2007, accessed 24 December 2007, http://allafrica.com/stories/200710180320.html.
485. Ibid.
486. Ibid.
487. Ibid.

488. Ibid.
489. See the statutory provisions on insolvent trading in sec. 588G of Australia's Corporations Act 2001. See also sec. 588H of that same statute, regarding the defences to breach of the insolvent trading provisions.
490. See, for example, A. Cloherty, 'Knowledge, Attribution and Fraudulent Trading', *Law Quarterly Review*, no. 25 (2006): 122; F. Oditah, 'Wrongful Trading', *Lloyds Maritime and Commercial Law Quarterly* (1990): 205; and S. Griffin, *Personal Liability and Disqualification of Company Directors* (Oxford: Hart Publishing, 1999).
491. See *Infra*. (n.507).
492. In the United States, for example, after the Enron scandal, the role of internal auditors in corporate governance has taken on a whole new meaning. The passage of the Sarbanes-Oxley Act and actions by the U.S. Securities and Exchange Commission have imposed new requirements on auditors, corporate boards, and management. Internal auditors now have an opportunity to work together with audit committees to help in the corporate governance mandate. For further insights into this discussion, see generally, for example, S. C. Rollins and R. B. Lanza, *Essential Project Investment Governance and Reporting: Preventing Project Fraud and Ensuring Sarbanes-Oxley Compliance* (Fort Lauderdale, FL: J. Ross Publishing, 2005) and A. M. Marchetti, *Sarbanes-Oxley Ongoing Compliance Guide: Key Processes and Summary Checklists* (Hoboken, NJ: Wiley, 2007).
493. See the World Bank, 'Report on the Observance of Standards and Codes (ROSC)—Corporate Governance Country Assessment: Armenia, April 2005', p. 2, accessed 8 November 2007, http://www.worldbank.org/ifa/Armenia%20ROSC%20(final).pdf.
494. See, for example, Re Brian D Pierson (Contractors) Ltd (1999) BCC 26; Re Oasis Merchandise Services Limited [1998] 1 Ch. 170; Re Floor Fourteen Ltd (2000) ETC 416; Re Continental Assurance Company of London plc [2001] BPIR 733; and Re Leyland Daf Ltd [2004] UKHL 9. See also generally P. James, I. M. Ramsay, and P. Siva, 'Insolvent Trading—An Empirical Study', *Insolvency Law Journal* 12 (2004).
495. See sec. 172 of the English Companies Act 2006.
496. 2003/HP/359, an unreported case in the High Court of Zambia (judgement delivered on 1 September 2004).
497. Cf. generally Griffin, *Personal Liability and Disqualification of Company Directors*.
498. See Center for International Private Enterprise, 'Institute of Directors', accessed 17 February 2007, http://www.cipe.org/programs/global/partners/

dispPartner.php?id=258. This article points out that 'the Institute of Directors of Zambia was launched on 7th April 2000 by the then Minister of Commerce, Trade and Industry, Honourable Mr. W. Harrington. The launch was a culmination of one and a half years' work of a task force, which was set up on 24th June 1998 during the first workshop on Corporate Governance jointly conducted in Lusaka by the Commonwealth Association for Corporate Governance based in New Zealand and the Institute of Chartered Secretaries and Administrators, Zambia Association. The Institute of Directors is a leadership forum, which helps members develop through education, information and communication and aims to have a positive influence on the larger business environment. The Institute of Directors is committed to improving and upgrading Corporate Governance in Zambia.'

499. See Re Chez Nico [1992] BCLC 192, establishing the possibility of the company owing duties to an individual member. Cf. *Foss v. Harbottle.* (1843) 2 Hare 461, 67 ER 189.

500. (1843) 2 Hare 461, 67 ER 189.

501. *Foss v. Harbottle.*
(1843) 2 Hare 461, 67 ER 189.

502. See Zambia's Companies Act 1994, secs. 383 and 384. Under English law, the penalty for fraudulent trading will be strengthened further by the coming into force of sec. 993 of the English Companies Act 2006.

503. Cf. Cloherty, 'Knowledge, Attribution and Fraudulent Trading'.

504. See Zambia's Companies Act 1994, secs. 383 and 384.

505. Ibid.

506. [1968] 2 All ER 1073.

507. [1987] Ch. 264 at 285.

508. [1983] BCLC 325. See also El Ajou v. Dollar Land Holdings plc [1993] 3 All ER 717 at 739; Polly Peck International plc v. Nadir (No. 2) [1992] 4 All ER 769; Karak Rubber Co Ltd v. Burden (No. 2) [1972] 1 WLR 602 at 632; Agip (Africa) Ltd v. Jackson [1992] 4 All ER 385; Eagle Trust plc v. SBC Securities Ltd [1992] 4 All ER 488 at 499; cf. *Belmont Finance Corporation v. Williams Furniture Limited* [1979] Ch 250; P. Birks, *Lloyd's MCLQ* (1989): 296; P. Birks, *Law Quarterly Review* 105 (1989): 352 at 355; C. E. F. Ricket, 11 *Oxford Journal of Legal Studies* 11 (1991): 598 at 602; and Powell v. Thompson [1991] 1 NZLR 597.

509. Per Peter Gibson J., [1983] BCLC 325.

510. Cf. the text supported by *Infra.* (n.525).

511. Cf. International Compliance Association, *International Diploma in Compliance* (Birmingham: International Compliance Training Ltd., 2002), 198.
512. [1948] 1 KB. 339 at 344.
513. (1968) Cr. App. 373 at 398.
514. R v. Moys (1984) 79 Cr. App. 72. See also R v. Sinclair [1986] 1 WLR 1246.
515. 523 F.2d 697 (9th Cir. 1976), as reproduced by A. Bowie, 'Criminal Law Outline Lecture Two: Chapter 7', accessed 20 November 2007, [http:// www.professorbowie.com/Lecture%20Two.htm. See also U.S. v. Hayden, 64 F.3d 126 (3d Cir. 1995); U.S. v. Caminos, 770 F.2d 361 (3d Cir. 1985); U.S. v. Rodriguez, 983 F.2d 455, 457 (2d Cir. 1993); Johnson & Towers, 741 F.2d at 670–671; and U.S. v. Self, 2 F.3d 1071 (10th Cir. 1993).
516. The term *mens rea* is a Latin expression, meaning 'guilty mind'. In criminal law, except in cases of strict liability, often the *mens rea* must be accompanied by an *actus reus* in order for there to have been a crime committed. In short, *mens rea* means 'guilty mind' and *actus reus* means the 'thing done.' Generally, a crime is committed when a person commits a guilty act accompanied by a guilty mind. In the United States, for example, the U.S. Model Penal Code does not use the Latin terms *mens rea* and *actus reus*. The code uses the following terms to describe a culpable person's state of mind: (a) *purpose*, (b) *knowledge*, (c) *recklessness*, and (d) *negligence*.
517. As reproduced by Bowie, 'Criminal Law Outline'.
518. Ibid.
519. See *Infra*. (n. 557).
520. See the text of this book under 4.2. Wrongful Trading.
521. See Mwenda, *Combating Financial Crime: The Legal, Regulatory and Institutional Framework*, 71–80.
522. In Zambia, there is no statutory definition of drug trafficking. Section 2 of the Narcotic Drugs and Psychotropic Substances Act 1993 refers simply to 'trafficking' and defines it as (a) being involved directly or indirectly in the unlawful buying or selling of narcotic drugs or psychotropic substances and includes the commission of an offence under the Narcotic Drugs and Psychotropic Substances Act 1993 in circumstances suggesting that the offence was being committed in connection with buying or selling, or (b) being found in possession of narcotic drugs or psychotropic substances in such amounts or quantities as the president may, by statutory instrument, declare to be trafficking for purposes of the Narcotic

Drugs and Psychotropic Substances Act 1993. But, this definition does not tell the full story about what constitutes drug trafficking because the definition refers only to trafficking. Part II of schedule II of Zambia's Narcotic Drugs and Psychotropic Substances Act 1993 provides a list of drugs that can be trafficked. This list refers to two categories of drugs, narcotic drugs and psychotropic substances. Closely related to this list is the statutory definition of trafficking in section 2 of the Narcotic Drugs and Psychotropic Substances Act 1993. I have already examined this definition. So, what then is drug trafficking? It is important to remember also that parts III, IV, and V of the Narcotic Drugs and Psychotropic Substances Act 1993 provide additional offences relating to the use of narcotic drugs and psychotropic substances. These offences include:

a. trafficking in narcotic drugs or psychotropic substances;
b. importing or exporting narcotic drugs or psychotropic substances;
c. possessing narcotic drugs or psychotropic substances;
d. cultivating plants for narcotic or psychotropic purposes;
e. using narcotic drugs and psychotropic substances;
f. attempting, abetting, or soliciting activities in contravention of provisions of the Narcotic Drugs and Psychotropic Substances Act 1993;
g. conspiring to commit drug offences;
h. unlawful manufacture of narcotic drugs or psychotropic substances;
i. inducing another to take narcotic drugs or psychotropic substances;
j. unlawful possession of instruments or utensils for administering narcotic drugs or psychotropic substances;
k. permitting premises to be used for the unlawful use of narcotic drugs or psychotropic substances;
l. unlawful supply of narcotic drugs or psychotropic substances;
m. double doctoring;
n. impersonating officers of the Drug Enforcement Commission;
o. unlawful use of property for narcotic drugs or psychotropic substances; and
p. possessing property obtained through trafficking.

For my immediate purposes, I shall treat the offences that are listed as falling within a broader definition of drug trafficking, which includes the unlawful and illegal importation, exportation, production, manufacturing, possession, sale, distribution, or use of narcotic drugs and psychotropic substances.

523. Section 2 of Zambia's Prohibition and Prevention of Money Laundering Act 2001 provides that '"money laundering" means—(a) engaging, *directly* or *indirectly*, in a business transaction that involves property acquired with *proceeds of crime*; (b) receiving, possessing, concealing, disguising, disposing of or bringing into Zambia, any property derived or realized directly or indirectly from *illegal activity*; or (c) the retention or acquisition of property knowing that the property is derived or realized, directly or indirectly from *illegal activity*.' (italics added)

524. See generally, for example, D. T. Johnson and R. A. Leo, 'The Yale White-Collar Crime Project: A Review and Critique', *Law and Society Inquiry* 18, no. 63 (1993); C. Pereyra-Suarez and C. A. Klove, 'Ring Around the White Collar: Defending Fraud and Abuse', *Whittier Law Review* 18, no. 31 (1996); and, E. S. Podgor, 'Criminal Fraud', *American University Law Review* 49, no. 3 (April 1999).

525. Dine, *Criminal Law in the Company Context*, 65.

526. Ibid. See also Re L. Todd (Swanscombe) Ltd [1990] BCC 125.

527. Podgor, 'Criminal Fraud', accessed 22 November 2007, http://www.wcl. american.edu/journal/lawrev/48/podgor.html.

528. Ibid.

529. Ibid.

530. Ibid.

531. *Supra*. (n.520-533).

532. See G. M. Lawrence and J. T. Wells, 'Basic Legal Concepts: The Fraud Beat', accessed 18 November 2007, http://www.aicpa.org/PUBS/JOFA/oct2004/lawrence.htm.

533. See Ferenc v. World Child, Inc. 977 F. Supp. 56 (D.D.C. 1997).

534. See the text of this book supported by the following endnotes: *Supra*. (n.520-533).

535. R. Goode, *Commercial Law* (London: Penguin Books, 1995), 112. See also *Caparo plc v. Dickman* [1990] 2 WLR 358; Hedley Byrne & Co. Ltd v. Heller & Partners Ltd [1964] A.C. 465; Esso Petroleum Ltd v. Mardon [1976] Q.B. 801; Amalgamated Investments & Property Co. Ltd v. Texas Commerce International Bank Ltd [1982] Q.B. 84; Car & Universal Finance Co. Ltd v. Caldwell [1965] 1 Q.B. 525; and generally R. Goode, *Commercial Law*, 3rd ed. (London: Penguin Books, 2004).

536. Companies Act 1994, sec. 383(2).

537. Ibid., sec. 383(3).

538. Ibid., secs. 357(1) and (2).

539. Ibid., sec. 357(1).

540. Cf. the statutory rule in the Companies Act 1994 prohibiting fraudulent trading.

541. Establishing the concept of shadow director in Zambia, section 203(4) of Zambia's Companies Act 1994 provides as follows: 'A person not being duly appointed director of a company, on whose directions or instructions the duly appointed directors are accustomed to act shall be deemed to be a director for the purposes of all duties and liabilities imposed on directors.' This statutory provision makes improvements to the law regarding directors' duties and liabilities in Zambia. The provision introduces the concept of a shadow director to company law in Zambia. Under the repealed Companies Act 1921 of Zambia, the concept of shadow directors was not covered to the same extent as it is covered under English law (see the English Companies Act 1985, sec. 741(2) on shadow directors). Indeed, before the enactment of Zambia's Companies Act 1994, no person influencing the decisions of a company's board of directors from outside of the board could be considered a shadow director. But today, a shadow director generally is seen as one who is normally acting through someone else. In contrast, a de facto director often holds out and acts in person. For a further reading on the concept of shadow directors, see Goode, *Principles of Corporate Insolvency Law*, 2nd ed., 444–468. See also generally R. M. Goode, *Principles of Corporate Insolvency Law*, 3rd ed. (London: Sweet and Maxwell, 2005).

542. Companies Act 1994, sec. 2.

543. Banking and Financial Services Act 1994, sec. 86.

544. See Bank of Australia v. Hall (1907) 4 C.L.R. 154 at p. 1528, which discusses the meaning of the comparable phrase 'as they become due' in Australian legislation. See also Expo International Ltd v. Chant [1979] 2 N.S.W.L.R. 820; Stooke v. Taylor (1880) 5 Q.B.D. 565, per Cockburn L.J. at 575; O'Driscoll v. Manchester Insurance Committee [1915] 3. K.B. 499; Re Bryant Investment Co Ltd [1974] 2 All E.R. 683; Re Globe New Patent Iron & Steel Co. (1875) L.R. 20 Eq. 337; Mann v. Goldstein [1968] 2 All E.R. 769; and Cornhill Insurance plc v. Improvement Services Ltd [1968] 1 W.L.R. 114.

545. *Cf.* the court rulings in the cases cited in *Infra.* (n. 560).

546. See Re a Debtor (No. 17 of 1966) [1967] Ch. 590; Re European Life Assurance Co. (1869) L.R. 9 Eq 122; Tottenham Hotspur plc v. Edennote plc [1995] 1 B.C.L.C. 65; Winter v. I.R.C [1961] 3 All E.R. 855; Re William Hockley Ltd [1962] 2 All E.R. 111; Stonegate Securities Ltd

v. Gregory [1980] 1 Ch. 576; Re British Equitable Bond and Mortgage Corp Ltd [1910] 1 Ch. 574; Re A Company (No. 001573 of 1983) (1983) 1. B.C.C. 98, 937; Re Dollar Land Holdings Ltd [1994] B.C.L.C. 404; and Re Primlaks (UK) Ltd [1989] B.C.L.C. 734.

547. *Cornhill Insurance plc v. Improvement Services Ltd* [1968] 1 W.L.R. 114.

548. Ibid.

549. See generally Goode, *Principles of Corporate Insolvency Law*, 2nd ed. See also generally H. Rajak, *Insolvency Law: Theory and Practice* (London: Sweet and Maxwell, 1993); D. Campbell, *International Corporate Insolvency Law* (London: Butterworths, 1992); R. Pennington, *Pennington's Corporate Insolvency Law* (London: Butterworths, 1991); A. Clarke, *Current Issues in Insolvency Law* (London: Stevens and Sons, 1991); and P. Smart, *Cross-border Insolvency* (London: Butterworths, 1991).

550. 2003/HP/359, an unreported case in the High Court of Zambia (judgement delivered on 1 September 2004).

551. See Bank of Zambia, 'Press Statement, January 14, 2003: BOZ Takes Possession of Access Financial Services and Access Leasing'.

552. Ibid.

553. See *Zambezi Times Online*, 'Access Finance Engaged in Crime'.

554. Ibid.

555. Ibid.

556. Ibid.

557. Section 77(1) of Zambia's Banking and Financial Services Act 1994, as amended by the Banking and Financial Services Act (Amendment) Act 2000.

558. Section 77(2) of Zambia's Banking and Financial Services Act 1994 is as follows: 'Where the Bank of Zambia is unable to obtain an agreement under subsection (1) within a time, and in a form and content, satisfactory to the Bank of Zambia, or where the Bank of Zambia considers that the need for prompt action makes the negotiating of such an agreement impractical, the Bank of Zambia may direct the bank or financial institution or any director, manager or other person concerned in its management to do either or both of the following: (a) cease or refrain from doing the act or pursuing the course of conduct; (b) perform such acts as, in the opinion of the Bank of Zambia are necessary to rectify the situation.' In particular, but without limiting the generality of subsection (2), the Bank of Zambia can, in accordance with section 77(3) of Zambia's Banking and Financial Services Act 1994, (a) direct the culpable bank or financial institution to refrain from adopting or pursuing a particular course of action

or to restrict the scope of its business in a particular way; (b) impose any limitation on the bank's acceptance of deposits or the payment of interest thereon, the granting of credit, the making of investments, or the payment of dividends; (c) prohibit the bank or financial institution from soliciting deposits or the payment of the interest thereon either generally or from specified persons or classes of persons; (d) prohibit the bank or financial institution from entering into any other transaction or class of transactions, or from commencing or continuing any activity which it is permitted under Zambia's Banking and Financial Services Act 1994 to carry on; or (e) require the suspension or removal from office of any director, officer, or other person.

559. Constant reference was made in the judgment to sections 81, 84, 86, and 101 of the Banking and Financial Services Act 1994.

560. 2003/HP/359, an unreported case in the High Court of Zambia (judgment delivered on 1 September 2004).

561. Banking and Financial Services Act 1994, sec. 87(1).

562. Ibid.

563. Ibid., sec. 87(2).

564. Ibid., sec. 87(3).

565. See the text of this book supported by the following endnotes: *Supra*. (n.520–533).

566. Companies Act 1994, sec. 357(2).

567. Ibid., sec. 357(3).

568. Ibid., sec. 357(4).

569. Dine, *Criminal Law in the Company Context*, 69–70.

570. Ibid., 70.

571. Ibid., 70–71.

572. Companies Act 1994, sec. 358(1).

573. Ibid.

574. Ibid.

575. Ibid., sec. 358(2).

576. Companies Act 1994, sec. 358(3). See also Companies Act 1994, sec. 359.

Chapter 5

577. See UNCITRAL, '1997—UNCITRAL Model Law on Cross-Border Insolvency with Guide to Enactment', accessed 20 February 2009, http://www.uncitral.org/uncitral/en/uncitral_texts/insolvency/1997Model.

html. See also Resolution A/RES/52/158, adopted by the UN General Assembly, 'Model Law on Cross-Border Insolvency of the United Nations Commission on International Trade Law', (further to the report of the Sixth Committee (A/52/649)), dated 30 January 1998.

578. See UNCITRAL, '1997'.

579. Ibid.

580. Ibid.

581. See Goode, *Principles of Corporate Insolvency Law*, 2nd ed., 495.

582. There are variants on this, such as the principal place of business or the centre of the debtor's main interests, but the underlying idea is the same—namely, the state with which the company has its closest juridical connection.

583. See Goode, *Principles of Corporate Insolvency Law*, 2nd ed., 495.

584. Ibid.

585. Ibid.

586. Re Oriental Inland Steam Co., ex p. Scinde Railway Co. (1874) L.R. 9 Ch. App. 557, per Mellish L.J. at 558, and Re Bank of Credit and Commerce International S.A. (No. 11) [1996] B.C.C. 980, per Sir Richard Scott V.-C at 998.

587. Goode, *Principles of Corporate Insolvency Law*, 2nd ed., 495–496.

588. Ibid., p. 496.

589. Ibid., pp. 496–497.

590. [1989] Q.B. 360.

591. See Goode, *Principles of Corporate Insolvency Law*, 2nd ed., 497.

592. See *Felixstowe Dock and Railway co. v. US Lines Inc* [1989] Q.B. 360. An extract from the opinion is set out in the judgment of Hirst J. at 368.

593. Goode, *Principles of Corporate Insolvency Law*, 2nd ed., 497.

594. Ibid. There is, however, some uncertainty regarding the relationship between *lex fori concursus* and the law governing the creation of security interests and other real rights in assets in the possession of the debtor company.

BIBLIOGRAPHY

BOOKS

Arora, A. *Practical Banking and Building Society Law*. London: Blackstone Press, 1997.

Asser, T. M. C. *Legal Aspects of Regulatory Treatment of Banks in Distress*. Washington, DC: IMF, 2001.

Bakibinga, D. J. *Company Law in Uganda*. Kampala: Fountain Publishers Ltd., 2001.

Barth, J. R., G. Caprio, and R. Levin. *Rethinking Banking Regulation: Till Angels Govern*. New York: Cambridge University Press, 2006.

Bederman, D. J. *International Law Frameworks*. New York, New York: Foundation Press, 2001.

Blair, M. *Ownership and Control*. Washington, DC: Brookings Institution, 1995.

Boschma, H. E., M. L. Lennarts, and J. N. Schulte-Veenstra. *Alternative Systems for Capital Protection*. Alphen aan den Rijn, Netherlands: Kluwer Law International, 2006.

Bradgate, R. *Commercial Law*. London: Butterworths, 1995.

Brealey, R. A., and S. C. Myers. *Principles of Corporate Finance*. New York: McGraw-Hill, 1991.

Campbell, A., J. R. La Brosse, D. G. Mayes, and D. Singh, eds. *Deposit Insurance*. New York: Palgrave Macmillan, 2007.

Campbell, A., and P. Cartwright. *Banks in Crisis: The Legal Response*. Aldershot: Ashgate Publishing, 2002.

Campbell, D. *International Corporate Insolvency Law*. London: Butterworths, 1992.

Clarke, A. *Current Issues in Insolvency Law*. London: Stevens and Sons, 1991.

Cranston, R. *Principles of Banking Law*. Oxford: Clarendon Press, 1997.

Davies, P. *Gower's Principles of Modern Company Law*. 6th ed. London: Sweet and Maxwell, 1997.

———. "Institutional Investors in the United Kingdom." In *Contemporary Issues in Corporate Governance*, edited by D. D. Prentice and P. R. J. Holland. Oxford: Clarendon Press, 1993.

Davis, E. W., and J. Pointon. *Finance and the Firm: An Introduction To Corporate Finance*. Oxford: Oxford University Press, 1994.

Dine, J. *Criminal Law in the Company Context*. Aldershot: Dartmouth Publishing, 1995.

Farrar, J. H., and B. M. Hannigan. *Farrar's Company Law*. 4th ed. London: Butterworths, 1998.

Faundez, J., ed. *Good Government and Law: Legal and Institutional Reform in Developing Countries*. London: MacMillan, 1996.

Ferran, E. *Company Law and Corporate Finance*. Oxford: Oxford University Press, 1999.

Goode, R. M. *Commercial Law*. 2nd ed. London: Penguin Books, 1995.

———. *Commercial Law*. 3rd ed. London: Penguin Books, 2004.

———. *Legal Problems of Credit and Security*. London: Sweet and Maxwell, 1988.

———. *Principles of Corporate Insolvency Law*. 2nd ed. London: Sweet and Maxwell, 1997.

———. *Principles of Corporate Insolvency Law*. 3rd ed. London: Sweet and Maxwell, 2005.

Gough, W. J. *Company Charges*. London: Butterworths, 1996.

Goulding, S. *Principles of Company Law*. London: Cavendish Publishing, 1996.

Griffin, S. *Personal Liability and Disqualification of Company Directors*. Oxford: Hart Publishing, 1999.

Hamilton, R. W. *Corporation Finance: Cases and Materials*. St. Paul, MN: West Publishing, 1989.

————. *Corporations*. 4th ed. St. Paul, MN: West Publishing, 1997.

International Compliance Association. *International Diploma in Compliance*. Birmingham: International Compliance Training Ltd., 2002.

Judge, S. *Company Law*. Oxford: Oxford University Press, 2008.

Loose, P., J. Yelland, and D. Impey. *The Company Director: Powers and Duties*. Bristol: Jordan Publishing, 1993.

Lücke, H. K. 'Good Faith and Contractual Performance'. In *Essays on Contract*, edited by P. Finn. Sydney: The Law Book Company Limited, 1987.

Manning, B., and J. J. Hanks Jr. *Legal Capital*. Westbury, NY: Foundation Press, 1990.

Marchetti, A. M. *Sarbanes-Oxley Ongoing Compliance Guide: Key Processes and Summary Checklists*. Hoboken, NJ: Wiley, 2007.

Mwenda, K. K., ed. *Banking and Micro-finance Regulation and Supervision: Lessons from Zambia*. Parkland, FL: Brown Walker Press, 2002.

————. *Banking Supervision and Systemic Bank Restructuring: An International and Comparative Legal Perspective*. London: Cavendish Publishing, 2000.

————. *Combating Financial Crime: The Legal, Regulatory and Institutional Frameworks*. Lewiston, NY: The Edwin Mellen Press, 2006.

————. *The Legal Administration of Financial Services in Common Law Jurisdictions: With Special Attention to the Dual Regulation System in Zambia*. Lewiston, NY: The Edwin Mellen Press, 2006.

————. *Legal Aspects of Combating Corruption: The Case of Zambia*. Youngstown, NY: Cambria Press, 2007.

————. *Legal Aspects of Corporate Capital and Finance*. Washington, DC: Penn Press, 1999.

————. *Legal Aspects of Financial Services Regulation and the Concept of a Unified Regulator*. Washington, DC: The World Bank, 2006.

————. *Zambia's Stock Exchange And Privatisation Programme: Corporate Finance Law in Emerging Markets*. Lewiston, NY: The Edwin Mellen Press, 2001.

Mwenda, K. K., and D. A. Ailola, eds. *Frontiers of Legal Knowledge: Business and Economic Law in Context*. Durham, NC: Carolina Academic Press, 2003.

Oditah, F. *Legal Aspects of Receivables Financing*. London: Sweet and Maxwell, 1991.

Parkinson, J. E. *Corporate Power and Responsibility: Issues in the Theory of Company Law*. Oxford: Oxford University Press, 1995.

Pennington, R. *Directors' Personal Liability*. Oxford: BSP Professional Books, 1987.

————. *Pennington's Company Law*. London: Butterworths, 1990.

————. *Pennington's Corporate Insolvency Law*. London: Butterworths, 1991.

Prentice, D. D. *Reform of the* Ultra Vires *Rules: A Consultative Document*. London: Department of Trade and Industry, 1986.

————. 'Some Aspects of the Corporate Governance Debate'. In *Contemporary Issues in Corporate Governance*, edited by D. D. Prentice and P. R. J. Holland. Oxford: Clarendon Press, 1993.

Proctor, G., and L. Miles. *Corporate Governance.* London: Cavendish Publishing, 2002.

Rajak, H. *Insolvency Law: Theory and Practice.* London: Sweet and Maxwell, 1993.

Rees, W. *Corporate Governance and Corporate Control.* London: Cavendish Publishing, 1995.

Rollins, S. C., and R. B. Lanza. *Essential Project Investment Governance and Reporting: Preventing Project Fraud and Ensuring Sarbanes-Oxley Compliance.* Fort Lauderdale, FL: J. Ross Publishing, 2005.

Rose, F. *Nutshells: Company Law.* London: Sweet & Maxwell, 1998.

Sealy, L. S. *Cases and Materials in Company Law.* London: Butterworths, 1996.

Sealy, L. S., and R. J. A. Hooley. *Text and Materials in Commercial Law.* London: Butterworths, 1994.

Shepperd, J. C. *Law of Fiduciaries.* Toronto: Carswell, 1981.

Singh, D. *Banking Regulation of UK and US Financial Markets.* Aldershot, UK: Ashgate Publishing Limited, 2007.

Smart, P. *Cross-border Insolvency.* London: Butterworths, 1991.

Stapledon, G. *Institutional Investors and Corporate Governance.* Oxford: Clarendon Press, 1996.

Wood, P. R. *Project Finance, Subordinated Debt and State Loans.* London: Sweet and Maxwell, 1995.

JOURNAL ARTICLES

Allen, C. 'Non Par Value Stock'. *Central Law Journal* 90 (1920).

Baxt, A. 'Companies, Powers, Objects in Memorandum and the Doctrine of Ultra Vires'. *Australian Law Journal,* 1969.

Berle, A. A. 'Problems of Non Par Stock'. *Columbia Law Review* 25 (1925).

Beuthin, R. C. 'The Ultra Vires Doctrine—An Obituary Notice'. *South African Law Journal* 83 (1966).

Birks, P. "Misdirected Funds: Restitution from the Recipient" *Lloyd's Maritime and Commercial Law Quarterly* 296 (1989).

———. "Misdirected Funds" *Law Quarterly Review* 105 (1989).

BonBright, J. C. 'The Dangers of Shares Without Par Value'. *Columbia Law Review* 24 (1924).

Budylin, S. 'Going Beyond: The Ultra Vires Problem in Russian Corporate Law'. *Columbia Journal of East European Law* 2, no. 1 (2008).

Care, J. C., and L. Haller. 'In Harmony or Out of Tune: Is Advocates' Immunity an Appropriate Principle in Common Law Countries?' *Journal of South Pacific Law* 8, no. 2 (2004). Accessed 8 October 2009. http://www.paclii.org/journals/fJSPL/vol08no2/5.shtml

Cheffins, B. R. 'Corporate Ownership Structure and the Evolution of Bankruptcy Law: Lessons from the United Kingdom'. *Vanderbilt Law Review* 55 (2002).

Cloherty, A. 'Knowledge, Attribution and Fraudulent Trading'. *Law Quarterly Review* 25 (2006).

Farnsworth, E. A. 'The Eason-Weinmann Colloquium on International and Comparative Law: Duties of Good Faith and Fair Dealing under the UNIDROIT Principles, Relevant International Conventions, and National Laws'. *Tulane Journal of International and Comparative Law* 3, no. 47 (1995).

Frederick, D. 'The Par Value of Stock'. *Yale Law Journal* 16 (1906–1907).

Goforth, C. 'Proxy Reform as a Means of Increasing Shareholder Participation in Corporate Governance: Too Little, But Not Too Late'. *The American University Law Review* 43 (1994).

Goodbar, J. E. 'No Par Value Stock—Its Nature And Use'. *Miami Law Quarterly* 3, no. 1 (1948).

Greenfield, K. 'Ultra Vires Lives? A Stakeholder Analysis of Corporate Illegality'. *Virginia Law Review* 87 (2001).

James, P., I. M. Ramsay, and P. Siva. 'Insolvent Trading—An Empirical Study'. *Insolvency Law Journal* 12 (2004).

Johnson, D. T., and R. A. Leo. 'The Yale White-Collar Crime Project: A Review and Critique'. *Law and Society Inquiry* 18, no. 63 (1993).

Keily, T. 'Good Faith and the Vienna Convention on Contracts for the International Sale of Goods (CISG)'. *Vindobona Journal of International Commercial Law and Arbitration* 3, no. 1 (1999). Accessed 28 July 2008. http://www.cisg.law.pace.edu/cisg/biblio/keily.html#faith.

Leigh, L. H. 'Objects, Powers and Ultra Vires'. *Modern Law Review* 33 (1970).

Ming, W. W. C. 'Ultra Vires and Corporate Capacity in Singapore'. *Singapore Academy Law Journal* 1 (1989).

Morawetz, V. 'Shares Without Nominal or Par Value'. *Harvard Law Review* 26 (1913).

Mwenda, K. K. 'Banks and the Use of Chinese Walls in Managing Conflict of Duties'. *University of Newcastle Web Journal of Current Legal Issues*, no. 2 (2000).

———. 'Can "Corruption" and "Good Governance" Be Defined in Legal Terms?' *Rutgers University Journal of Global Change and Governance* 2, no. 1 (Fall 2008).

———. 'Can Insider Trading Predicate the Offence of Money Laundering?' *Michigan State University Journal of Business and Securities Law* 6, no. 2 (Spring 2006).

———. 'A Company without a Memorandum of Association: Policy Implications'. *Southern Africa Journal of Comparative and International Law* 32, no. 1 (March 1999).

———. 'The Concept of "Conducting Business in an Unsound Manner" under Malawi's Banking Act 1989'. *Malawi Law Journal* 2, no. 2 (2008).

———. 'The Concept of "Unsafe and Sound Practice" under Lesotho's Financial Institutions Act 1999'. *Lesotho Law Journal* 15, no. 2 (2005).

———. 'The Concept of "Unsafe and Sound Practice" under Vanuatu's Financial Institutions Act 1999'. *Nyerere Law Journal* (previously *University of Dar-es-Salaam Law Journal*) 2 (2004).

———. 'Insider Dealing Law in Zambia: A Flawed Concept'. *University of Ghana Law Journal* 19 (1996–1999).

———. 'Intermediation and Investor Protection in Zambia'. *Zambia Law Journal* 25–28 (1993–96).

———. 'Legal Aspects of Banking and Financial Services Supervision in Zambia'. *International Business Law Journal* 2, no. 35 (October 2001).

———. 'Legal Construction of the Term "Bank": A Comparative Study'. *Tilburg Foreign Law Review* 8, no. 2 (2000).

———. 'Legal Problems of Financial Assistance: A Comparative Legal Study'. *The African Journal of International and Comparative Law* 9, pt. 4 (1997).

———. 'Redefining Insider Dealing Law for Emerging Markets: A Comparative Legal Study'. *University of Zimbabwe Law Review* 14 (1997).

———. 'The Regulation of Micro-finance Institutions for Rural Finance: An International and Comparative Perspective'. *Journal of International Banking Law* 17, no. 12 (2002).

———. 'The Regulatory and Institutional Framework for Unified Financial Services Supervision in the Baltic States'. *Columbia University Journal of East European Law* 9, no. 2 (2002).

———. 'The Regulatory and Institutional Framework for Unified Financial Services Supervision in the United Kingdom and Zambia'. *Michigan State University Journal of International Law* 14, no. 1 (Spring 2005).

———. 'Revisiting Common Law Fiduciary Duties of Financial Intermediaries: from Developed Stock Markets to an Emerging Stock Market'. *Journal for Juridical Science* 22, no. 1 (June 1997).

———. 'The Securities Act 1993 of Zambia: A Comment on the Defective Provisions for Controlling Insider Dealing In Zambia'. *University of Stellenbosch Law Review* 8, no. 2 (1997).

———. 'Wrongful Trading and Fraudulent Trading in Corporate Insolvency Law: The Case of Zambia'. *Oxford University Commonwealth Law Journal* 8, no. 1 (2008).

———. 'Zambia's Securities Act 1993 on Trial: The Case of Insider Dealing'. *Statute Law Review* 18, no. 2 (1997).

Mwenda, K. K., and A. Laszczynska. 'Legal Problems of Debt Subordination: A Comparative Study'. *African Journal of Comparative and International Law* 10, pt. 4 (December 1998).

Mwenda, K. K., and A. Wiseberg. 'Corporate Law Safeguards Against Oppression of Minority Shareholders'. *South African Mercantile Law Journal*, no. 1 (May 1999).

Mwenda, K. K., and D. Ailola. 'Legal Aspects of Corporate Finance: A Comparative Study of the Law on Financial Assistance'. *Southern Africa Journal of Comparative and International Law* 31, no. 2 (July 1998).

Mwenda K. K., and G. N. Muuka. 'Towards Best Practices for Micro-Finance Institutional Engagement in African Rural Areas: Selected Cases and Agenda for Action'. *International Journal of Social Economics* 31, no. 1/2 (2004).

Mwenda, K. K., and S. S. Silomba. 'Legal Aspects of Share Watering: A Comparative Study'. *Stellenbosch Law Review* (University of Stellenbosch, South Africa), no. 1 (2000).

Oditah, F. 'Wrongful Trading'. *Lloyds Maritime and Commercial Law Quarterly* 205 (1990).

Pereyra-Suarez, C., and C. A. Klove. 'Ring Around the White Collar: Defending Fraud and Abuse'. *Whittier Law Review* 18, no. 31 (1996).

Podgor, E. S. 'Criminal Fraud'. *American University Law Review* 49, no. 3 (April 1999). Accessed 22 November 2007. http://www.wcl. american.edu/journal/lawrev/48/podgor.html.

Prentice, D. D. 'Creditors' Interests and Directors' Duties'. *Oxford Journal of Legal Studies* 10, no. 2 (1990).

Ricket, C. E. F. 'Strangers as Constructive Trustees in New Zealand'. *Oxford Journal of Legal Studies* 11 (1991).

Ronald, J. G. 'Globalizing Corporate Governance: Convergence of Form or Function'. *American Journal of Comparative Law* 49 (2001).

Triantis, G. D., and R. J. Daniels. 'The Role of Debt in Interactive Corporate Governance'. *California Law Review* 83 (1995).

Vishny, R. W., and A. Shleifer. 'A Survey of Corporate Governance'. *Journal of Finance* 52 (2000).

Wedderburn, K. 'Shareholders' Rights and the Rule in *Foss v. Harbottle*'. *Cambridge Law Journal*, 1957.

Willis, J. 'Statute Interpretation in a Nutshell'. *Canada Bar Review* 16, no. 1 (1938).

Wolff, L. 'The Disappearance of the *Ultra Vires* Doctrine in Greater China: Harmonized Legislative Action or (Simply) an Accident of History?' *Northwestern Journal of International Law and Business* 23 (2003).

PUBLISHED GOVERNMENT REPORTS AND OTHER MATERIALS, INCLUDING SEMINAR PAPERS

Asser, T. M. C. *Regulatory Treatment of Banks In Distress*. Washington, DC: IMF, 1999.

Bank of Zambia. *Banking and Financial Services (Corporate Governance) Guidelines 2006*. Lusaka: Bank of Zambia, 2006.

———. *Financial Sector Development Plan (FSDP) (2004–2009)*. Lusaka: Bank of Zambia, 2004.

Committee of Inquiry into the Working and Administration of the Present Company Law of Ghana. *Final Report of the Committee of Inquiry into the Working and Administration of the Present Company Law of Ghana* (Gower's Report). Accra: Government Printers, 1961.

Freshfields, Bruckhaus and Deringer. *Consultation Study Concerning the Implications of Adopting a No-par Value Share Regime in Hong Kong: Final Report*. 29 November 2004. Accessed 8 February 2009. http://www.fstb.gov.hk/fsb/co_rewrite/eng/pub-press/doc/no-par_e.pdf.

Graham, J. 'The New Companies Act: (A) An Introduction to the New Act; and (B) Forming a Company'. Seminar paper, Companies Act Seminar, Pamodzi Hotel, Lusaka, 12 October 1994.

Harmen, M. C. 'Memorandum from the Council of the Chartered Institutes of Secretaries of Joint Stock Companies and Other Public Bodies to the Gedge Committee'. In *Report of the Committee on Shares of No Par Value*, the Gedge report. Board of Trade, Cmd 9112 of 1954.

U.K. Cohen Committee 1945, Cmnd. 6659.

U.K. Committee on Corporate Governance. *Report of the Committee on Corporate Governance* (Hampel report). London: Gee and Co., 1998.

U.K. Committee on Financial Aspects of Corporate Governance. *Report of the Committee on the Financial Aspects of Corporate Governance* (Cadbury report). London: Gee Publishing, 1992.

U.K. Jenkins Committee 1962, Cmnd 1749.

Waxman, M., and N. Annamalia. *Systemic Bank Insolvency: A Legal Framework For Early Crisis Containment.* Washington DC: The World Bank, 1999.

PhD Theses and Other Academic Dissertations

Chulu, J. M. 'Corporate Governance in Zambia'. PhD diss., University of Essex, 2008.

Liswaniso-Kampata, T. M. 'The Challenges of Corporate Governance in Banking Supervision: An Evaluation of Some Financial Sector Development Plan Recommendations'. LLM diss., University of Warwick, 2008.

Mulwila, J. M. 'Parastatal Companies and the Law in Zambia'. PhD diss., University of London, 1980.

Mwape, A. A. K. 'Bank Governance and Regulation in East and Southern African Countries'. PhD diss., SOAS, University of London, 2006.

Sameta, L. 'Directors' Liability for Insolvent Trading in Zambia'. LLM diss., University of Warwick, 1996.

Tarinyeba, W. M. 'Corporate Governance in Uganda: The Role of Bank Finance'. JSM thesis, Stanford University Law School, May 2006.

Web-based Articles

Bank of Zambia. 'Press Statement, January 14, 2003: BOZ Takes Possession of Access Financial Services and Access Leasing'. http://www.boz.zm/Media/Access_%20Financial_Services.htm. Accessed 17 April 2005.

Boone, K. 'Kevin's English Law Glossary: Statutory Interpretation'. http://www.kevinboone.com/lawglos_statutory_interpretation.html. Accessed 18 April 2005.

Bowie, A. 'Criminal Law Outline Lecture Two: Chapter 7'. http://www. professorbowie.com/Lecture%20Two.htm. Accessed 20 November 2007.

Center for International Private Enterprise. 'Institute of Directors'. http:// www.cipe.org/programs/global/partners/dispPartner.php?id=258. Accessed 17 February 2007.

Curd, R., and K. Hare. 'United Kingdom: Auditors' Negligence: Liability to Company and Shareholders'. 2 June 2008. http://www.mondaq. com/article.asp?articleid=61268. Accessed 3 May 2009.

FindLaw for Legal Professionals. http://caselaw.lp.findlaw.com/scripts/ getcase.pl?court=2nd&navby=case&no=007972v3&exact=1. Accessed 10 February 2005.

Fundanga, C. M. 'A Brief Look at Corporate Governance in Zambia'. http://www.bis.org/review/r061208d.pdf. Accessed 28 April 2009.

Hawaii Administrative Rules. Title 16, U.S. Department of Commerce and Consumer Affairs, Chapter 27, Supervisory and Enforcement Action Relating to Financial Institutions. http://www.hsba.org/hsba/ Legal_Research/Hawaii/Hawaii/Admin/DCCA/ch27.cfm. Accessed 17 April 2005.

International Chamber of Commerce. 'Corporate Governance Developments in Zambia'. May 2005. http://www.iccwbo.org/corporate-governance/id4937/index.html. Accessed 27 April 2009.

International Organization for Standardization. 'Committee Draft of ISO 31000 Risk Management'. http://www.nsai.ie/uploads/file/N047_ Committee_Draft_of_ISO_31000.pdf. Accessed 20 April 2009.

Jamaica's Companies Act 2004 (No. 10 of 2004). http://www.mct.gov. jm/Companies%20Act%20b.pdf. Accessed 11 January 2009.

Lawrence, G. M., and J. T. Wells. 'Basic Legal Concepts: The Fraud Beat'. http://www.aicpa.org/PUBS/JOFA/oct2004/lawrence.htm. Accessed 18 November 2007.

Mailafia, O. 'Nigeria: In Praise of the Judiciary'. *Daily Trust*, 7 July 2008. http://allafrica.com/stories/200807071608.html. Accessed 10 June 2009.

Malupenga, A. 'Ex-Chief Executive Challenges ZNOC's Liquidation in Court'. *The Post*, 6 November 2002. http://www.accessmylibrary. com/comsite5/bin/pdinventory.pl?pdlanding=1&referid=2930&purc hase_type=ITM&item_id=0286-27009281. Accessed 28 November 2007.

Mauritius' Companies Act 2001. http://www.gov.mu/portal/sites/ncb/ fsc/download/compact2001.doc. Accessed 11 January 2009.

Moonze, L. 'Account for $90m, Nonde Tells Government'. *The Post*, 15 December 2003. http://www.accessmylibrary.com/comsite5/bin/pdin-ventory.pl?pdlanding=1&referid=2930&purchase_type=ITM&item_ id=0286-19713310. Accessed 30 November 2007.

OECD. 'The OECD Principles of Corporate Governance'. http://www. oecd.org/dataoecd/41/32/33647763.pdf. Accessed 5 May 2009.

Shivji, I. 'The Life and Time of Babu: The Age of Revolution and Liber-ation'. *Law, Social Justice and Global Development (LGD)* 2 (2001). http://www2.warwick.ac.uk/fac/soc/law/elj/lgd/2001_2/shivji/. Accessed 25 June 2009.

Sulkowski, A., and K. Greenfield. 'A Bridle, a Pod and a Big Stick: An Evaluation of Class Actions, Shareholder Proposals and the Ultra Vires Doctrine as Methods for Controlling Corporate Behavior'. *Boston College of Law Faculty Papers*, paper no. 92, Boston College of Law, 2005. Accessed 31 December 2008. http://lsr.nellco.org/cgi/ viewcontent.cgi?article=1092&context=bc/bclsfp.

Times of Zambia. 'Zambia: Mwanawasa Prescribes Corruption Pana-cea'. 18 October 2007. http://allafrica.com/stories/200710180320. html. Accessed 24 December 2007.

Trade Compliance Center. 'Zambia: Trade Policy Review Summaries— 1996 (Zambia's Trade and Economic Reforms, 23 August 1996)'.

http://tcc.export.gov/Country_Market_Research/All_Research_ Reports/exp_005844.asp. Accessed 15 December 2007.

U.K. Department of Trade and Industry. 'Companies Act 2006: Explanatory Notes'. http://www.opsi.gov.uk/acts/acts2006/en/ukpgaen_20060046_ en.pdf. Accessed 20 December 2008.

UNCITRAL. '1997—UNCITRAL Model Law on Cross-Border Insolvency with Guide to Enactment'. http://www.uncitral.org/uncitral/ en/uncitral_texts/insolvency/1997Model.html. Accessed 20 February 2009. [See also Resolution A/RES/52/158, adopted by the UN General Assembly, 'Model Law on Cross-Border Insolvency of the United Nations Commission on International Trade Law' (further to the report of the Sixth Committee (A/52/649)), dated 30 January 1998.

U.S. Oklahoma State Banking Department. 'Statement on Unsafe and Unsound Banking Practices'. http://www.state.ok.us/~osbd/Banks/ Statutes/unsound.htm. Accessed 25 April 2005.

Woolf, E. 'A Return to Rational Concepts'. *Accountancy* (Institute of Chartered Accountants in England and Wales), 1993. http://www.faqs. org/abstracts/Business/A-return-to-rational-concepts-Whose-fault-is- it-anyway.html. Accessed 8 May 2009.

World Bank. 'Report on the Observance of Standards and Codes (ROSC)—Corporate Governance Country Assessment: Armenia, April 2005'. http://www.worldbank.org/ifa/Armenia%20ROSC%20 (final).pdf. Accessed 8 November 2007.

———. 'The World Bank Insolvency Initiative'. http://www4.world- bank.org/legal/insolvency_ini/overview.htm. Accessed 6 May 2002.

Zambezi Times Online. 'Access Finance Engaged in Crime'. http://www. zambezitimes.com/fulltxt.php?id_news=1879. Accessed 17 April 2005.

INDEX

www.ingramcontent.com/pod-product-compliance
Lightning Source LLC
Chambersburg PA
CBHW021948220326
41599CB00012BA/1374